Child Welfare Practice

A Guide to Providing
Effective Services
for Children and Families

Thelma Falk Baily
Walter Hampton Baily

❧ ❧ ❧ ❧ ❧ ❧ ❧ ❧ ❧ ❧ ❧ ❧ ❧ ❧ ❧ ❧

Child
Welfare
Practice

Jossey-Bass Publishers
San Francisco • Washington • London • 1983

CHILD WELFARE PRACTICE
A Guide to Providing Effective Services
for Children and Families
      by Thelma Falk Baily and Walter Hampton Baily

Copyright © 1983 by: Jossey-Bass Inc., Publishers
                      433 California Street
                      San Francisco, California 94104
                                          &
                      Jossey-Bass Limited
                      28 Banner Street
                      London EC1Y 8QE

Library of Congress Cataloging in Publication Data

Baily, Thelma Falk.
      Child welfare practice.

      Bibliography: p. 223
      Includes index.
      1. Social work with children—United States.
2. Child welfare—United States. 3. Children—Services
for—United States. 4. Family social work—United States.
I. Baily, Walter Hampton. II. Title.
HV741.B29   1983   362.7'0973   82-49034
ISBN 0-87589-558-1

Manufactured in the United States of America

The paper in this book meets the guidelines for
permanence and durability of the Committee on
Production Guidelines for Book Longevity of the
Council on Library Resources.

JACKET DESIGN BY WILLI BAUM

FIRST EDITION

Code 8304

The Jossey-Bass
Social and Behavioral Science Series

Preface

This book is addressed to the essential needs of child welfare workers in the performance of their jobs. It attempts to answer such questions as "What must I do?" "How can I best do it?" "What facts and skills do I need as a basis for what I do?" We do not concentrate on every theoretical study; rather, we focus on the crucial information and skills that the worker must have at his command in order to perform effectively in a child welfare setting.

The impetus for this book comes from several sources. First is the demand by workers themselves. With rare exception, practitioners are eager to improve their knowledge and skill in service delivery. Workers who have been in the field for many years often feel some deficiency because of the increasing proliferation of modes and theories of practice. In contrast, new practitioners in large, systematized, technologically advanced organizations find themselves caught up in systems analysis, operations theory, monitoring, accountability, management "style," policy development, and communications theory; as a result, some of the practice content, seemingly common and available ten to twenty years ago, has been lost.

There is, then, a hunger, sometimes a desperation, for practical skills and knowledge to do the job. Practitioners also want to have current theories, practice modalities, and human development concepts translated into daily practice. The gap between theory and practice is not a new one, but the multitude of theories in existence today are difficult to sort out and sometimes to apply. The problem is compounded by the fact that some supervisors have never practiced in the human services but, rather, have been moved into supervision from another agency because of their management skills. The new practitioner is often lost unless he or she has had previous, adequately supervised child welfare experience or an educational program clearly focused on practice. Some child welfare practitioners have obtained their jobs by transfer from another state agency and have minimal, if any, skills in performing their jobs. In addition, newly employed college graduate staff, prepared in any of the social sciences, social work, counseling, education, and related fields, are eager to translate their theoretical knowledge into practice. Furthermore, agencies themselves may provide minimum direction for practice, emphasizing instead the "delivery" of service. If we place this mix together—a multitude of theories, a supervisor who may never have practiced, an administration that must be primarily concerned with managing and monitoring, staff who may be outdated or whose education has stressed a practice theory that the agency may not support or understand—then there will be many questions and conflicts over how best to do the job. A practice that attempts to embody all theories may be a poor one, but there are still some basic ground rules for good performance, and it is these that we attempt to set forth in this book. In short, this book is an attempt to put in perspective the substance of practice, the flesh and bones often left behind in our preoccupation with the newer, and admittedly very essential, components of public welfare systems.

A second catalyst for this volume is the 1980 Adoption Assistance and Child Welfare Act, which is intended to provide additional funds for improved child welfare services. Even if funds are not forthcoming and provision is not made for additional practitioners and services, we must still be as efficient as possible in improving services and particularly in achieving a permanent status for more children.

A final impetus comes from our recognition that many practitioners effectively provide professional, responsive, caring service to families in spite of systemic/structural problems that often hamper and discourage them. Thus, high-quality service, whether in public or private agencies, is possible and achievable. This book will attempt to help all practitioners reach a high quality of service without denying that there are many impediments to the achievement of the standard for which we all strive.

This book is accordingly addressed to the new practitioner who is transferring to child welfare from other human service employment; to the experienced person who takes employment in child welfare but has never worked in a human service agency before; to the college student or graduate who is just beginning career practice; and to the seasoned practitioner who may find the book useful for confirmation and reminders about essential practice.

Overview

The opening chapter introduces the field of child welfare and identifies a number of characteristics that practitioners should have. Emphasis is placed on the rights of children and families who use services. An orientation toward the family, not the individual, is stressed throughout the book.

Chapter Two, on intake and initial assessment, stresses the crucial nature of the first contact with the consumer and the desirability of having highly skilled practitioners—practitioners who are responsive to the spoken and unspoken needs of the consumer—employed in this strategic part of service. Intake is a mutual process between client and practitioner; both have information to share with the other, so that a clear agreement can be secured at the end of the first meeting. Cases moving beyond the first interview require efficient and complete assessment.

Separation, the subject of Chapter Three, is a common life experience and is essential for growth and development. However, extended and disruptive separations of children from their primary caretakers can be painful and harmful. A practitioner cannot completely erase the pain, but she or he can take steps to minimize it for everyone associated with the event: natural parents, foster parents, the placed child, his siblings, and the practitioner herself. Practitioners should not hesitate to help all these persons recognize and manage their feelings about separation.

Day care, discussed in Chapter Four, is used as an extension of the family and is a highly valuable service to strengthen and maintain families during periods of crisis, during a transition, or when parents take employment. Practitioners in day care have opportunities to strengthen and improve parental skills, intervene and alert parents to emerging problems, support and protect the child when parents are particularly distressed, and involve parents in peer relationships for socializing and for sharing parental experiences.

Chapter Five focuses on foster family care, a major service for children. Here we describe the qualities that prospective foster parents must have if they are to function in the best interests of the foster child. We also discuss the practitioner's relationship with foster parents, natural parents, and the placed child. Even though a child is removed from his home, practitioners must remain committed to strengthening the parents' roles and to keeping them involved in decision making for their children. Finally, we describe recent efforts to establish children in permanent homes—through permanency planning and the Adoption Assistance and Child Welfare Act of 1980.

Residential treatment, the subject of Chapter Six, is an essential form of care for children who, for a variety of reasons, cannot remain at home. Service to children alone, however, may provide no benefit if they have to return to family members who have not changed any of their behaviors while they were away. Parents, whenever feasible, must be involved in the change effort.

Child protection, discussed in Chapter Seven, is a unique

service within child welfare, since the practitioner represents the authority of the state, must reach out to unmotivated clients, may testify in court against the parents, and may require the family members to change their parental performance. Service may be provided even when a parent maintains that it is not needed. The work with abusive and neglecting parents is often slow and thankless, but there is satisfaction when parents learn to provide not only physical comfort to children but psychological nurture as well.

In Chapter Eight termination of services—a significant episode in case activity—is covered. Termination, which can be described as a phase, not an event, should be planned and can be used as a very productive period of learning and consolidation of experience for the consumer. Consequently, practitioners should be ready to help persons move through, and make the best use of, the termination phase. Practitioners should never underestimate the feelings that clients have about terminating relationships, even when brief service has been provided. Of equal importance, practitioners must be aware of their own feelings about termination, since these feelings affect their performance in service termination.

As emphasized in Chapter Nine, practitioners have the obligation to advocate in behalf of their clients whenever practices and policies interfere with the receipt and use of service or when a service is unhelpful or outright harmful. Not every practitioner may be able to be *the* advocate, but every practitioner should be ready to participate in an advocacy effort, whether for a single client or for a group of consumers. Failure to advocate may result in the professional neglect of clients.

Chapter Ten underscores that children and families in need will continue to use child welfare programs and that there is no shortcut to serving families competently and compassionately. As important as it is to assure services to people after difficulties arise, policies and programs should also be directed to the prevention of family breakdown.

Brief annotated bibliographies follow each chapter, and a bibliography for the book includes both references cited and other recommended sources of information.

This book emphasizes practice behaviors and suggests many statements that practitioners can make and questions they can ask of consumers. Case illustrations highlight typical problems faced primarily in public child welfare services, including practitioner behaviors with both parents and children. Actual cases are analyzed to clarify what the practitioner did and what else might have been done. The frustrations and the satisfactions in child welfare are clearly portrayed in the case examples.

Acknowledgments

Inspiration to write this book came primarily from our colleagues in public child welfare agencies in many parts of the country. They shared cases, dilemmas, and solutions, as well as their talents and abilities. With spirits high through the most difficult tasks, they continue to stimulate thinking on practice issues, and we are grateful. Our respect for each practitioner and decision maker is enormous.

Thanks are extended to the staff of the library of the University of Southern Maine, Portland: Jerry Banner, Phyllis Locke, Becky Rose, and especially Sheila Johnson. They gave diligent help in locating, and sometimes relocating, sources of information.

William E. Henry, Gracia A. Alkema, and Dorothy Conway, editors at Jossey-Bass, provided many ideas and suggestions for the organization and presentation of material, and to them we are especially grateful.

We acknowledge the competent editing help provided by our son, Peter, and the many hours of research and clerical detail given by our son, Kenneth, and our daughter, Ingrid, as well as their unfailing support for this endeavor.

Parsonsfield, Maine   Thelma Falk Baily
February 1983   Walter Hampton Baily

Contents

xv

The Authors

Thelma Falk Baily is associate director of a protective services project at the Judge Baker Guidance Center, Boston, and a senior member of the American Humane Association faculty, Denver. She received her B.A. in sociology from the University of Pennsylvania in 1948 and her M.S.S. from the Bryn Mawr School of Social Work and Social Research in 1962. She has practiced in child protective services; foster care and adoption; residential programming; individual, group, and family treatment; and as a supervisor, administrator, and consultant. For seven years she was a social work professor and currently consults, lectures, and conducts workshops throughout the country.

Walter Hampton Baily is a part-time faculty member of the University of Maine, Augusta; a consultant; and a researcher. He received his B.A. in sociology from Temple University in 1951, his M.S.S. from the Bryn Mawr School of Social Work and Social Research in 1956, and his D.S.W. from the Catholic

University School of Social Service in 1979. After twenty years of social work practice, he served as a faculty member in B.S.W. programs at the University of Southern Maine and at Castleton State College, Vermont, where he was program chair. His dissertation research dealt with baccalaureate social worker performance levels, and the study was used in a national classification validation study by the National Association of Social Workers.

The authors collaborate on research and education for social service agencies. They are currently engaged in an analysis of the definitions of child abuse and neglect for a statewide network of public and private agencies.

Child Welfare Practice

A Guide to Providing
Effective Services
for Children and Families

CHAPTER ONE

Qualities and Skills of Effective Practitioners

Child welfare work is demanding and exhausting; it is also very rewarding. The following vignettes—some pleasing; others repellent, infuriating, or perplexing—give some notion of the joys and sorrows experienced by those who work with families and children.

Derek is getting along a lot better now. I don't think that would have happened if he didn't come here. He eats better and isn't as nervous as he was before. So thanks for helping us [mother of a five-year-old, to day care staff].

The mother glared at me and said, "I don't care what anyone thinks, but I hated that kid from the minute he was born. For one thing, he looked like his father, the man who left me stranded as soon as he knew I was pregnant. He did nothin' but spit up and have loose bowels. When he spit up, I was so mad that I just scooped it all up and made

1

him eat it again. I called him a bastard. That's what
he is, isn't he? He has no father and that's what
you call kids like that [part of social history on a
youth admitted to a residential treatment program].

They took my Timmy away from me, and
it's all your fault. Why did you tell those lies in
there? That's all they were—lies, lies, lies. You said
everything we talked about was secret, all between
us, you said. And now that judge took him away,
just because of what you said [statement made by
a parent to a Social and Rehabilitation Services
worker, following a court hearing].

The newborn "wouldn't die" when the moth-
er tried to drown it in a toilet. "I pushed the baby's
head down so it was under the water. . . . I just left
it there until I saw that its arms stopped moving."
The mother's sister, who assisted in the delivery,
helped hold the baby down, because the mother
was in physical pain. "The baby wouldn't die in
the water, so I took it out and banged its head on
the floor." The mother banged "the child's head
twice," and the sister told her "to bang it harder."
She finally threw the baby out the bathroom win-
dow. The mother had recently worked in a Head
Start program, teaching "little kids the alphabet,
numbers, and shapes." The mother stated, "I
hated the baby and the baby's father." Both wom-
en were held on a murder charge [Racher and Campisi, 1982].

Yeah, we were out in the field on a tractor,
just me and him by ourselves. It was unusual because generally all the rest of the kids are there,
too. But this one time he happened to be there by
himself. I get a bang out of him when I let him
steer the tractor. He gets a bang out of it, too, and
I just have to chuckle watching him do it [foster
father describing relationship with foster child;
quoted in Aldridge, Cautley, and Lichstein, 1974,
p. 24].

Clearly, the professionals who work with cases such as
these must acquire certain special skills and attitudes.

Requisite Abilities and Attitudes

The following selection of values, skills, and knowledge are central to the child welfare field. Without them the practitioner cannot do an effective and compassionate job.

Ability to Communicate. Greater demands in communication are placed on the child welfare practitioner than on those in other fields, since the worker must be able to communicate with all age groups—including very young children, who communicate nonverbally—and handle the messages sent and received among family members. Communication occurs in what the worker does, as well as in what he* says, and both forms of interchange are central to the child service role. The worker must be aware of the unintentional messages all of us send through body language and must learn both to control and to utilize this method of communication. Communication skill, in its broadest sense, involves the ability to listen to both the spoken and the unspoken words of consumers** and the ability to describe the practitioner's role and services in ways that are clear to the client.

Sensitivity to Feelings of Parents and Children. Child welfare practice, since it invariably deals with two generations of people, requires an accurate and heightened sensitivity to the emotions generated between a child and a parent in the course of their mutual growth and development and to the feelings generated during separation and reunion. The practitioner must encourage her clients to express their feelings verbally or through actions; and she must then help them grapple with

---

*The traditional use of the pronoun *he* has not yet been superseded by a convenient, generally accepted pronoun that refers to *he* or *she*. Therefore, we will alternately use *he* and *she* in referring to both clients and practitioners.

**The words *client* and *consumer* will be used interchangeably throughout the book to indicate the person or persons who are served by a human service agency. *Consumer* has a more neutral connotation than *client*, which may suggest dependency or reduced status. No derogatory intent is implied by the use of either word, and the two words are used only to reduce the repetition of a single term. A few authors have suggested the word *citizen* to refer to all service users.

and manage these feelings, which are often intense, enduring, and painful.

Recognition That Each Human Being Is Worthy of Help. Central to all human service practice is the respect and dignity accorded to the individual. This is more easily stated than accomplished in practice, and, in child welfare work, it often seems more natural to identify with the child than with the parent. When we meet an angry, hostile client, it is easy to forget that he began in the world as a totally dependent infant and responded first and foremost to love and to caring. He was not angry and offensive and resistant to offers of help. We know from experience that if one method of treatment is not successful, then another may be. If one practitioner is not helpful, another may be more effective. A person who does not use help and change in one time period may be ready for change at a later stage of life and development. Thus, the seemingly intransigent, offensive, and repulsive client may later become the giving and caring parent. As difficult as it may be at times, practitioners must look far beyond the exterior shell of each person, especially when that exterior is not particularly likeable, and respond to the person as one who is worthy of caring attention, responses, and aid. Attitudes of retaliation and rejection have no place in the practice repertoire of child welfare staff.

Willingness to Give Information to All Clients. The provision of information is at one and the same time an expression of caring, concern, acceptance, and support for the family and the child. When information is not given freely and fully, both the client's functioning and the practitioner's continued communication and relationship with the client may be impaired. What the client does not know may in fact hurt him. Information provided must be organized, coherent, and delivered in a way that the consumer understands. Age-appropriate information, given in terms children understand, must always be provided. Research on former foster children reveals that they knew far more than they were told about their parents and the reasons for placement and replacement.

Ability to Tolerate and Deal with Resistance. Similar to the understanding and compassion required in the attitude of acceptance of each person, we must look beyond the exterior of resistance and recognize that most people do want to improve their own lives and the lives of their children. Dealing with resistance requires patience, understanding, and occasionally endurance. Resistance cannot be handled by those who must control others, those who must expedite rapidly, or those who need quick gratification and immediate results. Child welfare workers must also recognize their own resistance to change and their need for sameness and stability.

Ability to Demonstrate That Adult Behavior Can Damage Children. Practitioners must be able to create doubt in the minds of parents about their behavior toward their children. That is, the practitioner must, without criticizing or shaming the parent, point out that certain parental actions, attitudes, and statements are not conducive to a child's healthful development. At the same time, she should point out parental behavior that has helped the child—thereby building on existing strengths, not on parental limits or deficits. In all instances the practitioner's statements should convey the expectation that the parent can perform in ways to enhance the child's development and, at the same time, bring more satisfaction to the parent.

Readiness to Insist on Cessation of Destructive Behaviors Toward the Child and to Make Environmental Shifts When Needed. The practitioner must have the conviction that behavior harmful to the constructive growth and development of children must be changed or modified; if it remains unchanged, the practitioner must insist that the child be removed from his present environment. When serious deprivation or damage is being inflicted on a child, the practitioner cannot equivocate about the need for change. The authority for such change may have to come not only from the practitioner's professional knowledge but from the agency, from other professions in the agency or community, and, finally, from the state itself, through the court system.

Ability to Teach Family Members How to Improve the Developmental Climate for Children. Once the parents admit, even though reluctantly, that their behavior needs to be changed, the child welfare practitioner must then assist them—through coaching, persuasion, encouragement, information, role modeling, and instruction in establishing different relationships with their children.

Willingness to Support Growth and Change in Parent and Child, No Matter How Small the Improvement. Practitioners whose clients have severe developmental disabilities are perhaps more tolerant of slow change than other child welfare personnel; thus, they provide a model of certain essential skills. They are able to perceive, understand, and give recognition to small changes in levels of personal functioning. They are also more readily able to tolerate regressions to previous levels of behavior. As practitioners examine some of their own habits and difficulties in making changes, they may develop increased tolerance and respect for the problems others have in initiating and sustaining changes. What may be defined by the practitioner as a small change may in fact be considered a substantial change by the consumer, and we must be quick to support and endorse improvements when they occur. Some circumstances in child welfare practice appear to have few, if any, commendable elements; it is, therefore, all the more important to look for, define, and support improvements in performance and family functioning. These small increments of improvement may be the base upon which larger behavioral gains are made.

Willingness to Use the Legal Authority Vested in Some Services. An increasing number of practitioners are legally responsible for some services to children and families, and they have the legal mandate, in conjunction with other authorities, to remove children from their homes or to conduct certain screening examinations. Although legal authority is not new for child welfare workers, what is new is that so many staff members are now accountable to courts, must implement the provisions of legally mandated services, and have the authority to initiate actions in behalf of children. Such actions are taken, with rare exceptions, only after the practitioner has consulted with other staff in the child welfare program or with authorities in other departments, such as the police, the courts, or the district attorney. Employing authority is invariably a last step; seldom is it the first action in behalf of children. Because it is a serious step and can have major ramifications for family integrity and the family's use of community services, it must not be put into practice casually; but when the indicators are clear that legal authority must be used, practitioners need the resolve to act forcefully.

Willingness to Work for Improvements in Agency Services and Community Policies. To the community at large, employment in a child welfare service means that the practitioner stands for effective and caring policies and practices in behalf of children. Thus, the practitioner has an obligation as well as an opportunity in the performance of his job. Unfortunately, many public child services, as well as private agencies, are overextended and have only limited resources; thus, the services they provide may not be of high quality. Although practitioners may be weary of fighting the bureaucracy merely to accomplish a day's work, they must try to bring about changes in their own services and in community policies that do not speak to the best interests of children. The process of change is often slow and may have to be accomplished through committees or other organizations, but the responsible practitioner should recognize the need for agency policy modification and the need for improved community attitudes toward children and families.

Ability to Function Adequately Within the Agency and Carry Out Its Mission and Goals. Child welfare services all have essentially the same mission: to strengthen family life wherever possible, to protect children from abuse and neglect, and to provide supplemental, supportive, or substitute nurturing care for the child when the family cannot be kept together. Practitioners work within the boundaries of policies and programs established through a legislated and organized structure, yet they may not always endorse all policies and procedures. Specific program goals within an agency may be deficient in implementing the overall mission. For example, agencies may place too many children in foster care, may consistently overlook children who are being neglected, or may be less than vigorous in locating permanent placement plans for minority or handicapped children. Both small and large bureaucracies are society's major vehicles to assist people, and even though practitioners should advocate for improvements in practice and search for policy changes to ensure the best services to consumers, they should also, within reason, adapt to agency practices.

Ability to Accept and Express Feelings of Joy and Sorrow. Child welfare practice exposes the worker to some of the most joyous and upsetting experiences in human relationships. When he encounters offensive and difficult situations, such as in cases of child neglect or sexual abuse, he must be able to balance these experiences with more "normal" and pleasurable social contacts in his own family or in other significant relationships. "Burnout" is an understandable consequence when practitioners engage in depleting and exhausting work, and social workers must find satisfying ways to express their feelings and to get replenishment—for instance, through group meetings sanctioned by the agency, through informal groups, or through an individual's own methods of relaxation and expression.

Ability to Understand One's Own Feelings About Separations and Personal Loss. Separations occur frequently in child welfare programs, perhaps more often than we would like to recognize. The loss from death, especially accidental death, is a traumatic experience. However, the separations and losses from a *chosen* separation, or the loss that a child feels when a parent abandons him or excludes him from home, or when a court terminates parental rights, can have powerful and lasting impact on the parties involved, especially the children. Practitioners often have to help parents make such a choice, be with them when a court decides for placement, counsel parents prior to and after termination of parental rights, and help the child through the separation. Child welfare workers are sometimes accused by parents of causing the separation. Practitioners should know which aspects of separations and losses are most difficult for them in order to be able to handle themselves comfortably when clients must be helped through the process. This does not mean that the worker should be unsympathetic and cold to the suffering of the participants, but he must be careful not to be immobilized or shattered by the strength of the emotions expressed. In times of such devastating stress, clients need security and stability.

Ability to Recognize That Parenting Is a Difficult Job. Parenting is a major job for which the vast majority of parents receive no training, negligible support, and little recognition. The infant demands constant care. The young child's emotional and learning needs are great, and if they are not adequately met, the child may protest, placing more pressure on the parent. The older child is a different challenge, with his beginning participation in peer groups and exposure to many community influences. The adolescent brings additional demands, related to independence, physical changes, emerging expressions of sexuality, a mixture of childlike and adult behavior, and criticism, sometimes severe, of family values. Many parents in our society, through either extended families or through financial assets, can have others share in, or substitute for, the parental role. Many of the families who are served in child welfare programs do not have access to these supplemental resources. Finklestein (1981, p. 102) states that residential treatment staff need to have a "tolerance for and understanding of the imperfections of their own parents and the parenting potential in themselves." We believe this characterization can be applied to all staff who work in child welfare. It provides us with an additional perspective and humility in serving parents.

Recognition That Child and Family Consumers Will Not Meet One's Own Emotional Needs. Practitioners must obtain their needs for nurture from persons other than the clients they serve. This does not mean that there cannot be a social conversation within the framework of practitioner-client contacts. Discussions of subjects other than the child welfare issue may strengthen clients, since such conversations allow the client to move away from any feelings of helplessness or dependency he may have. Again, the purpose of the conversation is to improve the consumer's ability to function socially, rather than to meet the practitioner's needs for nurture. It is not to be suggested that the social worker should find no satisfaction in his work, but rather that his personal needs must be sought in other realms of life experience: from the employing agency, from peer groups, from family and friends, and from various organizations.

Recognition That the Agency and the Practitioner May Be Only a Small Part of the Child's or Family's Total Experi-

ences. In some aspects of service, such as adoption or permanency planning, practitioners admittedly can make a major contribution to the consumer's life and direction; in many other
aspects of service, however, the worker may exert a relatively
small influence on the client, whose social networks and life experiences are often far more significant to him. Research shows
that we tend to place too high a value on ourselves and our accomplishments with clients, whereas clients assign greater credit
for positive changes to those social resources and environmental
assets available to them (Maluccio, 1979; Maluccio and Sinanoglu, 1981). Working relationships that are developed with consumers are important, but of greater significance are the connections and relationships that clients can develop and use in the
wider community. This means that attention must be given to
organized community social support systems and to the consumer's best use of his own networks.

. *Persistence.* In the professional literature, persistence is
conveyed in terms such as *encouraging, motivating,* and *advocating.* The idea here is to persevere and maintain a stand obsti-
nately, or to carry out an uninterrupted course with the consumer. Many families with whom we work, especially at first,
are unmotivated and fatalistic—particularly families that manifest the "apathy-futility syndrome." Such families are emotionally numb, lonely, committed to virtually nothing, and verbally
inaccessible; they lack competence in many areas of living and
feel that nothing is worth doing. Their feelings of futility are so
pervasive that they infect those who work with these families
(Polansky, 1981, p. 40). The idea of persistence does not mean
taking over another's life—not that we can do that anyway—but·
it also does not mean yielding to the resistance or lack of motivation of consumers when it is apparent that some change can
be made, however small. If the practitioner gives up, then discouraged and distressed persons will have one more piece of evidence to confirm their distorted beliefs.

Some Preliminary Definitions

Child Welfare and Child Welfare Services. Kadushin (1978,
p. 4) defines child welfare as the "broad range of activities de-

signed to benefit children, promote their well-being, and strengthen or assure provision for meeting their physical, social, emotional, educational, and moral needs." Child welfare, then, is concerned with the well-being of all children. In contrast, "child welfare services speak to the special needs of particular groups of children"; they are "specifically designated as social services, a configuration of special programs having special functions, engaging in special activities." Child welfare services include, for example, foster care, adoption, day care, homemaker, residential, and group home programs; "runaway" programs; and crisis intervention services to keep families together. Tax-supported child welfare services dominate the field, and many of the private or nongovernmental service agencies often have contractual arrangements with public agencies to carry certain program responsibilities.

Child welfare services are usually categorized as (1) supportive services, such as counseling and crisis intervention—services that strengthen the parents so that the family and child roles can be improved or sustained; (2) supplementary services, such as day care—services that assume certain parental responsibilities; and (3) substitute services, such as foster care—services that replace the parental role for a temporary or extended period.

Child Welfare Practitioners. Social work methods are the generally accepted modes of providing services to children and parents in child welfare. Persons trained as social workers are by no means the only practitioners. Staff members of child welfare agencies have often completed educational programs in psychology, education, nursing, and many other human service specialties. Agencies choose from a range of models of practice, such as reality therapy or behavior modification, and some organizations permit units or divisions to select their own practice modes. For specialized programs, such as day care for the emotionally disturbed child, professionals from fields such as medicine, public health nursing, rehabilitation, psychiatry, and psychology may be used; and professionals other than the social worker often give direct service to families. However, the person providing the bulk of case and group services to families and individuals, and the staff member carrying case management responsibilities, is usually considered a social worker.

Social Work. Baer and Federico (1978, p. 61), synthesizing the work of many previous analysts, define social work as an activity concerned and involved with "the interactions between people and the institutions of society that affect the ability of people to accomplish life tasks, realize aspirations and values, and alleviate distress." Social work, as they define it, has three purposes: "(a) to enhance the problem-solving, coping, and developmental capacities of people; (b) to promote the effective and humane operation of the systems that provide people with resources and services; and (c) to link people with systems that provide them with resources, services, and opportunities."

Family Orientation in Child Welfare

As long as family members show some motivation and capacity to retain or rebuild the family unit, child welfare programs, instead of focusing on the child as an individual, should focus on the child as part of a family; that is, they should attempt to maintain, support, and strengthen the family: "The first task in both education and practice is to put the severed child back into the family and the severed family back into its network of extended kin, friends, neighbors, community, and neighborhood" (Germaine, 1981, p. 326). Emphasis on the family requires practitioners to be "more committed to values of fairness, cooperation, mutuality, and harmony than to values of self-actualization, individual success, and unlimited freedom" (Halleck, 1976, p. 493). According to Hartman (1981b, pp. 8-10), a family "consists of two or more individuals who define themselves as a family and who, over time, assume those obligations to one another that are generally considered an essential component of family systems. [Even if a] 'family' is connected by neither blood nor legal ties, policy and practice in child welfare and in all areas of service should support and sustain these kinds of family systems, which are not biologically determined or legally recognized but are socially and emotionally important." Humans are by nature social creatures and "are nourished within a network of intimate human connections." Individualistic approaches tend to disregard the importance of intimate attachments to families. "Social programs . . . tend to take over family tasks and roles rather than enhancing the family's resources and capacities to perform its functions."

In short, Hartman stresses that the "individual cannot be considered apart from his or her intimate human connections." Therefore, "practice should model itself after life, should utilize natural systems as sources of help and change, and should protect and nurture the sources of support and opportunities for growth and self-realization that exist in a client's human environment." Such an approach, in Hartman's view, changes social work practice, "since family members become important participants in helping efforts, rather than being locked out of them." In addition, it requires that practitioners be involved with the network of people who can help the child and family.

Consistent with the above emphasis on family in child welfare, the "life model" of practice is currently gaining considerable interest in social work. Germaine and Gitterman (1980, p. 28) state that "problems represent the stress generated by discrepancies between people's needs and capacities, on the one hand, and environmental qualities, on the other." Stress arises in three interrelated areas of living: life transitions, environmental pressures, and maladaptive interpersonal processes. Life transitions include the movement from childhood to adolescence or from adolescence to adulthood, status changes such as from unmarried to married or from employee to supervisor, and crisis events such as the onset of a chronic disease or death of a spouse. Environmental pressures include unresponsive organizations such as a racist employer, an educational system that expects all students to behave and perform at the same levels, and physical structures that are too congested and restrictive for healthful human activity, whether in the home or workplace. Maladaptive interpersonal processes include problems that people have in relating to and communicating with others, including family and friends and those representing different age, racial, ethnic, or religious groups. As indicated by Hartman, this life model shapes the direction of social work practice: the way in which the problem is defined; the roles of clients and workers; the steps or phases of helping; the assessment of change possibilities in people, networks and organizations; and the activities of professionals.

Ewalt (1982, p. 194) adds still another dimension to this concept of practice. In reviewing several books, she points out the difficulties of clearly defining, initiating, and effecting environmental changes. She notes that much more "is involved in the social situation than relationships with significant others" and suggests that something broader than interpersonal relationships is required—not only for assessment but sometimes for intervention. Perhaps "intervention in the environment might sometimes be *preferable* to 'treatment,' even by a clinical social worker." Ewalt believes that social workers are instructed in "*how* to do various procedures of counseling but not *whether* to do them."

Consumer Rights and Practitioner Obligations

A 1978 *New Yorker* cartoon shows a small boy sitting at mealtime with his parents. The boy glares at his father with an angry frown, and the father, with astonishment on his face, looks at his son and asks, "If I make you drink your milk you'll sue me?" Amusing at first glance, it is a serious reminder of the marked changes in parent-child relationships and the increased rights that children now have under the law. The legal rights of children and adults who use human service programs—rights established by court decisions, as well as by public laws enacted by Congress—have also increased markedly in the past decade and probably will continue to increase. These rights have emerged as clients of public services began to be recognized not just as "recipients" but as citizens with rights no different from those of any other person.

Rights of consumers are important to consider not simply because of the legal constraints and requirements on agencies and workers but because there is a match between assuring service users their legal rights and according them dignity, respect, and equitable treatment. Such treatment is inherent in quality services based on humanitarian values and delivered by skilled practitioners.

Martin (1981, pp. 4-9), in discussing the preservation of

client rights, notes that clients are stigmatized through the concept of "handicapism"—that is, discrimination on the basis of handicap. Most of those served in public programs are considered handicapped or limited in some way. If consumers are consequently considered different, then we tend to treat them that way. Our attitudes must be changed; moreover, as Martin points out, we must continue to receive information on the legal and therapeutic rights of clients. There is "no contest between rights and therapy, and professionals must recognize that appropriate therapeutic interventions *include* client rights." Martin reviews recent court cases and statutes and concludes that the following rights are accorded to individuals receiving social services:

1. *Privacy*—the right to be left alone. Only an overt behavior justifies one's inclusion in a program.
2. *Psychological Autonomy*—the right to be free to speak and think. The First Amendment protects the "free flow of ideas from unwarranted interference with one's mental processes," and there is a "trend to respect the client's psychological autonomy."
3. *Due Process.* If life, liberty, or property is threatened, then the due process of law must take place before any one of them is removed. Educational opportunity is now considered a property, and "due process is required for almost any intervention by the state." Change of a client's status in a program now requires an official notice and an opportunity for a hearing.
4. *Protection Against Harm.* Even though an agency intervenes with the intention to help, it may harm the individual. Dysfunctional behavior as a result of intervention or service "has been found to be violative of the . . . prohibition against cruel and unusual punishment." Foster care is sometimes considered potentially worse than the care provided by the natural parent.
5. *Involuntary Servitude.* Work assignments must be compensated or must be a valid part of a therapeutic program.
6. *Least Restrictive Alternative.* Choices of programs must exist, and the least restrictive one must be used.
7. *Individualized Treatment.* Individual service plans must be

made. Such plans must state the goals and the short-term
objectives of treatment and must identify the person who
will implement the actions.
8. *Minimum Standards.* Treatment programs, especially in
residential settings, must provide adequate nutrition, clothing, reading material, privacy, and the like.

Client rights and agency/practitioner obligations are clearly described by Kuehn and Christophersen (1981, pp. 54-55).
Although their material was prepared for situations of abuse
and neglect, it applies equally well to many other services.

1. Parents have a right to know what approach
    [such as behavior modification or psychother-
    apy] will be used in treatment.
2. The client has a right to know approximately
    how long the treatment will last.
3. The client has a right to know in advance ap-
    proximately how much the therapy will cost
    [and whether there are any subsidies to help
    pay the cost].
4. The client must be informed that he does have
    the right to refuse treatment [and the possible
    consequences of refusal].
5. The client has a right to know what, if any,
    consequences there may be for terminating
    therapy prior to its completion.
6. The client has a right to know what the scope
    of confidentiality will be regarding therapy.
7. The client has a right to input in deciding the
    treatment goals.
8. The client has a right to know what the cri-
    teria for completion of his therapy will be.

Kuehn and Christophersen (1981, pp. 55-57) then identify nine additional rights after the client has signed an agreement for treatment. These are crucial because parents who
abuse or neglect are often not voluntary clients, and the treatment may be concerned with the separation or preservation of
the family unit. Again, even though this listing applies to abuse
and neglect, the agency obligations can readily be applied to

other treatments or services, and clients can demand thorough, professional services, based on sound knowledge and experience. Patients expect nothing less from medical personnel in treatment, and it is apparent that recipients of social services are entitled to similar quality of service.

1. Therapists should understand the dynamics of abuse and neglect, and consumers "have a right to . . . educated and trained therapists."
2. The client must be comfortable with the methods and techniques of treatment and has the right to approve the treatment modality.
3. The treatment should be proven to be effective in making the environment safer for children.
4. "Clients have a right to a periodic review of their treatment progress," with the equivalent right to request a change in therapy staff if there is no progress.
5. General principles of initiating behavioral change are not sufficient; clients have a right to be provided with specific methods, words, and actions to initiate change.
6. The practitioner must be able to model and demonstrate how to change one's own or a child's behavior.
7. "Clients have a right to be given procedures for handling specific situations where problems typically occur." In abuse cases parents are entitled to have instructions on how to handle high-stress situations away from home—for instance, in stores and restaurants.
8. If modeling is not effective in the office, then the therapist has the obligation to make home visits, to model the management of difficult situations, and to help the parent handle them.
9. Consumers have the right to acquire skills that will help them in the future.

The rights and obligations spelled out in the preceding lists are related primarily to the correction of deficiencies in interpersonal processes. However, as previously noted, many analysts emphasize that environmental pressures—"unresponsive organizations, social networks, or physical structures" (Germaine and Gitterman, 1980, p. 28)—also need to be modified. As this problem area becomes more clearly defined and delineated, clients may seek environmental modifications as a routine process. Major environmental changes have occurred for large groups of citizens, such as through the deinstitutionalization movement, but efforts at achieving a reduction of environmental pressures for a single person or family may also emerge as a right.

Liberman (1981, p. x) summarizes the concept of legal and professional obligations to and with consumers in the following: "Informed consent for intervention should include the responsibilities of both clients and treatment agents as well as the potential benefits for them. An ideal example of giving clients the power to change their own behavior—which may be approximated with all handicapped populations—occurs when clients choose their own goals, monitor their own behavior, arrange the conditions of their environment to facilitate progress toward the goals, and instruct, evaluate, and reward themselves."

Summary

Child welfare practice is rewarding and exhausting. Human service employment requires that the practitioner have and develop a wide range of skills, values, and knowledge that will help consumers make the best use of their own assets, as well as the formal and informal services and networks available to them. Child welfare practitioners, because they serve adults, children, and families, require characteristics and skills that include: sensitivity to feelings of parents and children, recognition that each person is worthy of help, willingness to give information to all clients, ability to tolerate and deal with resistance, ability to demonstrate that adult behavior can damage children, readiness to insist on a cessation of harmful behaviors toward children, ability to teach family members how to improve children's development, willingness to support growth and change in parent and child, willingness to use legal authority when necessary, willingness to work for improvements in social services, ability to function within the agency and to carry out its mission, ability to accept and express feelings of joy and sorrow, ability to understand one's own feelings about separation and loss, ability to recognize that parenting is a difficult job, recognition that child and family consumers will not meet one's own emotional needs, recognition that the practitioner may be only a small part of the child's or family's total experiences, and persistence.

Child welfare services are designed to meet the special needs of particular groups of children. They include some core services, such as foster care, adoption, day care, and residential care, plus some very specialized programs. The body of knowledge and skills represented in the profession of social work is the one most followed by child welfare services, although many modalities of treatment and practice may be used. Social work is concerned with the relationships between people and the societal institutions that affect people's abilities to pursue life tasks, achieve their aspirations, and reduce stress. Child welfare should have a family, rather than an individualistic, orientation, and efforts should be made to restore, support and strengthen the family unless all indications show that this is not possible. Stress for families may result from life transitions, environmental pressures, and deficient interpersonal processes. Practitioners need to be aware of all three areas as service is provided.

Clients of human service agencies have achieved a substantial number of rights and entitlements in the past decade. These rights will continue to increase and to be implemented, and they will have a marked impact on the way that services are provided and on practitioner activities. There is a match between the assurance of a person's rights and the provision of a highly skilled, dignified, responsible, and effective service.

Special Annotated Bibliography

Crouch, R. E. "International Declaration/Convention Efforts and the Current Status of Children's Rights in the United States." In R. B. Lillich (Ed.), *The Family in International Law: Some Emerging Problems.* Third Sokol Colloquium. Charlottesville, Va.: Michie, 1981. An excellent update and analysis of children's rights.

Hartman, A. "The Family: A Central Focus for Practice." *Social Work,* 1981, *26* (1), 7-13. A clear and convincing statement for a family emphasis in child welfare.

Kuehn, B. S., and Christophersen, E. R. "Preserving the Rights of Clients in Child Abuse and Neglect." In G. T. Hannah, W. P. Christian, and H. B. Clark (Eds.), *Preservation of Client Rights.* New York: Free Press, 1981. An exceptional analysis of client rights. Other articles in the book are equally thorough and well documented.

CHAPTER TWO

Conducting the
Initial Interview
and Assessment

All social agencies have policies and procedures to determine whether services can be provided to an applicant. Depending on whether the agencies are supported by public or private
funds, the services will vary considerably, and different criteria
will be set up to screen applicants. Eligibility factors in both
public and private agencies also vary widely and include such
items as the person's ability to pay for service, age, disability,
extent of problem, and willingness to become involved in the
program. Although some services—for example, child protection programs—are given to people whether they want them or
not, the assessment process is discounted if certain criteria are
not met—for example, if there is no finding of neglect or abuse.
    Public agencies differ from private or voluntary agencies
in at least two important ways. A public agency must perform
an intake service to determine the client's eligibility and, if the
person is eligible, must render some service. A private agency
may offer either a brief or extended intake, but it has no legal
obligation to render a service. This agency can, for good reasons,

state that it has insufficient staff or other resources to meet a client's need or that its services are not suitable for the consumer's problems. Private agencies can also develop waiting lists, offering the consumer the choice of waiting or of seeking help elsewhere. Public agencies are less likely to develop waiting lists, though they too may delay the onset of service.

Jenkins and Schroeder (1980) list the following activities of a child welfare intake service: provision of information, referral, acceptance of a service application, acceptance of an abuse report, determination of a client's next contact with the agency, and acceptance of a financial application. They also list two activities that occur after an application is received—what is usually called intake: (1) initial decision to accept a case and (2) determination of eligibility for social services, including decision to provide temporary social services.

The following steps are considered under diagnosis—more often called assessment: (1) diagnosis of child/family case and offer of continuing services, (2) referral to another agency, (3) contact with agency to which client is referred, (4) provision of information to client on referral to another agency, and (5) monitoring of referral to another agency.

Jenkins and Schroeder note that about half of the protective services have rotating staff for the intake and assessment functions. In services such as requests for foster care, day care, or counseling, one third have rotating intake. Many agencies provide backup functions for emergencies, and staff with specialized skills are sometimes available for intake in particular cases.

Holder and Mohr (1980, p. 100), discussing cases of neglect and abuse, provide a more specific listing of the steps during intake and assessment:

Intake of Referral

Receive referral
Explore appropriateness of referral
Departmental acceptance of referral as a report of neglect or
    abuse
Check local records

May make collateral contacts with professionals (police, medical, and school personnel)
Document record
Referral elsewhere, if necessary
Assess need for service to reporter
Validate referral

Initial Assessment

Initial contact with family/child
Subsequent assessment visits
Collateral contacts
Assess damage to child
Assess continued risk to child
Evaluate family indicators of abuse or neglect
Determine if abuse or neglect exists and continue case as open
Determine need to invoke authority of the court
Provide emergency services as needed
Provide feedback information to appropriate persons
Document record
(At this point, the case moves into ongoing service.)

Intake Activities

Generally speaking, a child welfare agency must provide intake services that will allow staff to evaluate the need for service, select an appropriate resource to respond to an identified need, and deliver the service or refer the client to a more suitable source of assistance. If no service is indicated, the agency member responsible for intake must state clearly why service will not be provided. In other words, the intake process is a working period during which both client and agency worker focus on solutions to a crisis or problem.

Neither the client nor the staff person can make responsible choices if the intake study is only a quick, superficial review of the problem. Both the agency and the client need data from each other before they can proceed further in the problem-solving process. The agency must acquire information in order to determine whether services can be offered, and the client must have adequate information in order to decide whether to use this service. Consequently, the intake practitioner must be open and direct in stating what the particular service consists of, how it is provided, by whom, where, how often, what it costs, and what obligations are placed on the client. The client must be helped to understand that the service may change over time according to his changed needs. Consumers often do not know what questions to ask, and the intake practitioner must give information that may elicit questions and must offer facts that may not occur to the user. In short, the client must know what he is getting into and what he is going to get out of it.

Inadequate intake service can destroy an agency's public image and add to community feelings of frustration and anger. Consequently, the agency must choose competent intake workers who command respect both in the agency and in the community and are able to interact with clients and with colleagues. They must also be adept at establishing referral contacts, in order to provide the network support essential for both long-term and emergency aid.

The initial contact will set the tone for ongoing service to the caller, and the staff member must be prepared to reach out to a multitude of organizations in the community service network. If a caller is clearly demonstrating mental pathology and if the agency has no mental health service, a strong relationship should exist with a facility so that a request for evaluation will be accepted as valid, and service will be made quickly available to the caller. This capacity for referral can best be achieved through a mutual trust built on a collaborative working relationship that has continuity. If a different person makes the calls each month, no matter how acute the situation, responsiveness is delayed while a new determination is made: "Does this person know what he is talking about, and does he have the authority to commit his agency resources and to request the collaboration of our services?"

Intake staff should have the knowledge and skill to cut through barriers and to produce emergency responses if they are needed. If a client walks into the reception area of an agency and announces an intention of suicide, the intake staff must know how to reach a mental health professional, even if the telephone operator responds, "I'm sorry, they're all in a meeting" or "I'm sorry, he's with a client" or "I'm sorry, they're out to lunch." With knowledge of how agencies operate or by remembering some personal contact, the intake staff will be able to reach help: "I know that Dr. Jones will not mind being interrupted; we've worked together on many cases." "Please tell Dr. Jones I'm the person he meets on the jogging trail in the morning and that now I need help immediately." "Please page them in the lunchroom; I know they won't mind." This aggressive outreach can be accomplished only by a staff member who has demonstrated competence both inside and outside the agency.

Intake staff must have the skill to enable each caller to give the necessary facts for determining a need for service. If facts are not elicited at the initial call, other staff members must gather the information. This is a great waste of agency resources and certainly produces frustration among staff members who are sent out on the basis of incomplete or unfounded information. In addition, clients may be harassed as a result. If initial information is limited, intake staff might call or write to the referring source or to the prospective client and ask for more information before reaching a decision about the need for assessment.

Intake is basically a desk-bound assignment that requires the capacity to listen carefully, to ask appropriate questions, to enable the caller to share both his concern and all known information, and then to make a judgment regarding needed follow-up. If this is a protective service intake, the judgment regarding follow-up must be based on the intake worker's belief that neglect or abuse is occurring, not on whether the worker knows or can prove who is neglecting or harming the child. The goal of the worker is to provide agency intervention before a crisis occurs.

The following referral was made to a child welfare service by a friend of the parents. The information was received the day after Thanksgiving:

John, age seven months, male. Parents: Doreen and John. Referent stated that child is sleeping in drawer and receives poor care. Child may be underfed but did visit doctor this week. Referent saw mother slap child for throwing a bottle on floor. Child has rash all over body, and it is alleged that there is no food in the house. This case is known to the welfare board.

Perhaps the friend was not willing to give additional information, but the data are indeed meager. The large gaps are perhaps more important than the content supplied. What would a worker want to know? Is sleeping in a drawer neglect? It is if the drawer is small and is closed into the bureau: the child will probably suffocate. If the drawer is large enough to hold the child and is suitably padded and located in a safe place, then it is more than adequate. Which doctor saw the child? Perhaps the physician saw the child because of the rash, and the parents have medication for it. If there is no food in the house on the day after Thanksgiving, the situation may be more serious than at another time of the year. However, we do not know when the friend visited the parents. The call came in at 9:10 A.M., but the visit may have been a week ago. What events, if any, preceded the slap when the child threw his bottle? Did the slap cause any apparent injury to John? Is the friend aware of the type of aid the parents receive from the welfare board? Can the friend be of any aid to the family if it appears that some service may be needed to improve parenting?

The social worker assigned to this assessment probably will want to contact the referent again, assuming that the friend will cooperate in supplying information. Preferably, however, the worker should have obtained additional information on the first contact, or at least should have determined that the referent was unable to answer any of the above questions, thereby giving the worker a better sense of the priority for seeing this family.

At the outset, intake workers should gather information on all persons involved in a family system, including age, sex, relationship, school or occupation, and living arrangement. The following questions also should be asked: What is going on now, why is it a problem, who thinks it is a problem, what attempts have been made to do something about it, and why is a call being made now? What resources are personally available to the family through their own network of friends, neighbors, and relatives? Are the family members exposed to outside pressures? Specifically, do relatives place undue demands on them? Is there a lack of transit in a rural area? Does the family have minority status, resulting in communication problems or discrimination? If the caller is not a member of the family, how does he happen to know the family, and what responsibility does he have for the family? What motivated the call at this particular time, and what ongoing resource might this person be? It is important to tell the caller what the agency's next steps will be: "We cannot proceed unless we have the following information. How do you think we can get the necessary information?" Or "I will be reviewing any prior information we may have about this family and then follow up to determine if some service is indicated. Please call us if you remember or learn additional facts that will increase our knowledge about this family. Thank you for being concerned and for calling."

After the initial call, the worker should check computer and other files to determine the availability of prior data. If concerns have been expressed either by or for this family on a repeated basis, perhaps the assessment has never been adequate. The caller or the family members then need to be told: "You have called us four times in the last fifteen months, and we have never identified your need or provided a service. You clearly believe there is some problem, or you would not repeat your request for help. This time we are going to work together to determine what is happening and what should or can be done to change your situation." "Your daughter has run away four times, and we have never figured out what is causing the running. Something causes all running, so this time we are going to work together and find out how we can change the running." "Your mother has called us three times in the last three months to say that your baby cries a lot and is not properly cared for. When babies cry constantly, something is the matter. This time we are going to work with you until we find out how to help reduce the crying, for your sake as well as the baby's. It isn't easy to listen to a baby cry and not know how to help it or how to stop it."

Assessment Activities

There is no absolute line or separation between the intake or referral and the initial assessment phases. The assessment is a more detailed interview with the person or persons identified as having a problem or as requesting assistance. This interview may take place in the office if the client has transportation and is not suspicious of an out-of-the-home experience. If there are young children in the family, the agency should provide an appropriate facility for child care during interviews, such as a clean, safe spot to place an infant, a clear floor and toys for toddlers, a low chair or table and books or drawing material for preschoolers. Most agencies cannot provide a separate playroom with supervision, but an area in an interviewing booth or room is absolutely essential. Parents cannot be expected to focus on their problems or on the agency's need for information if they must have an active child on their laps during an interview. Neither can a staff member observe, interview, or gather information when concerned about a child's comfort or when chasing him about an office.

Some interviewers elect to take diverting toys or materials—a puppet or paper and pen or colorful magazines—with them for their in-home interviews. Such equipment is not necessary, however, when parents have provided play equipment for children. Food items, such as crackers or candy, should not be distributed, since they are messy and can represent an intrusion on the parents' rights to provide for children. There is no magic way to produce a cooperative child in an interview, but careful planning is both a courtesy to the child and an example for the parents.

Interviews should be arranged to mesh with the client's schedule as well as the staff member's. If the report is urgent (father has just been taken to prison, children are alone, mother is in uncontrolled rage), the agency must respond promptly. If there is a telephone and if there is someone to notify, a staff member should call and state that he expects to visit the house within two hours.

Even if a person has requested service such as "I need day

care for three children," she may feel apprehensive about the agency's response to her request. Perhaps her prior experience with helping persons has been rejection or disapproval of behavior or living arrangements. Perhaps she has never requested help and so must base her expectations on her past experiences with relationships or on reports about services from the experiences of family members or friends. People rarely expect to get help, even if they request it. Furthermore, a request for help does not mean a willingness to accept it. People fear that others may thereby learn of their misfortunes. They also fear that they will be blamed for the problem, will be expected to make most or all of the changes to solve the problem, will lose their autonomy or be manipulated by others, will be forced by other family members to make changes, and will have to admit behavior that is unacceptable even to themselves. Moreover, some people find dependency unacceptable, since it revives unpleasant experiences of being a child. The person who is unable to be flexible about role behavior will also find it difficult to move from independence to some dependence on others.

If someone outside the family has reported a need for help, this individual is even less likely to expect something positive from the interaction. Fear and anxiety are normal responses to the staff member's announced intention to conduct an interview. All persons develop a system of defenses to protect themselves against physical or emotional assault. Therefore, it is solid practice to conduct the initial interview as soon as possible after the announcement of the plan. This reduces the time of anxiety and also allows the worker to observe and gather information before the person's defenses are fully mobilized. If the time interval is too long between announcement and arrival, the worker will be observing the defense system rather than the family situation. It is rarely useful, however, to make unannounced visits "to catch the person off guard."

At the initial interview, the staff member should introduce herself, give the name of the agency she represents, and then state the purpose of the visit. She should try to enter the situation with an open mind, without prior assumptions. In a child abuse referral, the client should be asked to describe the situation that might have prompted the referral. Some clients will deny that there is a problem, even if they themselves have contacted the agency. In such instances the interviewer must be firm: "You were troubled when you called me, so it will be best if we talk for a while about what was happening when you called." Or "Someone thinks you need help and took the time to call us. We find that if someone thinks there is a crisis, it is important to find out what is happening." Or "We have a report that John is hurt. It is my job to find out what is going on." Some clients will insist that everything is all right now: "You are right. There was a terrible fight here last night. John did get a black eye and went to school looking horrible today. We were drinking, and we should have stopped. It has never happened before and won't happen again." There is no better way to get rid of a child welfare worker than to describe the scene, admit guilt, and promise to refrain from any further trouble. It wraps up a process in five minutes. The worker should persist, however, and not allow the client to manipulate her into dropping the interview prematurely.

Other clients may manifest apathy or depression: "Do what you want. You're going to do that anyhow. What chance do I have?" Others may express outright hostility. They may be angry because someone has exposed their family situation to the outside world; or they may be angry at any type of interference, and the child welfare worker represents an authority that interferes; or they may be asking for help and take for granted the agency's rejection.

Many parents express the fear of legal consequences and will promptly ask, "Are you going to take my child away?" Someone with no decision-making power has probably given them an answer to that question, with comments such as "If you don't stop running around, the state will take your children" or "Don't worry, the state doesn't want your children, and we'll do everything to help you keep the children. We'll vouch for you." At this point the worker might fall into the trap of dodging the client's question by reciting the purpose of the agency: "We believe that families are the most important unit for raising children. . . . We will do everything in our power to help your family to stay together." Later the worker may conclude that the children are in jeopardy. If a court hearing is then required, the parents' attorney may say, "I understand that during your first visit you said that you would do everything in your power to hold this family together. Please list for this court the action you have taken and the resources you have used to keep the family intact." The worker may be hard pressed to respond and thus may be giving poor protection to children. There is only one answer to the question of whether the children will be taken away: "To be honest, I don't know." As assessment progresses, it is the worker's obligation to inform the client of the process: "I am concerned that our plan is not working, your behavior hasn't changed, and we may need to move John for a while." If the agency does decide to move the child, the parent must immediately be informed of the decision.

During an initial visit to the applicant's home, the social worker will observe the neighborhood—its apparent safety, environmental health and hazards, public transit, access to stores and community facilities, and adequacy of public services; the house—privacy, adequate heat, water supply, safety, and cooking and bathing facilities; the appearance and behavior of family members; the resistance to or motivation for service; and the nature, extent, and seriousness of the problem presented. If agency intervention seems warranted, the worker will commit resources to a mutually agreed-upon plan: "It is apparent to me that you do care about your children but that you need some help to care for them. First, we must plan to have a doctor see the children. Then I will ask Mrs. Smith, who works with our agency, to give day care. I would like to take you to meet her and to discuss your children's needs and activities with her. Also, if you agree, I will help you call your landlord so we can find out about screens for some windows. It isn't easy to handle babies or food or to sleep with all these flies and mosquitoes."

If there is no community resource to meet the applicant's need, the social worker should show sympathetic understanding and possibly direct the client to family, church, or friends. "I know that you want a service for your children after school, but we have no one who cares for school-age children. Do you know any local group that may take on such a project? If you are concerned, there may be other parents who have the same concern. Perhaps you could take turns with the children after school." This response to the lack of community resources is not meant to place burdens on the person asking help, or to expect the client to solve his own problems. It is an attempt to assess whether the client does know of others with similar needs and whether the consumer may be able to initiate a self-help program. Staff must practice within the limits of what any community can provide. They must also use imagination in asking for service from agencies, including requests for exceptions to stated policies.

The service plan must take into account the current situation, the short- and long-range needs of the client; his own view of the problem, including causes and solutions; the assets and resources of the agency and other community resources in meeting the specified needs; and an assessment of the long- and short-range advantages and disadvantages of this service for the consumer. In certain instances, however, action may need to be taken—for example, regarding the placement of a child—even though only minimum information is available. The urgency of the service provision may be due to several factors, especially the lack of other community services, the desertion or death of a parent, or the sudden emotional breakdown of a member of the family.

Intake and assessment in some types of service and situations do not need to be lengthy. For example, the admission of a child to a day care program for a trial period may be an easy transition for both parent and child. If the child has received adequate parenting and is mature enough in his development to make the change, and if the parents support the child in the program, then the use of the service may be very rewarding for both parent and child. This may not be so for the neglected, abused, or troubled child whose parents are facing a crisis. A longer intake process, with the collection of additional data, may be required in order to understand the child's particular needs, the readiness of the parents to accept and support the child's needs, and the capacity of the agency staff to supply the child's needs by engaging him in a special group or program. The intake process, including assessment of the child in the program, may result in referral to a more specialized program, including possible placement away from home.

Even though the intake process may be shortened when the child and his parents display strengths and assets, staff must still be prepared to assess in more detail if problems in the transition develop. We would like to believe that all the dynamics of a family can be observed and defined during the intake process, but the following case shows that this is not always possible.

Willard C., age four, was brought to the day care center by his mother, a young woman who seemed quite at ease in her request for care for her son. She wished to try the program, since one of her friends had used the center about two years ago and was well pleased with it. Mrs. C. was contemplating part-time work and would be looking for employment as soon as Willard felt comfortable. Willard was described as a healthy child, relaxed around other children, sleeping well, no eating problems, although he was occasionally withdrawn and shy. The father, who did not come for the interview, was reported as favoring day care so that the mother could work. A sister, age nine, in the fourth grade, was doing satisfactorily in school.

Willard came three days later for a visit and then attended for five hours regularly every day. The mother's description of Willard was basically accurate, and he moved fairly easily into the program, showing no more than the usual signs of discomfort in transition from home to center. After about ten days, however, the mother seemed to have considerable discomfort about his adjustment, and he began to cling to her more and more when she left him off and picked him up. At the same time, his behavior in the program became erratic. Several times a day, he would anxiously inquire about his mother—he needed her; when would she arrive? The brief discussions with Mrs. C. at the beginning and end of his day did not sufficiently help the staff understand the reasons for his distress. Consequently, she was asked to come in for a longer interview.

After a considerable review of Willard's behavior elsewhere, and the staff's recognition that she seemed harassed when she left him and picked him up, the mother revealed that she had not found work and really did not want to work. This pressure came mostly from her husband, who believed that it would be helpful to both Willard and the mother for him to be in a preschool program. She admitted that she might be too close to Willard, and "maybe he depends too much on me." However, she did not see her employment as an answer to the problems. It was apparent that her own anxiety over the separation, which she was able to conceal with great effort, had broken out and was affecting Willard. She decided, after a second interview, that they should try to work on this problem now, rather than have it continue. Willard remained in the program, and the parents attended a family counseling program affiliated with the center. In about two months, Willard's behavior improved as his mother became less anxious about releasing him. She did locate part-time employment about two months after that.

The staff of this agency realized that Willard's problem was not his alone but, instead, involved the whole family. Other agencies might have continued to attempt to relieve Willard's stress with minimum involvement from the parents. If so, the underlying problem—the mother's resistance to employment and the effect of her feelings on Willard—might never have been resolved or might have been poorly resolved. His lack of adjustment justified her avoidance of employment, and soon she could have him removed from care. At the same time, she did want to help Willard and herself become more separate and therefore was willing to have him in day care. Although she feared the separation, she also hoped that it would help to produce the needed change in their relationship. She may not have realized that such a change would require a greater effort on her part. This realization initially caused anxiety but probably also brought a feeling of relief, since she was partly aware that things had to be different. The fact that a healthy separation ultimately was achieved in a short length of time suggests this mother's capacity and readiness to deal with the issue.

Part of intake responsibility is to make use of other services to supplement one's own service. In the above case, the counseling program, which was related to the day care center, supplied a supplemental service to the family. (The Thames, Grace, and Loren cases in Chapter Four should also be reviewed, since they contain illustrations of intake service.)

Workers should not unduly blame themselves if important dynamics or problems emerge soon after the delivery of service starts. The initiation of service, by itself, may activate problems that were lying just below the surface of consciousness, ready to emerge, and that would have occurred whether service was begun or not.

Not all problems can be resolved at once. In fact, an applicant may not be able to describe or even list all his problems. These problems may have taken a long time to develop and may be imbedded in family life, in community problems, or in business or governmental policies and practices. The worker should help the applicant list his major problems and then should take a single problem at a time, starting with the one most critical to the family's need for survival as well as the one that the consumer is most able to work on. In some instances the agency may be unable to respond to any of the presenting problems. For example, the consumer may believe that his problem can be solved by the placement of a child when, in fact, he really needs to apply for income maintenance and to secure extensive health care for the child. If the family agrees, then the major service the agency provides is referral to assure that the parents obtain the needed services.

What the client *wants* may not be what the client *needs*. Although we must respect and seriously consider the client's solution to a problem, the solution may not benefit the family in either the short or the long run. When we are desperate, we make decisions too quickly, and they may not be constructive. The intake-assessment process encourages thoughtful decision making. When there appears to be a clear discrepancy between what the consumer wants and what will benefit the family, the social worker must present his observations and propose an area of agreement over how they will begin to work together. There can be no mutual assessment if the two parties cannot agree on either the nature of the problem or the first steps to resolve it.

Mrs. Barnett came to the child welfare agency asking that her three-year-old son, Larry, be placed in a foster home. Her neighbor had had a daughter placed after she could no longer put up with the child's behavior. Mrs. B. expressed willingness "to sign anything, even a permanent release form," to get some relief from this child's demands. Mrs. B. has three older children. Home visits and further discussion revealed that Mrs. B. was highly disorganized but essentially adequate in caring for all the children. A day care service was available for Larry. In addition, a homemaker service was used to help the mother plan and organize, and counseling sessions were begun to help the mother sort out why this particular child represented such an impossible burden. Data from the day care provider regarding his provocative behavior increased understanding of the dynamic. The mother agreed to try this arrangement for six months and then reconsider the need for foster care.

It was tempting to accept voluntary placement of a preschool child who had no described handicaps. However, exploration of the total situation allowed the agency to develop a service delivery plan that did not respond to the client's request but did respond to the problems that prompted the request. Beginning interviews do not always reveal the extent of family difficulties, nor do they readily produce appropriate solutions. The interviewer needs "to formulate a notion of the problem and its meaning" (Compton and Galaway, 1975, p. 280). He also needs to be alert to all possibilities, so that a family does not become locked into one service, such as foster care, when other options might be available.

Coordination of Intake and Assessment

The Celia Rhoads case below reveals the benefit of early and intensive intervention to improve a mother's parenting skills. It also shows some gaps in information and an omission in reaching out to significant persons in the family's network. We can only guess at whether outreach would have significantly affected the case outcome. Six events, which may take place during an intake and initial assessment, are illustrated: (1) agency collaboration in service delivery; (2) joint agency assessment of the family problem; (3) direct casework service to the parent; (4) referral to other services; (5) administrative manipulation to expedite service; (6) case acceptance, after six weeks, in a coordinative role.

Marilyn Rhoads, age forty-three, mother
Anthony Marsha, age thirty-six, father
Celia Rhoads, age one month

Background Information: Marilyn's parents are both in their eighties and live in Halltown, about thirty miles away. Marilyn's mother is placing pressure on Marilyn to marry Tony. Tony's father and stepmother both live in Phoenix, about ten miles away. Tony's father told Marilyn that he would take Celia away and place her for adoption if she does not marry Tony. The stepmother stays out of it.

Tony is employed as a laborer in a shoe factory, and he is Marilyn's sole source of support. He complains of chest pains frequently, is described as having a very short temper, and is probably mentally retarded.

Marilyn is markedly obese, has a history of hypertension and depression, and her family has a history of diabetes. She and Tony live in his poorly constructed cabin with minimum toilet facilities. Her husband died eighteen months ago. He was a heavy drinker and died in bed following a very intense, short period of drunkenness. They had no children.

This family was brought to the attention of the child protective services (CPS) unit by the public health nursing agency (PHNA) and the community hospital in an adjoining town. The hospital had initially referred the case to the PHNA following Celia's birth as an emergency caesarian section. The mother had entered the emergency service complaining of abdominal pains. She denied any knowledge of pregnancy, did not relate to the child in the hospital, stated that she did not want the child, and revealed no knowledge of parenting an infant. The hospital staff and the public health nurse had also ascertained that the home conditions were marginal for a young child. During the mother's confinement in the hospital, options of care for the child were discussed. The mother initially agreed to adoption, then changed her mind after her parents insisted that she must raise the child herself. Risk factors at the point of hospital discharge were considered as follows: age and inadequacy of the parents, poor living conditions, high risk for health problems, mother's lack of knowledge of pregnancy and rejection of child, mother's lack of experience with children.

Initially, the case was not accepted for CPS because the PHNA was active. Two days after the mother went home, the PHNA asked for homemaker service, but the request would be given low priority unless the case were open to CPS. Therefore, the case was accepted for CPS, which facilitated the immediate assignment of a homemaker.

Ten days after case opening, the mother was providing
only marginal care to Celia, and she still refused all care arrangements except keeping the baby. The public health nurse and the
homemaker had made three visits to the mother to teach her
child care methods. The nurse's concerns at this time included
poor bonding between mother and child, inappropriate feeding
techniques, inadequate formula preparation, and the mother's
leaving Celia unattended. In addition, during the last visit four
days previous, the cabin was filled with flies, and there were
feces from seven cats scattered over the floor. Marilyn did clean
these up when requested to do so by the nurse. However, she
refused instruction in bathing Celia, preparation of formula, and
other child care tasks. A physician at the Family Practice Center
will see Celia, and Marilyn sees her own physician in Halltown,
where her parents live. Both the public health nurse and a
homemaker will visit Marilyn twice a week, each on different
days. A social worker assigned for further assessment submitted
the following report:

I made my initial visit with the public health
nurse, who introduced me to Marilyn. Marilyn was
polite, but her affect was very flat. She told us she
was going to tell Tony on this date that he could
no longer stay with her. She expressed worry about
this because he has a violent temper and hits her
when he becomes angry.

Marilyn had obtained an application for Aid
to Families with Dependent Children (AFDC), and
I helped her fill it out. I made certain that she was
aware that she would be eligible only if Tony was
not living there or visiting every night.

Celia appeared healthy, but Marilyn did not
show a great deal of interest in her. She held Celia
awkwardly and far away from her. There was no
interaction between her and her baby.

A few days before the next home visit, I
learned from the public health nurse that Marilyn
has been doing well with the baby. Her improvement has been more than was expected, and the
nurse is no longer as worried about the care Celia is
receiving. She stated that Marilyn has been expressing a desire to move but is afraid because Tony has
threatened to use "hit men" if Marilyn leaves with
the baby.

Home visit three and a half weeks later: During this visit, Marilyn was less flat in affect than she had been during the previous visit. I observed limited interaction between her and Celia. She told me she didn't know what to do about moving away from Tony. I had informed her that I had not yet submitted her AFDC application, since Tony was still living there. Marilyn said she was afraid of Tony, as well as his brother. She had had a big fight with Tony last Sunday, and he had attempted to choke her. I talked with her about the women's shelter, which provides counselors for women in her circumstances. She agreed to see a counselor there if I arranged it.

Celia's breathing sounded congested, very labored, and raspy. Marilyn said she had an appointment in five days with the physician. She said Celia's cold had just started getting worse.

Following this visit I called the public health nurse, telling her how congested Celia was. She decided to make a visit today. She called back later to state that the congestion was confined to the upper respiratory tract. She felt that Celia would be all right, since she would be seeing the physician next week.

Home visit one week later: During this visit I found Marilyn's affect totally appropriate. She was also interacting spontaneously with Celia. Celia was gurgling and cooing and no longer appeared ill. Marilyn told me that Celia had received her first series of shots two days ago.

Marilyn said that she has had no further fights with Tony but has been thinking more about leaving him and moving to Arbortown. Tony's friend will be released from jail in a couple of months, and she believes that Tony will live with him. She expressed anger that he would leave her without resources but expected her to stay until he left. I told Marilyn that I had talked with the women's shelter, and we made plans to visit there next week.

I learned from Marilyn that she has had problems in the past with sugar in her urine. She also told me that there is a history of diabetes in her family.

Marilyn seemed more comfortable with me

during this visit. Since the involvement stage seemed to be completed, I began making small demands. I told her that she would have to decide how she was going to get rid of her cats if she really wanted to get into the shelter. I also told her that she should be thinking about the land and cabin that Tony had signed over to her when he was having financial problems. This asset is keeping her from receiving food stamps.

One week later an interagency conference was held. Following that, it was agreed that this referral was warranted and that the family is in need of ongoing casework. The extent of jeopardy has decreased since the referral date. The case objective is to continue to reduce jeopardy while maintaining the family unit; that is, the mother and child.

This case is typical of those received by public child welfare agencies. In this instance the family was referred to the child protective services unit, but the family could have been referred to the generalized social service intake unit of a public social and rehabilitation program.

Very little information was obtained on the father, and no attempt was made to meet with him after work hours, nor was an appointment even offered to him. The practitioners were apparently following the lead of the mother. However, he was supporting her financially and had signed over his cabin and land to her (admittedly to protect his assets). He might have been in need of medical care, and treatment might have reduced some of his violent behavior. The extent of his limitations was not known, but it was clear that he could hold employment and support three people. Stated simply, he was a resource that had been ignored. If his attitude toward his wife had changed, she might have bonded more quickly to the child. As it was, his withdrawal from her probably enabled her to become more engaged to the child. But we did not know this when the case was first referred, and violent fathers do not always remain violent. The cabin, as limited as it was, still belonged to him in principle, yet his wife was asking him to leave. In reality therapy, the treatment of choice in the agency, some consideration should have been given to this fact. However, the mother's use of an AFDC application was fairly strong evidence of her desire to live separately from her husband. The referral to the women's shelter might eventually result in the mother and father's reuniting.

In this case—unlike cases where no other service is being provided and where the family is unknown to any other program—the social worker had the luxury of depending on the observations and services of other practitioners in making an assessment. Consequently, she could balance her own observations against those of people who had known the mother over a longer period of time and in greater depth. The positive information about the family, received just prior to the social worker's second visit, indicated that the jeopardy to the child was reduced and also revealed Marilyn's ambivalence over leaving Tony. However, Celia's congested breathing alarmed the social worker sufficiently to make her call the public health nurse. Should she have told Marilyn that she was going to call the nurse? She may not have decided to do so until after leaving the mother. Did she thereby violate any part of her relationship with Marilyn? Remember that this family was referred to a child protective services unit.

In the last assessment interview, it is clear that positive changes have taken place between mother and daughter, and these can probably be attributed primarily to the public health nurse and the homemaker. The mother is also ready to meet with the staff of the women's shelter, especially since the possibility of abuse continues and it appears that Tony will leave. The social worker has not encouraged any pursuit of the possible diabetic problem but, instead, encourages the mother to consider the more concrete matter of a move to the shelter. Not everything can be done at one time, and the studies for possible diabetes may have to be delayed until more pressing living problems are settled. If Marilyn had had symptoms of disease, then diagnosis and medical treatment may have taken priority and affected case activity. Notice that there is minimum medical data about Celia, and there is no clear report of a telephone contact or other communication with the physician.

In thorough intake practice, all the forces working on a family or person must be considered. Therefore, it was probably a serious omission not to talk with Marilyn's parents. They obviously have great influence over her, even though she is in middle age, and seemed to be the crucial factor in her decision to keep Celia. They are a "significant other" to Marilyn, an important part of her network, and they have been overlooked as a resource. One might say that they were negative in demanding that she keep Celia; nevertheless, they should have been contacted to see what positive influence they could wield in helping her to respond to Celia. Their further contact with Marilyn and the agency could have resulted in the release of Celia for adoption, or in Marilyn's more rapidly accepting Celia as her daughter.

Summary

All social agencies have policies and methods of collecting data in order to determine whether services can be provided to applicants. The intake and assessment process must evaluate the need for service, select the appropriate resources to respond to identified need, and either deliver the service or refer the consumer to the resource that can provide the service. The intake process can be viewed as a shared activity between two persons; both agency and consumer need data from each other in order to make sound decisions for reduction of problems. The intake process should not be a casual or superficial review of the situation; otherwise, it can be a disservice to the client. Inadequate problem and solution formulation may result in use of the wrong service, possibly increasing the problems.

Knowledgeable, competent, and respected staff should be assigned to intake. They must know their own agency and community services, must be able to elicit complete information quickly and sensitively, and must be able to cut through barriers to service acquisition. A wide range of information needs to be obtained about family members, family network, causes of current stress, the abilities of applicants to handle stress, the urgency of the request, the family's use of its own network and of other community resources, and environmental pressures on the applicants. Not all needs and requests can be met, and the agency must be clear in explaining the reasons that service cannot be provided. Intake staff must be prepared for a range of emotions and behaviors that may be expressed in the initial interviews: hostility, fear, denial of problem, overdependence, distress, guilt, and depression. Intake and assessment in selected situations, especially emergencies, may not have to be extensive, but staff must always be alert to a redefinition of the problem and the need for another service.

Special Annotated Bibliography

Compton, B. R., and Galaway, B. *Social Work Processes.* Homewood, Ill.: Dorsey Press, 1975. Chapter 7, "The Contact Phase," and Chapter 8, "The Contract Phase," are both very useful for the theory and practice of intake.

Shulman, L. *The Skills of Helping.* Itasca, Ill.: Peacock, 1979. This entire book on relationship and task accomplishment is outstanding, and many examples of practice are provided. The chapters on "The Preliminary Phase of Work" and "The Beginnings and the Contracting Skills" are excellent for the intake practitioner. The findings for practice are based on extensive research.

CHAPTER THREE

Helping Families Cope with Separation

Separation—the loss of a loved person or persons—does not take place in every child welfare service, but it occurs often enough to warrant examination of the event and of the activities that will reduce its negative impact on both children and adults. Separation invokes strong feelings—fear, anger, guilt, sadness, depression, loneliness, helplessness, relief—on the part of foster parents, siblings, and social worker, as well as the child. Prolonged separations related to child welfare services are often traumatic for several reasons: family members have been experiencing severe strains prior to separation; the parents have minimum control over the plan; the child has almost no choices; and authorities, such as the social agency and the courts, may intervene and change plans in unanticipated ways. In short, placement can be a smooth process, but it is often chaotic.

Separations are not always undesirable. People may be glad to separate from a spouse, a job, or a community, but they may still have feelings of loss and loneliness, which may in turn bring feelings of disconnectedness, barrenness, and emptiness, including self-rejection and self-alienation. The common factor seems to be an absence of emotional relatedness. Three kinds of loneliness can occur; if all three are experienced, the person may feel an overwhelming sense of loneliness. The first is existential, the recognition that each of us is ultimately alone in the universe. Part of existential loss is the separation we have from our previous selves, our childhood or adolescence, and the nostalgia we may have to return to an earlier period in our lives. The second loneliness is reactive, the response we have to any recent loss. The third type is pervasive loneliness, a serious problem for those who have lifelong patterns of difficulty in forming lasting and permanent relationships but who can still relate to others. If a person cannot resolve existential loneliness, then there will be an added problem in handling reactive loneliness. If both existential and pervasive loneliness are present, then a person will have greater difficulty in resolving a reactive loneliness (Applebaum, 1978).

Loneliness following separation often is accompanied by anxiety, possibly because one fears continued isolation and even, though irrationally, total obliteration of the self. A person who fears obliteration probably has regressed to an earlier emotional state, where separation meant death or a life-threatening danger. Such a person suffers not only a loss of emotional connectedness but a lack or reduction of cognitive abilities and a reduction in reason and judgment.

A loss usually requires a period of mourning. Mourning is a necessary process if individuals are to deal with the trauma of loss and to adapt to a changed situation. The several stages in the mourning process for adults have been fairly well accepted by practitioners, but they disagree about the ability of children to use the process—specifically, about the minimum age at which one is capable of mourning. Some believe that infants can mourn, others maintain that a child must be three or four years old to mourn, and others state that only after adolescence can a person truly mourn. Young children may need periodic discussion of a death to complete the mourning process (Furman, 1964; Bowlby, 1960; Krugman, 1971; Wallinga, 1966). Too frequently in practice, we do not allow children or adults adequate time for mourning; thus, they may carry unresolved emotional burdens indefinitely.

Separation Responses Among Children

Infants separated from their primary caretakers may develop a condition called "hospitalism," manifested by physical and mental retardation and a lack of responsiveness resulting from prolonged institutional care (Spitz, 1945, 1946b). They may suffer from "anaclitic depression," characterized first by weepiness and withdrawal, then by rigid behavior, and ultimately by insomnia, illness, and emaciation (Spitz, 1946a). A three-phase sequence of protest, despair, and detachment has also been identified. In the first phase, the child cries loudly, searches for the parent and is restless. If the parent does not return, noisy demands slowly discontinue, and the child lapses into apathy. If a substitute caretaker arrives, the child will usually relate and recover. Without a reliable parent, the apathetic phase lasts about three weeks, and then the third phase begins. In this phase, the child has a vacant stare and becomes oblivious to events around him: he often seeks satisfactions from his own body, loses his appetite for food, and shows little emotion (Bowlby, 1960).

Brief and more normal separations experienced by young children do not result in such stressful responses. The toddler or preschool child becomes more capable of managing separation from parents for longer periods of time. The control of bowel and bladder functions enhances self-esteem and feelings of independence. The development of or increase in abilities or functions such as mobility, speech, memory, and reality testing enhances the child's capacity to accept or endure some separation. The child can feel safe in even initiating his own separation, for short periods, from the parent. This independence and the gratification received from persons other than the parent further increase his sense of security. Satisfactory relationships with other adults enable the child to learn that persons besides the parents can be trusted; however, if his parents leave him—even for short periods—in the care of persons he does not like, he probably will protest (Spitz, 1945, 1946a; Bowlby, 1960; Simsen, n.d.).

When the child begins to develop a sense of time, or of certain daily events, he will be able to understand that the parents plan to return at a certain time—assuming, of course, that there have been reliable separations before. "We will be home after naptime" or "We will be home just as you are having lunch" or similar statements with meaning for the child will enable him to tolerate absences. But young children are sensitive to the loss of the parent for several days, and they may retaliate with a cold, indifferent response when parents return. When a major loss or separation occurs, such as placement in a foster home, toddlers will often regress in their development. They may become demanding and dependent on others, requesting to be fed, wanting pureed foods rather than table food, losing full or partial control of bowels and bladder, calling for drinks of water at night, and making other demands. The requests, which may seem totally illogical to the substitute caretaker, probably represent the child's desperate internal needs and calls for help. The substitute caretaker may have spent the entire day with the child, preparing favorite foods and reading favorite stories, and is expecting a relaxed bedtime. He is startled when the child runs about the room, or laughs uncontrollably, or breaks a favorite toy by smashing it deliberately. The usual response is to stop the child with physical control or to let him know that "This isn't very nice when we've been nice to you all day." Better responses to the emotion that prompts the behavior might include: "It isn't easy to be away from home." "Most children worry when they don't see their parents." "When children are frightened, it is often so hard to talk about it that they show their pain by hurting something special." "I think you are hurting, and I want to comfort that hurt." "You might think that if you scare me away by your actions, then you are loyal to your mommy."

When toddlers experience lengthy separations, apathy may take place, including withdrawal, fearfulness, and a reduction of food intake. Tearfulness and crying are common, especially in the early stage of separation, and elements of the mourning process may be evident. The hospitalized child becomes very anxious with strangers and often shows fear and anger when parents depart. He may manifest restlessness, hyper-

activity, rhythmic rocking, and regressive behaviors such as soil-
ing and a refusal to chew solid food; diarrhea and vomiting may
also occur.

As the child approaches the age of six, he begins to inter-
nalize parental standards and values. He has acquired a sexual
identification, can function with some independence, and shows
an interest in objects and activities around him (Wallinga,
1966). Practitioners and auxiliary caretakers, relieved at the
child's apparent interest in things around him, may try to divert
him from an impending or recent separation by remarks such as
"I want to tell you about the fine playground at this school."
"You always talked about having a dog, and this family has two
friendly dogs. I think they are even allowed to sleep in the bed-
rooms." "This father drives a bakery truck, and I think he will
be glad to take you with him to deliver the baked goods." "I
saw you looking at the fish tank in the doctor's office. Do you
think you would like to have fish and take care of them?" Similarly, a day care provider may tell a parent, "Don't linger over
the goodbyes. When you go, he cries briefly, but then we find
something to attract his attention." Or a foster parent may say,
"It's better if she doesn't see her mother. Then she is not upset
so often."

If the child's feelings of pain are not addressed, however,
these feelings will continue to consume energy that could be
used more productively for the healing process. It is important
to make remarks such as "We could talk about the friendly dogs
at this house, but I think it is more important to talk about how
scary it is to go to a strange place" or ". . . how you must be
wondering what is happening now with your family" or ". . .
how you must be wondering about what you could have done
to change this day" or ". . . how it might feel good to cry or
scream or tell me how mad you are at me."

To address and invite pain in this way requires the courage and stamina to face and deal with one's own pain, to acknowledge that the child welfare role does produce separation
pain, and to develop methods to identify painful feelings. Every
practitioner must be clear about how he deals with personal
pain. Some professionals garden; it releases tension to dig in the

dirt. Some split logs, some hit tennis balls, some meditate or jog. Some bury pain and cry when something lovely occurs. The important accomplishment is to acknowledge that we produce pain and that we experience pain. Thus, there must be a method to cope with the pain produced and experienced. Many professionals are making use of staff meeting time to address this issue, and this is enhancing their practice energy and skill as well as reducing overwhelming feelings.

Although the child up to age six has developed some independence, regressive behavior may still occur on separation: enuresis, theft, lying; magical, irrational thoughts; fears, depression, hostility, and withdrawal; setbacks in school performance; nightmares and other somatic problems. The older school-age child generally is more self-reliant and has acquired more skills and learned better body control. Since he has had more experience in relating to adults such as teachers and clergy, he may have a better ability to endure separation than the younger child. He will also be better able to understand the reason for separation, although the emotional trauma will still be severe. Practitioners should work with a child in this age group at his developmental level, rather than according to chronological age. One ten-year-old can still be very dependent; another can be more like an adolescent in emotional maturation.

In adolescence a major conflict is the dependence/independence struggle. If a child is placed away from home, or separated from parents, the normal transition to adulthood may be delayed, since the adolescent now must become independent without the parents' support and must face the loss of dependency. Furthermore, if separation from family occurs, the adolescent's development of internal controls may be damaged, resulting in runaway activities, defiance of societal and peer group codes, taunting and testing those in authority, truancy, shoplifting, sexual acting out, and the like. If his behavior becomes unacceptable, the practitioner must recognize that the separation may have interrupted the normal development of internalizing controls and be prepared to focus discussions not only on the unacceptable behavior but on the difficulty of control: "It isn't easy when everyone expects you to remember limits and you keep forgetting what is expected. Sometimes people forget because they have too many other things on their minds. One thing that some people worry about is whether they will ever be able to be in charge of themselves. That is especially difficult if someone has just separated you from a familiar place, showing that someone else is in charge anyhow. So why try to control behavior?"

Effects of Separation on Natural Parents

The feelings of natural parents when confronted by foster placement of their child are as complex and as broad in range as the reasons for the placement itself. Among the emotions which parents most often experience are insecurity, shame, guilt, and mourning. On a practical level, parents must face the loss of a member of the family and a familiar routine, but, more important, they must face a set of ambiguous and inconsistent reactions. On the day of actual placement, for example, parents may experience such feelings as sadness, emptiness, anger, guilt, bitterness, relief, and thankfulness. They must adjust to a new status and a new conception of themselves, and they are aware of the changed light in which others—friends, relatives, colleagues—will view them. The failures of natural parents become public with the event of foster placement; family problems are opened up to the scrutiny of caseworkers and perhaps to that of others in the community. Parents may lose esteem in the eyes of their peers and may feel inadequate, shameful, rejected by both child and society, and censured.

If parents are feeling useless and censured, it is perfectly logical that they may struggle to recover some autonomy— sometimes by active or subtle attempts to sabotage the new caretaker with messages such as these: "You won't have to stay very long." "We'll get a lawyer working on this, and then we'll see who can take you away." "You're our kid, and we'll get you back. You don't have to listen to those other people." "When you come home, we're going to get you new furniture."

Practitioners should make clear to parents that they understand the parents' strong feelings about the loss of autonomy: "It isn't easy to have someone else making decisions about your child's life." "Sometimes parents have a need to let their children know they are still in charge, and we can understand that you may have that need." "We must try to work out a way for you to assure your child of your continuing love even though you need to separate for a while." "It's important to talk about how terrible you must feel. You have a right to feel that way." Sometimes comments such as these reduce the parents' need to prove autonomy in sabotaging placement. At the very least, they send a message that the practitioner recognizes and accepts the feelings that parents are having.

Guilt may be an accompanying emotion at separation, resulting from a parent's request or acceptance that the child must be placed or his relief once the child has departed. Conversely, a parent may regard the placement as a punishment for the child and be secretly pleased at the child's supposed pain in leaving his family. The overriding feeling of natural parents, however, is likely to be grief at the loss of their child and at their inability to share in his future growth and development.

Effects of Separation on Foster Parents

Feelings of sorrow and loss by foster parents at the departure of a child must not be underestimated. Practice reveals that foster parents often react strongly to the separation. New and inexperienced foster parents may agree verbally with the social worker that it "will be difficult" to see a foster child leave their home and return to natural parents or move on to an adoptive placement. Yet, when the actual event or separation is introduced, the emotional reality of the situation is far different from the intellectual discussion prior to placement. Even experienced foster parents have difficulty at the point of separation.

The extent of distress for foster parents will be related to at least four variables. One of these is the maturity of the couple and their capacity to give without expecting too much in return and to recognize, both emotionally and cognitively, that the foster parent's function is to provide temporary parenting to a child in need. A second factor is the length of time that the child has been with them and the age of the child on admission. The foster parents of a child who is supposedly abandoned with no likelihood of natural parents' ever showing up may assume a larger natural parent role; they may invest more emotionally because they believe that the child will never see his natural parents and probably will never leave the foster home. If the parents suddenly appear and are able to obtain the release of the child, this separation may be more difficult for the foster parents. A third variable is the adjustment that the child has made in the home; if, for example, the child has become a close companion and playmate for a natural child in the home, the foster parents can understandably miss his extra contribution to family life. The fourth variable is the situation to which the child is going. If the foster parents are totally opposed to the plan, they may resist the change, attempt to undermine it, and carry anger over the transfer as well as sorrow in their perception of the inadequacy of the placement plan. In contrast, if the plan meets their standards, their happiness for the child will ease and counterbalance their feelings of distress over his departure.

If the child has presented unmanageable problems for the foster parents, the child's departure may produce more relief than distress. All practitioners have had calls from foster parents demanding removal of a child because of behavior that they could not tolerate. Sometimes the feelings of relief prompt foster parents to say that they want no more children. In such cases practitioners should try to identify the separation feelings the foster parents may be having: "It isn't easy to care for a child and have that care rejected." "You may wonder for a long time how Joan is and whether or not other families can deal with her." "Some people tell me that they feel guilty about being glad when a child leaves. This is a job that doesn't always bring success, and that can mean we see ourselves as failures."

If the child and family have never bonded, staff might plead for more time. This may intensify the foster parents' feelings of distress about separation, because the agency expected something that they could not produce. A relationship that does not materialize usually represents failure for the foster parents; the actual moment of separation documents the failure.

Practitioners sometimes assume that foster parents, because they have chosen a child-caring role and receive payment for it, may not have emotions similar to those of natural parents. This simply is not true, and social workers must be prepared to discuss separation with foster parents as with natural parents. They may carry guilt and shame over their perceived failures to provide adequate care, and the feelings of failure may be accurate. And when a child is removed because the foster parents have not performed adequately, their self-image of competence in parenting may be severely damaged. Feelings of anger toward the agency and social worker may be mixed with guilt for inadequate parenting. The conflicting feelings over separation will often parallel the natural parents' feelings of loss, although the intensity may be less.

Effects of Separation on the Placed Child

The effects of separation through foster placement are likely to be similarly complex in the case of the child. While the repercussions of placement vary according to the child's age and other characteristics, certain basic patterns can be expected. Just as the parents must adjust to an absence in their household, the placed child reacts to becoming an addition to his foster family. He must accustom himself to a totally different physical and social environment, and must shift his loyalties and affections to his foster parents. The child is expected to accept new forms of parenting, and this inevitably leads to anxiety and fear at a time when the child may still be living in his old home psychologically even as he inhabits his new home physically. Finally, the child mourns for his parents, just as his parents mourn for him.

Mishne (1979) has found important differences between children who were abandoned by their parents and those who lost a parent through death. The abandoned child demonstrates more emotional problems; less empathy for others and less ability to relate to others; less capacity to learn, to perceive accurately, and to handle feelings; and more concern with self than the child of a deceased parent. The disturbance most noticeable

in children who have been psychologically or actually abandoned is described as pathological narcissism. This disturbance
may be expressed in an inordinate inflation of the self, a need
to be first or best, and an apprehensiveness about one's needs
being met. The child who can understand death, or who can be
helped to grasp the concept of a deceased parent, can accomplish some or all of the mourning process. That child can move
on. But the child who is abandoned by a parent can feed the
fantasy of return and reunion. The child who longs for a lost
parent may make a persistent quest for the parent and may rage
at everyone; as a result, he undergoes frequent replacements in
different homes or facilities. Moreover, in Mishne's view, the
abandoned child suffers a greater personal assault than the child
of a deceased parent. The child of a dead parent may feel that
he had something to do with the parent's death. But the abandoned child knows, or learns through longer and longer separation, that "I have been given up, put aside, left, or lost, and my
parent is still out there somewhere" (p. 32). Thus, he faces the
additional blow to self-esteem: there must be some personal de-
fect, or reunion could take place.

Because foster placement gives institutional confirmation
of some inadequacy in a given family's life, the child, too, may
view his placement as confirmation of his "badness" and may
express this through his feelings or behavior. He may see separation from his parents as a personal defeat or failure, and may
seek reasons for his apparent rejection in his own behavior or
personality. Conversely, he may become angry with his parents
for abandoning him; this anger may turn to guilt on the part of
the child in his attempt to negate or deny feelings of hostility
(Wallinga, 1966). Anger toward parents may lead to death
wishes for parents, which may subsequently elicit fears for their
safety and health.

The child's feelings about relationships with adults in general and parent figures in particular are usually as confused as
his feelings about the separation. His primary worries may be
characterized by withdrawal and feelings of fear: because one
close relationship has been brought into question, he may be
suspicious and hesitant about initiating others. His anger toward,

and distrust of, his own parents may lead him to react in a similar way toward foster parents. In an attempt to comprehend his new situation clearly, the child may ask for, and respond to, clear-cut rules by which he must live. Later on, after the child has become acclimated to his new home, he may fear a second rejection and act to precipitate it by testing the limits of rules and the strength of foster parents themselves.

If an adolescent has been unmanageable in a situation, and if this behavior contributes to the process of a separation from familiar caretakers, this youth might well bind his own anxiety about the new situation by asking for a clear set of expectations. Practitioners may mistakenly look on such a request as evidence that "All he really needed was a set of defined limits. His parents were loose and of course he didn't know what to expect." Similarly, the new caretakers may assume a position of great superiority: "You see, children need limits. Just hold them in line and they can be managed. It takes work, but see how it pays off to be firm." It is important, however, for the practitioner to respond to the adolescent's feelings, particularly if the request represents a shift in behavior: "Sometimes when people ask for rules, they are so frightened about a new situation that they think rules will help. And sometimes they do help to hold a person together. But they usually don't work after a while. So we need to plan to talk many times about how difficult it is to take on new people and new ways of living."

Elements of fantasy may also accompany separation. Some young children may feel that they have been kidnapped and thus have no control over their situation; they fear that they may never find or rejoin their natural parents. Even children who have stable early relationships fantasize that they really belong with the wealthy family in town or that they were born to royalty and the cribs were switched by mistake in the hospital nursery. It is, therefore, easy to comprehend that separated children believe that they have been snatched and are being hidden from their parents. After all, parents who love them would surely come to rescue them if they knew where they were.

Not all the social and emotional behaviors of the foster

child are related to the act of separation or placement itself. Many of the behaviors evidenced may spring from patterns or concerns that predate the placement. Therefore, the placement worker must carefully assess the child's behavior prior to placement, so that subsequent situations can be analyzed and dealt with in light of what has gone before.

Effects of Separation on Siblings

The repercussions of a child's placement affect not only the child and his parents; they extend to the siblings remaining with the natural family as well. Like the other family members, siblings grieve for the lost relationship with the placed child. They also have more intricate and ambiguous feelings: distress or anger at the placement of the sibling, satisfaction at the placement of the child, and fear of being placed themselves. Specifically, the siblings may feel hostile toward parents for placing the child, and guilty because of their anger and also because they may believe that their own unstated wishes or desires in some way resulted in the placement. They may feel that their parents did not give them complete or accurate information about the placement. If they were not fond of the placed child, gratification and subsequent guilt may occur, particularly where they had shown considerable hostility toward the child. Their fear of being placed themselves, perhaps for capricious reasons, may be expressed openly or indirectly—by statements that they wish to be placed, with accompanying guilt and ambivalence about wanting to leave home. In any case, the sibling is almost certain to experience a degree of withdrawal from, and suspicion of, the natural parents. Suspicion may result in compensatory behavior such as staying close to the parents, both to simulate affection and to watch the parents and prevent them from placing him. A younger sibling may believe that she too will be placed when she reaches the requisite age. She may fear that the child has been moved as a result of secret plans or plots and that she is also included in the plan in some way. Finally, the sibling may believe that some harm or calamity may befall the placed child if she is unable to join him.

Separation and the Practitioner

Because the social worker is the initiator of foster placement, he may experience stress stemming from a number of
sources. He is, in his profession, continually exposed to the un-
repressed feelings of clients—an occupational hazard unique to
the task of helping. The particular area of foster placement provides no exception to this pattern; in fact, the stresses associated with foster placement work may be particularly intense.
The child welfare worker, therefore, must be settled and secure
about his own separation experiences in order to remain steady
and stable with those facing the difficulties of separation, as
the following case attests:

A supervisor was reviewing the case of a mother who
wanted to place one of her two children. The social worker assigned to this case was black, experienced, and competent. For
three previous interviews, the mother had made it clear that she
was exhausted over this boy and that placement was her choice;
she had rejected all alternatives. (On another case carried by this
same practitioner, child placement had been effected only after
a lengthy process, with the worker slow to respond to the
need.) In a case conference to decide on further planning for
the boy, the supervisor raised the question of placement, since
the record seemed clear. After a lengthy discussion, the real
issue emerged: The worker was "sick and tired" of seeing so
many black parents place their children. She felt that all black
parents, including herself, had to resist the constant placement
of children, since such placements damaged the children and
perpetuated the image in America that black families had an
unusually high incidence of separations.

Child welfare practitioners must not be cavalier or callous
in recommending placement; at the same time, as Wilkes (1980,
p. 29) points out, they cannot be entirely negative and resistive
about placement and separation:

1. The worker who contends that separation is always to be
    avoided will lose credibility with the family if placement
    must occur.

2. The worker opposed to placement may deny or repress evidence that separation would be the most beneficial plan. Deterioration of family relationships may occur, and then there is not sufficient time to work out a constructive separation.
3. Placement is not an end in itself but is a process, and it gives everyone a chance to work through the steps necessary to accomplish the change.
4. Practitioners who oppose placement can become casual about the need for replacement, which requires the same working-through process as the original placement did.
5. If the placement experience has been a negative one or was poorly handled by the worker because of the worker's negative feelings about separation, then later work with the family may be difficult.

The stresses placed on the practitioner in a foster placement hearing are likely to come from the child's attorney, the parents' attorney, the court, the foster child, the natural parents, the worker's supervisor, and on occasion the foster parents. Demands made on the worker, and criticisms of him, are often unrealistic and irrational—making them all the more difficult to cope with in a logical and steady manner. Accusations from both children and parents are frequent: "You took me away from my parents." "You took my child away." "You didn't tell me this was going to happen." "You didn't tell the truth in court." Sometimes the worker may find that he is both cursed and blessed by the same family, and he will come to realize that, in such situations, expressions of appreciation and gratitude are rarely forthcoming.

It is the worker's task to share and to attempt to alleviate the pain and grief of separation, as well as to prepare family members to cope with the demands of the situation and to interpret the accompanying emotions and family dynamics. In addition, the worker must assist the foster parents in handling the impact of placement on the child's emotions and behavior. Because of the unusually powerful stresses placed on all concerned, the worker must prepare himself to approach these tasks even though he himself may feel emotionally drained.

The Child Welfare League of America (1959) lists five steps that the practitioner may take to alleviate the stress of separation:

1. Let the child know as quickly as possible that change will occur.
2. Help establish the belief that something will be positive about the change.
3. Allow the child to express anxiety and concern about the change.
4. Provide the child with an opportunity for reality testing in the new situation.
5. Look for evidence that the child is moving toward acceptance of placement.

The worker should begin discussion of the possibility of foster placement in small doses; in other words, planning and discussion should take the form of separate and tactful steps. As the child gains acceptance of each step, he will be emotionally prepared to move to the next. The worker must pace the placement process according to the child's ability to comprehend and accept it, without losing sight of any urgency that may spring from the natural parents' inability to sustain care of the child.

The discussion with the child regarding his placement must cover several important areas of concern. The child's natural home must be discussed realistically, not romanticized. The child must be permitted to express hostility, fear, and other emotions associated with separation; and the worker should be prepared and willing to discuss both realistic and illogical reasons for his placement: mental illness, illegitimacy, desertion, alcoholism, abuse, and "bad" (magical or primitive) thoughts, for example.

Workers should not assume that a child who has been neglected or abused by her parents therefore regards them as insufficient. Instead, children are likely to blame themselves and be sure that their behavior has prompted the rejection or need for separation. Children believe that their parents love them and could give care if they, the children, were worthy of the care.

A relatively new child welfare practitioner worked with an eight-year-old boy and his father, who lived in a shack on the city dump. In spite of the worker's best efforts, the father refused to move from the dump or to see that the boy attended school. Eventually the worker also learned that the boy, Joe, was often beaten over the back with a shovel that stayed conveniently at the shack doorway.

The court ordered agency custody, and during the next three months Joe was taken to eight foster homes. Each time he ran home, he was placed in a foster home that was farther away. At last the worker grew wise to the process and expended no energy on following Joe's trail. When a foster parent reported him missing, the worker drove to the dump and waited. After the eighth placement, she stated wearily, "Joe, no one is allowed to live on the dump. All children your age must go to school. Parents are not allowed to beat children with shovels. Soon you will be permanently harmed." The young boy turned an adorable face up to the worker and said, "My father doesn't mean to hurt me. He loves me." This statement of trust was then used to convince Mr. B. that he could respond to his son by setting up a nonneglectful and nonabusive living situation. Joe had demonstrated his commitment to his father, so the worker could now enable Mr. B. to reciprocate with acceptable parenting: he moved from the dump.

Finally, the worker must offer no false assurances during the course of placement discussions. Reassurance may only lead to further distrust by the child, because he has already learned that in trusting his parents he is now placed away from home. Too many false reassurances are given by parents, and social workers must not compound this error.

Once the child has been engaged in preliminary talk about placement, he may visit his new neighborhood and foster parents, perhaps taking special objects or toys to the new home. During this time, the child must be involved in the planning process as much as possible. He must be allowed to exercise as many choices as he can, so that he is able to maintain a sense of control over his own life. Too many choices, however, can overwhelm the child. Obvious choices include which toys to take, which clothing or item of clothing is to be worn, which snack shop to stop at for refreshment, which personal items stay in the child's hand and which go in the suitcase, and other choices unique to the situation.

Similarly, the natural parents, in spite of any inadequacies and the worker's potential dislike for them, must be involved in planning and executing the placement. This process strengthens both parents and child and improves the bonds between them. Foster parents also should be included and, depending on their skill level and previous foster care experience, should be kept apprised of separation problems and included in case-planning steps. The wise practitioner will use a variety of measures to individualize the separation process to each child's particular needs. As with all human relations practice, there is no exact formula for work with persons separating from each other; every situation requires the imaginative application of sound practice knowledge.

Separation Adjustments with a Preschool Child: A Case Example

The following case shows social service staff, foster parents, and natural parent working together to help a child achieve a temporary separation from the father.

Mr. Karlson, age thirty-five, divorced, requested temporary placement of his son, Harold, age four and a half. The father was planning to enter an alcoholic rehabilitation program for six weeks and could arrange no other plan for Harold. Mr. K. was employed, although having difficulty doing his work because of his drinking, and he was able to take a leave to try this treatment program. He and Harold were currently living with the father's girlfriend, but Mr. K. did not wish to leave Harold with her, since he was attempting to become less dependent on her. He also tended to blame her for his drinking. The father would enter the program in two weeks if an opening became available, and he expressed the hope that this was sufficient time to make plans. When asked by the social worker, he said that he had already told Harold that he was sick and needed to be in a special hospital for a month or so. Daddy would not see him during that time, Mr. K. had told his son, but they would get together again after he left the hospital. Harold had seemed to grasp the idea that "Daddy needed a nurse and doctor" but asked why the doctor could not see him at work or at home and give him medicine. He also wanted to wait at home while his father went to the hospital.

A few days later Mr. K. was notified that a foster home had been selected, and a plan was made for the father to bring Harold to the home and meet the parents. When the father arrived, it was obvious that he had been drinking, but he was still in control of himself and did show affection and concern for Harold. The social worker and Mr. K. had discussed some of the reactions Harold might have to this visit and to the impending separation, now scheduled for one week from the date of the visit.

Harold brought two of his favorite toys to the foster home, and the foster parents were quietly solicitous of him. He spent much of the time sitting on his father's lap, but a canary and a sturdy rocking horse attracted his interest briefly. The foster parents offered him milk and his favorite cookie. Harold was cautious around the parents, and he looked at many things with a guarded eye. The father later reported that Harold had not said much on the way home, had made a few negative comments about the house, but admitted he liked the swing in the side yard.

Harold's move to the foster home on the day before Mr. K.'s admission to the rehabilitation center was not too difficult for either of them. The father helped Harold move in, and the foster parents had prepared his choice of a luncheon sandwich. Since the social worker had agreed to bring Harold to the rehabilitation center after three weeks, Mr. K. was able to tell Harold exactly when they would see each other again.

Harold's adjustment was not unusual; he wet the bed several nights and was listless and somewhat withdrawn after the first week. He also woke up at night about five times, asking for a glass of milk and wanting to be reassured. When he talked about his father, he usually said that he would get well very quickly.

On the day of Harold's visit to see his father, he carried an old medicine kit that had been used by other foster children. Harold was delighted to see his father, and Mr. K. was very responsive to him and introduced Harold to a few of his friends. Harold's primary concern was about his father's health, and he insisted, very early in the visit, on giving his father "a shot to make him better." He was also enthusiastic enough about the results of his treatment that he told several people, including a staff member, that his "Daddy would leave soon, since I gave him a big shot."

Mr. K. picked up Harold the day after he left the center, and it was a happy reunion. Mr. K. told Harold how much he had missed him, and Harold was smiling and active. The foster parents joined the celebration, said goodbye, and wished them well.

Two months later Mr. K. called the agency again, because he was unable to discontinue alcohol use. His care of Harold had begun to deteriorate shortly after his treatment at the center. He had also been having arguments with his girlfriend over the drinking, and they were going to separate. Placement was arranged in the same home; but this time the separation was more difficult for Harold, and his father had more difficulty in supporting him through this transition. He gave conflicting stories about how long Harold would be in care. He was also unable to be direct with Harold about his illness, stating instead that he would have to work away from home and could not be with him every night. In addition, Mr. K. promised to visit Harold on specified days, but he would fail to show up. On the day of the third broken visit, Harold ran away from the home and was located about seven hours later. He ran away a second time after another one of his father's broken appointments and was found about three hours later.

In this case we see some of the common reactions to a separation experience. Harold's apparent denial of the father's illness and need for long treatment is a typical denial of the fear of losing his father. The use of the medical kit to heal his father is a fine example of the fantasy that a child can cure a disease and quickly bring his parent back. Children need some way to assure themselves that they can control their own lives, especially when faced with such an overwhelming loss. Harold's running away from the foster home was a more desperate attempt to locate a father who had, in the past, been quite reliable and a steady force in his life. Following both of the running episodes, Harold stated that his father was sick but would be better very soon, adding that "the doctors took him back to the hospital." Harold was experiencing what children feel when they are abandoned; they know that a parent is out there somewhere and absolutely will return again. Furthermore, father has not returned for a very good reason: he has been taken to the hospital by someone; otherwise, he would surely be coming to see his son.

Mr. Karlson was able to help his son through the first separation. During the second placement, Mr. Karlson's feelings about himself interfered with his capacity to inform Harold of the real reason for the separation. Harold certainly had some sense that the information offered was not accurate. We do know, from information provided by adults who, as children, were placed away from home, that children often have a fairly reasonable idea of why they are being separated from parents. Misinformation only creates more confusion and impairs a child's developing sense of perceiving reality. The misinformation probably increased Harold's pain over the need for a second placement and left him in greater panic, since he had to fantasize the "real" reasons for his placement. The social worker's attempts to relieve this distress may have helped somewhat, but the counseling was insufficient to reduce Harold's panic responses to this additional distress. A child must have accurate and age-related information from the parent.

Summary

In child welfare practice, separation usually refers to the loss of a parent or child. Several kinds of loneliness may be evoked by loss: existential, reactive, and pervasive. A loss of a loved one requires a period of adjustment. Adults go through several stages of mourning, but there is minimum agreement about the ability of children, especially younger ones, to work through the stages. Very young children who lose their parents and are institutionalized will usually have severe lacks in social and emotional development, whereas the child reared in his own family learns to adapt to brief separations. As the child grows older he can tolerate longer separations, but the loss of the primary caretaker will usually result in some regressive behaviors.

Natural parents can experience insecurity, shame, guilt, and grief on losing their children to someone else's care. The feelings of sorrow and loss by foster parents must not be underestimated when a child leaves them. Their reactions are usually related to four factors: the maturity of the caretaker, the length of time in care, the child's adjustment to the home, and the situation to which the child is going. The placed child will mourn for his parents, have anxiety and fear about living elsewhere, and may have many misperceptions about the reasons for placement. Children whose parents have died can often make a better adjustment than those whose parents have abandoned them. When only one child in a family is placed, attention must be given to the siblings, since they often have fears and concerns about the placement.

The social worker is not immune from the stresses of participating in the separation of family members; practitioners must be reasonably secure in their own feelings about separations. Staff must not be cavalier in utilizing placement, and must support placement when it is necessary. Specific practitioner actions aimed at reducing the stress of separation include: letting the child know when change will occur, indicating that something will be positive about the change, permitting the child to express concern and fear, helping the child to reality test the new situation, and watching for signs of the child's acceptance of the change. Sound practice during separation will not eliminate the pain, but it will help participants work through the trauma and have some choice and control over feelings and events.

Special Annotated Bibliography

Applebaum, F. "Loneliness: A Taxonomy and Psychodynamic View." *Clinical Social Work Journal,* 1978, *6* (1), 13-20. A clear statement of the causes of, and problems associated with, loneliness.

Edelstein, S. "When Foster Children Leave: Helping Foster Parents to Grieve." *Child Welfare,* 1981, *60* (7), 467-473. Recognizes the strong feelings of foster parents when losing a foster child.

Littner, N. *Some Traumatic Effects of Separation and Placement.* New York: Child Welfare League of America, 1956. A basic and well-accepted statement on the problems of separation.

Mishne, J. "Parental Abandonment: A Unique Form of Loss and Narcissistic Injury." *Clinical Social Work Journal,* 1979, 7 (1), 15-33. Shows that the abandoned child has more conflicts than the child whose parents are deceased; describes the different reactions to different types of losses.

Wilkes, J. R. "Separation Can Be a Therapeutic Option." *Child Welfare,* 1980, *59* (1), 27-31. Helps practitioners understand how negative attitudes toward placement may contribute to poor practice and working relationships.

CHAPTER FOUR

Day Care: Enhancing Children's Growth and Family Functioning

✿ ✿ ✿ ✿ ✿ ✿ ✿ ✿ ✿ ✿ ✿ ✿ ✿ ✿ ✿ ✿ ✿ ✿

Day care is the care of a child by a person other than the child's regular caretaker, for a period of less than twenty-four hours a day. It includes (1) care in someone else's home, (2) care in the child's own home, and (3) care in a public or private center. Although federal funding cuts have reduced the number of day care programs—some centers have closed, and many agencies still operating have had to limit services to the most disadvantaged groups, such as children who have been abused or neglected—day care remains a major component of the human services system, since we know that quality day care programs can enhance the development of many children and that parents want, need, and will use quality programs. We also know that good-quality service to parents will often result in good parenting for children.

Two decades ago day care was usually designed for the resolution of family problems, whereas recent statements define day care as a comprehensive service for the child, the family, and the community.

Day care programs can serve several purposes and, in fact, seldom have a single purpose. For example, they can educate and otherwise enhance the health and welfare of children, facilitate a parent's employment outside the home and increase family income, subsidize costs for mothers who are already in the work force, and identify children at "high risk." The programs provide challenging experiences for healthy and constructive children, as well as intensive and early remediation and training for handicapped or disabled children. Some children are placed in care because their parents, especially their mothers, need help in coping with their personal problems. In such instances the parent may voluntarily bring in the child, or a social agency may facilitate the placement. Other programs may set out to provide one need and then may prove to meet other needs as well. For example, a program organized and directed by a minority group, with the express purpose of improving the self-image and identity of minority children, may be equally effective in benefiting the working mother and in improving the child's social and cognitive skills.

The need for day care is hotly disputed. Some analysts (Hill, 1978; Bruce-Briggs, 1977; Woolsey, 1977) maintain that there are enough centers and homes for children; others (Kamerman and Kahn, 1976, 1979; Nolan, 1975; Hill-Scott, 1979) estimate that only 10 to 20 percent of the real need is being met and that services are least available to the economically disadvantaged and are unevenly distributed throughout the country.

Costs of day care services vary widely and are related to factors such as child/adult ratio; group size; location; salaries; extent and quality of other services, such as health, social services, and remedial programs; and extent and condition of physical facilities. Bruce-Briggs (1977) reports costs in centers with good-quality services of $3,250 to $4,000 a year. The most extensive study, conducted by Abt Associates (1979), found an average yearly cost, in 1977, of $1,884 per child. The range was from $960 to $3,372. Public centers usually maintain higher adult/child ratios, pay higher wages, and offer more services; consequently, costs are greater at these centers. If standards of care increase, costs will follow close behind. Furthermore, day care is a labor-intensive industry with very low wages, and staff salary increases will directly affect costs.

Licensing throughout the United States is becoming more standardized. Most federally funded programs must comply with the 1968 Federal Interagency Day Care Requirements and the 1980 Health, Education and Welfare Day Care Regulations. State laws affect all facilities, both public and private, serving more than three children. Licenses do not guarantee compliance, however, since monitoring staff are so burdened with complaints that little time is left for routine visits and program enhancement. Many municipalities and private organizations such as the Child Welfare League of America have also set day care standards.

Effects of Day Care on Children's Health

Parents, policy makers, and practitioners all have questions about the effects of day care on the young child: Does early separation from parents impair the mother-child relationship? Will emotional problems emerge later as a result of separation from the security of home? Will cognitive development be impaired or enhanced? Findings of recent studies are briefly summarized here.

1. Most children under age six who were of average or below average intelligence showed IQ and other cognitive gains during the first year of day care programs in group settings. One or two years after the program, however, they showed a progressive decline. This decline continued even after the children entered regular school, unless offset by special home-based programs in which parents were involved. The most severely deprived and disadvantaged children were those who profited least and who also lost the gains most quickly (Bronfenbrenner, 1974).

2. Group size is related to the extent of healthy child development. Children in groups composed of sixteen to eighteen children, regardless of staff/child ratio, do better than children in larger groups (Abt Associates, 1979).

3. In any program of early intervention for children, the

parent must not be placed in a subordinate role, since this weakens the parent-child relationship (Bronfenbrenner, 1974).

4. The findings of Belsky and Steinberg (1978, p. 944) contrast with those of Bronfenbrenner: "The day care experience has neither salutary nor adverse effects on the intellectual development (as assessed by standardized tests) of most children. For economically disadvantaged children, however, day care may have an enduring positive effect, for it appears that such day care experience may attenuate declines in test scores typically associated with high-risk populations after eighteen months of age." One other study, analyzed by the authors, suggests that positive results from day care may persist into the school-age years.

5. Does child care affect or influence the mother-child bond? Blehar (1974), in a sample of day care and home-reared children, found many positives for child care but noted that day care may have fostered anxious and ambivalent, as opposed to secure, attachments to mothers. However, Belsky and Steinberg (1978, p. 939), reviewing "the total body of evidence . . . regarding the effect of day care on the child's attachment to his mother," conclude that the studies offer "little support for the claim that day care disrupts the child's ties to his mother. . . . With the exception of Blehar's report, *not a single study provided evidence documenting the existence of substantial, systematic differences* between day care and home-reared children." The authors caution that the research was conducted in high-quality services, not necessarily typical of many child care programs. They add that the only justifiable conclusion is that day care need not disrupt the child's emotional bond with the mother.

6. Murray (1975, p. 787) studied the influence of maternal employment on children under age three and found that a child's "emotional adjustment and intellectual development" may be hindered if the mother's employment operates against the development of "a close, enduring relationship" between mother and child.

7. Children's social development also may be affected: "When compared with age mates reared at home, day care chil-

dren tend to interact more with peers in both positive and negative ways. That is, they are more likely to cooperate [with] as well as aggress against their age mates. Some evidence suggests, moreover, that children enrolled in day care for extended periods of time show increased apprehension toward adults and decreased cooperation with them, as well as a lessened involvement in educational activities once they enter school" (Belsky and Steinberg, 1979, p. 23). These conclusions may reflect socialization values in the United States, since, according to Belsky and Steinberg, day care studies in other countries do not show similar findings.

9. Kamerman and Kahn (1976), after reviewing research on day care, concluded that services do not seem to harm a child but that other programs are invariably needed later to solidify social and developmental gains made in the programs. They advocate day care as an important adjunct to other community efforts to support and enhance family life. In another study, of day care programs in Sweden and the United States, Kahn and Kamerman (1975, p. 946) found that these programs benefit children only if the parents also participate in them.

Social Services in Day Care

Practitioners with baccalaureate and associate degrees are often employed in day care centers, either as providers of care or as social workers. The percentage of staff employed exclusively for the social work role in centers is quite small (6 to 8 percent). In those centers that have social workers, there is invariably some overlap between the roles of teacher, social worker, and director. Along with parents and other socially active persons, a practitioner may be involved in establishing a center or a network of family day care homes. He may conduct educational programs on family life and child development. Or he may provide case services to families or individuals with problems related to child care. He may also help a parent locate and obtain other community services; or, if the necessary services do not exist, he may try to get them established.

Within a day care program, social workers participate as

team members with educators, nutritionists, psychologists, physicians, and others. That is, the social workers may serve as consultants to the other team members, in matters concerning the child's and parents' needs, or they may use information from other team members for ongoing services to child and family. Social work staff often serve an intake function, helping parents decide on the use of a day care service.

The case examples below suggest a few activities for a practitioner in day care.

Mrs. Thames, mother of two-and-a-half-year-old Tracy, applied to the center for immediate admission of her daughter. A young mother who separated from her husband six months ago, she was frantic about her situation. The cost of care was not a major problem for her, but the immediate placement of her daughter was, since she was working part time and taking three college courses. She had just removed her daughter abruptly from a licensed family day care home that was not to her liking, even though located near her apartment. Mrs. Thames asked the usual questions about the center, but she also asked a number of very direct questions about discipline and control, seeming almost possessed about wanting assurance that children were treated kindly. She needed detailed information about the teachers. Forthright responses by the social worker did not seem to allay her fears; even meeting several staff did not comfort her.

When the social worker expressed her interest in Mrs. Thames's strong concerns, the mother reported that Tracy had been treated harshly by the previous day care provider. For the past week, she explained, her daughter had seemed fearful of going to the home. But the mother failed to sense what was happening to the girl, even though she had found a welt mark on Tracy's back when she was giving her a bath. The proprietor said that the girl had slipped off a swing and become bruised. Finally, a barely noticeable bruise on her daughter's arm two days ago convinced her that mistreatment was taking place. Tracy fearfully revealed that "Aunt Lonny hit me," and Mrs. Thames removed her promptly.

Mrs. Thames was tense because her seasonal work demands were heavy, final exams were approaching, and a safe, secure arrangement for her daughter was essential. The social worker asked her whether other children in the day care home had also been treated harshly, but Mrs. Thames was too upset to discuss the subject further; her only need was to get a safe day care program immediately.

Tracy, a frail-looking, small child, did not adjust easily to the new environment, although her mother played as supportive a role as she could. After an initial settling in took place, the social worker consulted with the mother again about the previous day care home, stating that the occurrence of such strong discipline might suggest potential abuse. Mrs. Thames agreed but wanted to forget the event. A short time later, at the practitioner's initiative, Mrs. Thames agreed to assist with notification of the licensing agency, and she also contacted another mother of a child in the same home who had her own questions about harsh discipline. Both parents met with the licensing agency and learned that a complaint had been lodged with the previous state licensing person but that no action had been initiated. An investigation ensued; Mrs. Thames and another mother attended the hearing; and, nine months after Mrs. Thames came to the center, the day care home had its license revoked.

This case shows intake process with a visibly upset mother who felt guilty about what she regarded as her inability to perceive harmful treatment of her child. Her inability to lodge an immediate complaint against a previous caretaker is understandable. The social worker pursued the issue when the crisis had subsided; as the mother's guilt shifted to anger, she was able to take action. As a result, a caretaker who could be harmful to many children was no longer allowed to practice.

Mrs. Grace, mother of a three-year-old daughter and a two-year-old boy, went to the center with two friends who had children already enrolled in the program. Her friends encouraged her to visit and consider having the children enrolled there, since she had a part-time job and her current babysitter sometimes did not meet her expectations. She described her daughter, Alison, as a quiet child who was content to play quietly with others or by herself and who seemed fairly self-sufficient, whereas her son, Gerald, was an active boy "who has a lot of push to him."

Mrs. Grace observed the center activities carefully, remarking that the children were "very active" and that she hadn't realized how much went on at the center. At one point in discussion, she declared that she was very close to both her friends but that she did have some differences from them—for

instance, she still liked to know that her children were home rather than in a public building a half mile away. The social worker, by encouraging Mrs. Grace to describe the current child care
plan and what she hoped would be different in another placement, learned that the sitter was an old family friend who sometimes acted like a "bossy mother" to her. Mrs. Grace was also
concerned about the sitter's casualness with meal preparation
and nap arrangements. After further discussion Mrs. Grace decided that she would talk with the sitter, which would not be
easy, and see whether changes could be made in the kind of care
her children were receiving. If not, she might try to locate another sitter or might be willing to come back to the center and
discuss admission.

The Grace case illustrates the role of the social worker in
helping a parent decide on an appropriate child care plan. The
discussion enabled the mother to perceive more clearly what she
was looking for, as well as listing the steps she might take to improve her existing care arrangements. Mrs. Grace was clear
about her values and her friends' values, and her direct observation of the center helped to clarify what type of care was available at this center and what her options were.

Mr. and Mrs. Loren dropped into the center late one
afternoon to inquire about placement of their two sons—one,
three years old; the other, four. The parents met briefly with
the head teacher and, because of their numerous questions and
apparent conflict over whether to use a day care program, were
invited to meet with the social worker. Mrs. Loren, who had recently taken full-time employment, wanted to have the children
in part-time care even though the father was home for most of
the day to care for them. The father had lost his full-time job
and currently worked part time at another. Mrs. Loren implied
that her husband was not skillful in child care—an implication
that clearly offended him. From his various comments about
the children, however, the social worker concluded that his
wife was probably correct and that his approach to their care
was not very constructive. Over the period of a long interview,
the social worker also was able to recognize that Mr. Loren felt
threatened by the sudden role shift from full-time complete
provider to part-time supplemental income provider and active
caretaker to two young boys. The social worker did not criticize

the parents but, instead, assured them that "no parent is perfect" and encouraged them to consider a temporary child care plan. Mr. Loren then admitted some aggravation with their care at home and used his own need to seek other full-time employment as a justification for testing a short period of day care. He was initially critical of "not enough discipline" in the center, but this appeared to be more his need to feel in control of his children and the center than his need to discipline his sons. For the first two weeks of their stay at the center, he was not relaxed when he occasionally picked them up. He did attend several informal child development programs, developed friendships with two other fathers in the group, and became more accepting of the program and its usefulness to his family. After several months he volunteered to the social worker that he and his sons got along fairly well, but he was cautious about giving any credit to the center.

This situation shows family need for day care as it relates to employment and the assumption of rapid role changes for both parents. Here the father was brought into the program with as little threat as possible to his integrity, even though the staff recognized that he was an aloof parent expecting high performance but contributing little to the children's well-being. The program served several purposes for this family: (1) relief for the mother that the children would receive adequate, consistent care; (2) respite for the father, who was experiencing a personal crisis and found care of his boys a burden; (3) protection for the children from a father whose behavior under stress might have deteriorated; and (4) exposure to more constructive parenting skills for the father.

These three cases illustrate specific "problems" that clearly are not encountered by all children and families who use day care. Enrollment in day care programs can be a smooth process: the parent helps the child's transition to care, the parent does not feel guilty, the child separates easily, there are no health problems, the child profits from the program, and no crisis occurs in the parents' situation. When social breakdown does occur, however, social workers in day care centers will try to help families ameliorate the problem.

Communication with Parents: Specific Guidelines

Social workers in day care centers must be sensitive to the needs and distress of parents who seek a child care service. Responsive, caring service to parents results, in the long run, in good-quality parental care for children. When talking with parents regarding any aspect of the child's experience in day care, workers must help the parents feel as comfortable as possible and must give them a clear understanding of what the center expects from parents, how the staff will provide care, and what parents can expect from day to day. Even if the practices and policies of the care provider are written in a brochure, parents still must hear all this directly from the person who cares for the child. Staff must be able to recognize their own attitudes and responses toward both the child and the parents. If staff do not approve of a parent's actions, they should not express disapproval of the parent as a human being. For example, the statement "John is cold when we go outside to play, so I must have a warmer jacket for him" does not accuse the parent of doing a poor job. It does place a very realistic expectation on the parent to meet the child's need for proper clothing. If the parent does not have a warmer piece of clothing, the practitioner's unemotional statement may enable the parent to state that he cannot meet the need. The worker may then have to seek the services of another agency to solve the problem.

When any person is accused, typical responses include anger, defensiveness, or withdrawal. These responses do not produce a solution to the problem of keeping John warm. If parents are uncomfortable with the worker, they will manage to avoid her. If they cannot avoid her physically, because they must deliver and pick up their child, they will at least give quick, simple, or evasive answers. Some parents react to their discomfort by suspiciousness or by reporting the worker to a board member or the director. Other parents demonstrate bravado: "You can't tell me what to do." Until their discomfort is eased, they will not cooperate to ensure that their child's needs are met.

Whenever a worker becomes aware that a child is having

problems, she should take time to tell the parent, pointing out patterns of behavior that indicate strain and suggesting ways that the child might be helped. When a normally contented child begins to cry easily, seems irritable, or has sudden bursts of anger, something is wrong. Signs of extreme fatigue, loss of appetite, lack of interest in play, a desire to sleep an unusual length of time—all are signals of distress. It could be the beginning of an illness, a nutritional imbalance, a reaction to a family problem, an emotional disturbance, or a reaction to a problem in day care service.

Parents who demonstrate solid parenting should be praised, but an uncooperative parent should not be openly censured. The parent must never be placed in a subordinate role, since this undermines the parent-child relationship. To criticize the parents is to criticize and shame the child. Instead, the day care worker must give auxiliary strength to parents in order to promote adequate care for children. This task must be performed without anger and without evidence of annoyance. It is never helpful to make attacking or accusing statements to parents: "You are late again." Instead, one can say: "I am concerned because I cannot find any way to help you understand that John must be picked up at five o'clock every day." Workers must make sure, however, that parents are capable of performing as expected.

A provider in northern New England had been bathing two young children daily, because they were always dirty and malodorous when they arrived. She was about to increase her daily work substantially with the arrival of three new children. Since she would not have time to give daily baths, she instructed the mother to give them. The mother, a woman of limited intelligence, was not told when to give the baths, such as directly before bedtime, and was not specifically instructed to keep the children warm. The next morning the mother arrived, proud that she had bathed an infant and a toddler and delivered them, hatless and unblanketed, by 7 A.M. in zero-degree weather. The parent, doing her very best to follow instructions, could not possibly comprehend the distress of the provider.

Some parents display pervasive rage. Other parents are

angry only at certain people and in certain situations. If a practitioner can discover what provokes a parent's anger, it will be easier to predict explosions and to avoid confrontations. Statements such as "This may make you angry, but it is important for you to have this information" or "I know it makes you angry when I remind you of this, but I must have a sweater for Lisa" suggest that the parent has a right to the feeling of anger but at the same time make it clear that certain behavior will not be accepted. No matter how calmly and carefully parents are engaged, some will express anger in outbursts—predictable or unpredictable. This becomes tiring or perhaps even frightening. Although no one expects practitioners to accept assaults or other behavior that is harmful or upsetting, accepting the feeling of anger is part of child care provision: "I know you are angry, but we cannot solve anything until you stop shouting."

Day care is used sometimes to provide a buffer for children whose parents cannot handle their personal or family problems and therefore cannot give adequate care to their children. The children served may have been seriously damaged emotionally or physically. Staff members may find it discouraging to provide good day care when parents do not change or improve. It may appear that the service is useless, that the parents handily escape the responsibility of child care and do not even try to do a good job of parenting. One provider grew angry because she saw a parent relaxing on the beach while she was giving child care. She made a judgment, based on her value system, that anyone relaxing on a beach was just lazy, and she was not going to work for a lazy woman. It was necessary to move the child, because no one could help this provider understand the protective element of her service. Some families need long-term continuing support in order to function. They may never remake themselves, and a community agency may be needed until children grow up. Change may be brought about by working relationships with, and encouragement from, homemakers, and through the use of very concrete assistance, but some parents will keep all professionals at a distance. They will remain detached and unable to connect. If a person cannot tolerate closeness, he manages to find people who will reject him regularly.

These parents cannot be excluded just because their behavior is unacceptable. Excluding parents, in fact, does not protect or serve children. Many parents believe that eventually they will be let down. It is very important to send the clear message of persistence and tenacity.

Reports to the child welfare department are required if there is reason to believe that a parent abuses or neglects a child. It is not necessary to produce evidence of danger, but reports are more useful if specific observations about the behavior of child and parent are included: "Mrs. A. slams the brakes on her car, stomps out, bangs the door, drags John out of the car, pushes him in my door, does not speak to anyone, bangs her door again, and drives off without looking in any direction." If a child talks about parental behavior that is abusive or neglectful, a day care worker should listen and assure the child of staff interest in how he lives: "How does it make you feel when Mom hits you?" This question should not imply disapproval of the parent. It is an additional burden for any child to hear distress about a parent's shortcomings as perceived by others or as he already feels them. However, it is also important for children to reflect on their feelings about punishment. If they can think about how it feels when punishment is harsh and not deny and bury that feeling, they may recall the feeling when they become adults and have the urge to use harsh punishment on their own children.

When parents are accepted and children are encouraged to reflect on their feelings, another influence is provided for children's growth. Day care staff have the opportunity to influence the quality of life these children will have as adults. Staff may also indirectly influence how the succeeding generation will be cared for and grow. (Chapter Seven, on child protective services, gives many details on reporting abuse and on services to parents and children.) The following cases illustrate other guidelines.

Ensuring Parent Involvement in Planning. Each parent should be encouraged to take an active part in evaluating or selecting the day care provider or facility. This may reduce the ordeal of separation, and it may commit the parent to the ongoing responsibility of using the service selected or, if necessary, of changing to a more suitable service. Parents need to be assured that seeking and selecting good care is a part of responsible parenting. In the following case, the parents left the center with a greater understanding of child care than when they arrived. The change occurred because the assistant director was quietly persistent in walking them through the facility.

Mr. and Mrs. Largrave arrived at the center and announced that they wanted to bring their two young children in for care, starting tomorrow. No vacancy was available, and the parents were informed that admission would be likely in about two weeks. The assistant director offered to show them around the center, but they showed no interest. The assistant nevertheless invited them to walk around the center as they talked about the current activities of the Largraves' two boys. This elicited some questions from the father about the jungle house and a small climbing rack. The assistant described meals, reading, and other parts of the program. The mother said she hoped there was a television, since the boys were glued to it. The assistant explained that television was used to start programs with children and then showed the parents a few muppets and hand puppets that children could use to put on their own plays. Mrs. Largrave asked whether the children were also taught "not to be so smart." The assistant was then able to obtain more detailed information about the children's adjustment as well as the parents' needs and expectations for child care.

Defining Day Care as an Extension of Home. Parents should be helped to see child care as an extension of the home or as an auxiliary to the parent's care. If there is no mutuality in the decision-making process, the parent will not convey positive feelings about the arrangement to the child. If the parent sabotages the plan, overtly or subtly, the child will not be able to function as contentedly in the program.

At the end of the interview to make arrangements for Tony's care, Mrs. Donato, his mother, said tearfully: "Five months ago I ceased being a wife by getting a divorce, and today I'm giving up being a mother by this decision." Mrs. Cleone, the social worker, said that the mother might perceive it that way but that the staff saw it as a shared arrangement for Tony's best care. She reminded the mother of the many bits of behavioral information that had been asked for, so that the staff could do their best in helping Tony to adapt here: "We are absolutely counting on you to keep telling us about his behavior at home, so that we can be mindful of his needs when he is here; and we will give you facts about Tony's adjustment to the program." Mrs. Cleone also discussed with Mrs. Donato the difference between the mother's distress at separating from her husband and her later distress at relinquishing some of Tony's care to the center—two losses in a row, as she saw it. The social worker accepted the mother's feelings of loss but assured her that "the center has no intention of supplanting you as the parent. Children always want their own parents before they want child care staff." Mrs. Cleone added that the mother had shown that she was a responsible parent by investing so much energy and concern in the selection of a child care program.

Informing the Child About Parent Activities. Parents should be encouraged to let their children know where they go each day and what they do during the time the child is not with them. One parent stated it this way: "Debbie, you stay here while I go to the shoe factory. I use a machine that is as big as this table and it attaches parts of shoes together. See these two parts of the shoe here? If I don't put them together right, then the shoe doesn't feel very good on your foot. It hurts and you don't want to wear it. When I am finished each day, I will come for you and then we will go home to have supper." Day care staff should repeat the story. Their knowledge of family circumstances helps to reduce any feelings of strangeness that the child may have in the center. By talking about a parent's work, the staff may convey approval of the parent and recognition of her contribution to society.

Identifying the Anxious Child and Parent. If parents are anxious or overprotective, and have done most of a child's thinking for him, the separation will be difficult for both child and parent. Parents should be shown that anxiety can handicap the child physically and emotionally; that constant fear for a child's safety can cause a child to be overcautious, timid, or inactive. In the following case, the mother's observation of other children's behavior enabled her to recognize her preoccupation about her daughter and to get help for herself.

Adele, age five, had never been permitted to use any cutting device, such as a pair of scissors. When Adele's mother observed some of the activities of the center, she saw children using scissors and paste and became upset over Adele's being exposed to "dangerous things that can hurt her or someone else." The mother then asked whether band-aids were readily available and what the staff did when a child was injured. The teacher was very reassuring, showing her the blunt-edge points and commenting that the children had never been injured. Although the mother was not reassured, she still permitted Adele to enter the program. Once in the program, the child was very apprehensive about many activities, especially at cut-and-paste time. The teacher invited the mother in on several occasions to reduce her distress over the use of scissors and to enable Adele to be more free in using equipment. Adele lost her apprehension more quickly than the mother, who eventually was referred to the mental health center to help reduce many of her preoccupations and fears about normal activities.

Accepting and Analyzing Parental Criticism. Parents' feelings of discomfort or distress should be identified and discussed. The social worker should be prepared to accept valid criticism of himself, other staff, or the program and to make program revisions based on a child's needs or on the needs of different children, such as those from a new ethnic or religious group or social class. Parents' self-image and their ability to communicate and to protect and defend their children are improved when their concerns are heeded.

Jenny's stepmother, Mrs. Gordon, stopped the head teacher and was critical of the amount of time that was apparently available for lunch. She said that Jenny had told her almost every day for the past few weeks that she could not eat all her lunch. The teacher said she would plan to observe Jenny more carefully, since the other children seemed to finish their meals. The teacher learned that Jenny often left much of her meal, stating that she could not eat it all. Jenny never seemed to be hungry later in the day, and she never asked for additional snacks in the late afternoon. She was observed over the next week, and she always had some reason to be late to get to the table and to leave the table. She would want to use the bathroom again or find another urgent reason to depart. Staff were too lenient in permitting her to make this a daily habit, not noticing that it was cutting into the time available to eat. When the staff paid more attention to her at mealtime, discouraging or delaying trips from the table, the problem was resolved within a week.

Responding to Parental Threats. Staff must neutralize and modify threats made by parents to their children. Day care staff often have a higher investment in the child's well-being than in the parents; however, they must exercise caution in their selection of words and the feeling conveyed when they disagree with a parent's threats.

Allen, age three, was being dragged into the center by his mother. She looked harassed as she pushed him into a chair. He was not openly crying but was kicking his feet high to show his resistance. The teacher walked over to receive them, and the mother announced, "It was a hell of a job to get him here, but he's here." When the boy made a quick lurch from the chair, his mother sharply told him that he was to stop it now or "You can stay here forever in the center." The teacher said that they must be mad at each other; she then moved quickly to touch Allen while still looking at the mother and stated, so that the mother could hear: "Mommy wants you to get along and feel happy. She wants that so much that she would like you to stay here all the time. But we know that it would make you feel bad not to be with Mommy, even though you fight with her sometimes. People do fight with each other, but they also like to be together. Remember the fight you had yesterday with Alicia? Later you were playing together at the sink. I like you a lot and want to have you here. But we would never keep you here; Mommy will be back later today." Allen continued to have a defiant look as this was going on; he slowly became engaged with the group, and the teacher met briefly with the mother to explain why she could not support the mother's statement. They then talked briefly about the fight that the mother and Allen had had just before they left for the center.

Responding to Parental Approval of Aggression. Staff must be clear and unequivocal with parents when their child's behavior, before and after the center activities, poses clear hazards to other children. Consistent with child care policy of the importance of parents in the child's life, the expectation or requirement should not demean or embarrass the parent but should, whenever possible, enhance parental ability. Some events strain the ability of staff to respond without anger and to be supportive. In the following case, there was little that the teacher could do to involve the mother favorably. He had to take command quickly, since Billy was a hazard to the others. After the incident, however, he was able to spend some time with the mother.

Billy, age four, strode rapidly into the center while his mother strolled slowly behind. He was carrying a stick with a sharpened end and, immediately after entering the play area, began to jab it quickly toward other children. His mother passively watched as Billy pushed the sharp end close to other children's faces. The teacher, Mr. Sparks, moved rapidly toward him, sensing that Billy was out of control in his crude attempts to get the other children to play with him. The teacher held the stick firmly for a few moments, commenting on how long and thin it was, and then invited the other children to look at the colors of the bark. He asked Billy to tell everyone about the stick, and Billy became less tense and began to tell where he had found it. Mr. Sparks said that they would now place the stick in a safe place, so that Billy could take it home later. All this occurred in the presence of the mother. When Mr. Sparks asked her about Billy's behavior at home, she described him as being "ratty" both last night and this morning, adding that she had had to punish him several times yesterday. Mr. Sparks observed that she looked tired today and might not have felt up to managing her son's burliness: "I know that it's hard to cope with him when you are tired, but I have to ask you to prevent Billy from bringing anything hazardous like a sharp stick to the center." He suggested that she try to substitute something soft for Billy to bring to the group, a fluffy animal or a bathtub animal sponge, which the other children would be more interested in than a sharp stick. Billy would then gain more satisfaction, since he would be sharing something that others enjoy. Mr. Sparks also assured the mother that the staff at the center would try to help Billy with his tension and work with her to reduce it.

Resolving Parent-Staff Conflicts. Honest and realistic differences between parents and staff—sometimes the result of cultural or value differences—may be difficult, if not impossible, to resolve. For example, some families value courtesy, hard work, and attentiveness to adults, whereas the program may stress spontaneity, independence, and full expression of emotions. Issues such as these have to be resolved with the policy-making group and with the staff, but they also must be satisfactorily settled between parent and staff.

Mr. Franklin requested a meeting with the center director and announced that he did not like the way his daughter had been behaving since she started to come to the center. He wanted to know what they were letting her do or "telling her to do." He said that she had thrown some food at the table and was not as obedient as she used to be. After consulting with the head teacher, the director reminded the father that he and his wife had been concerned about their daughter's withdrawn, overquiet behavior and had agreed that an effort should be made to encourage her to express herself more freely. The director then pointed out that the transition might not be smooth as a child changes and tries new behavior. The father replied that he had not expected this much change, adding that another parent also was concerned about some recent overactivity and "snappiness" by her son. A plan was made to observe his daughter more carefully and see whether changes in her program might be made, but the father was unsatisfied and three days later placed his daughter in a day care home.

Giving Recognition to Parents. Staff working in day care often have, or may develop, a primary concern for children, and when a child arrives each day, full attention and a warm welcome are given to him. Such treatment helps the child leave the parent and get involved in activities and also assures him that he is wanted. However, it very effectively excludes the parent and in a practical way says, "You are unimportant." It is desirable for the staff to strike a balance between a warm response to the child and an effective response to the parent. This approach not only recognizes the importance of the parent but conveys the fact that the service is an auxiliary to the child's development.

Cindy arrived at the center with both eyes downcast, and Mrs. Sang, her mother, looked drab and tired. The teacher reached out first to touch Cindy and, at the same time, looked at the mother, who gave a faint smile. Cindy was willing to be picked up, and the teacher held her and patted her shoulder while still smiling at Mrs. Sang. She knew that the mother had had an important job interview the day before and said she hoped it had been all right. The mother said it had, but she still had to meet one other official. She expected to get the job but was worried that she might not.

Encouraging Peer Problem Solving. Whenever possible, parents should be encouraged to share their problems and ideas with other parents, informally or in structured discussion groups. Parents who will not accept advice or even entertain ideas from center staff may respond more positively to the views of other parents.

Mrs. Garland said to the teacher, almost with contempt, "I can see that you're not having much success in getting Ashanti to leave the play area. You should see the trouble I sometimes have in getting him to go to bed." Mr. Lyon asked about the bedtime routine, and the mother made a casual remark about what usually happened. She then said, "We'll just keep fighting it out, and I'll win eventually." At that moment another parent, Mrs. LaBreque, walked in. Recalling that Mrs. LaBreque had successfully solved a similar problem with her son, the teacher asked her to tell Mrs. Garland about her experiences. She said that she now offered clear choices to her son about *how* he wanted to go to bed, not *whether* he wanted to go to bed. Mrs. Garland was quite taken by the mother's directions, including stricter rules about the use of TV near bedtime and doing more relaxing things prior to bedtime. Mrs. Garland said that she was not sure her child would listen to anything she said, but she agreed to try these ideas. She looked at the teacher and, with a little humor in her voice, said, "It even might help Jack Lyon here, since he was having a problem today."

Identifying and Supporting Parental Strengths. Practitioners are accustomed to identifying limits. It is also important to define and support strengths, so that parents can increase their capacities to meet the responsibilities that accompany the use of day care.

Lena, age two, was premature at birth and also had an orthopedic handicap, which had been surgically corrected a few months ago. Mrs. Arenti, her mother, also had had extensive orthopedic care when she was young and attributed her own experience to her improved understanding of Lena's needs. This identification with Lena did not have any elements of overprotection but did detract from the mother's attention to Sergei, age six, and Alex, age three. All three children were admitted to the center while the mother worked almost full time; the father's work took him away from home all week. It became clear that Sergei was behind in development, and Alex was overdependent on the staff, often regressing in bladder control and in feeding himself at meals. By defining the older children's developmental needs with the mother, the staff were able to help her transfer some of the extra concern for Lena to the siblings. Staff and mother worked on a plan so that Lena did not feel left out as more attention was directed to the others. Day care itself was a help to Sergei and Alex, but now that Lena did not need as much attention as before, it was important that Mrs. Arenti devote more energy to the siblings.

Reassuring Threatened Parents. Some parents feel threatened by or jealous of their child's affection for the provider or staff. In fact, a child's happiness and progress can be very threatening to some parents. This jealousy will be especially evident when there is an unusually skilled and magnetic teacher who is capable and at ease in almost every situation. Parents need to be reassured that their place is not being usurped and that the person who appears unusually capable in handling children still cannot replace the parents' own skills. In addition, research shows that children in day care, when given a choice between parent and staff, always choose the parent.

Mrs. Rice was talking with the social worker about David, age five, and the difficulty she often had in soliciting his cooperation at home. She then referred to her observation of David's teacher, who seemed to have a magic influence over David and the other children in the group when she asked for clean-up assistance. Mrs. Rice commented somewhat bitterly that "David looks as if he adores her," something she never felt from her son. She did admit, however, that he was cooperating more at home, and for that she was grateful. The social worker suggested that David might be reaching out early to learn from and idolize other adults: "If he is attracted to and cooperates with others, that does not mean he thinks less of his mother." The social worker also reminded Mrs. Rice of the initial problems she had had with David when he came into care eight months ago: "You are now much better at taking care of David than you were before, aren't you?"

Understanding Parents' Reasons for Failure to Cooperate. There are many realistic, understandable reasons why parents are unable to meet reasonable agency expectations. Day care staff should look for such explanations before searching for subtle psychodynamic ones.

Ralph's mother, Mrs. Lester, age twenty-three, who was pregnant for the second time, was seldom if ever on time to pick up her son. Although her employment ended in sufficient time for her to arrange to be at the center, she was sometimes as much as two hours late. Her constant lateness became a problem for Ralph, since several other children in the group had parents who worked in the same industry and were fairly prompt in arriving to pick up the children. As he watched the other children leaving, Ralph became listless and distressed.

The mother, in a discussion of the problem, revealed that she was spending time with two men whom she had recently met, and it was very important to her to keep these relationships. She was in conflict over how to resolve the necessity to meet Ralph's needs and also meet her own needs for male companionship. She did not want Ralph around yet while she was starting to "meet a man." She did agree to a plan over the next six weeks to decide ahead of time which days she would be on time. Then staff could be more supportive of Ralph and help to keep him engaged with a program. He would also gain more status with peers by stating that he would be leaving on time today, later on Wednesday, and the like. She agreed to inform her friends more clearly about Ralph and her need to pick him up on time. This agreement worked well the first week, failed the next two weeks, but stabilized thereafter and became a fairly consistent plan. About three months later, she was keeping steady company with one of the men and was prompt in picking up Ralph.

Encouraging Growth in Children. Workers should not compete for a child's affection but should encourage each child's growth, demonstrating pleasure to parents when growth occurs—especially if the child has emerged from a stage where problem behavior was expressed. When the worker recognizes everything positive or helpful that a parent does for a child, she conveys the message that she respects the parent and has no wish to take over or prove that she can be a better parent. Comments such as the following usually increase a parent's confidence and pleasure: "I was so pleased to hear John using many new words; you must be spending additional time with him at home to help him learn so much" or "I wish you could have seen Amy offer her toy to Jennifer today and ask if she would like to play with it first. Later on she and Jennifer played together, sharing the water and dishes, and Amy was the one who initiated the play. She has changed so much in the past week, and you should have the credit for being so patient with her."

Summary

Day care has been designed to supplement family day care of children for some part of the day. It is a service for the child, the family, and the community, and it often includes educational, health, and social services. The licensing of day care services is now universal, but not uniform, in all states. Social science research shows few social, emotional, and cognitive differences between children reared at home and those enrolled in day care programs, but day care is probably more helpful for the economically and socially disadvantaged. Studies reveal no negative influence on the mother-child bond. Subsequent participation in educational and social programs helps children solidify developmental gains made in day care.

It is important to maintain communication with parents, even though some are fearful of staff, unsure of their own parental skills, show minimum cooperation with the program, and seem to have little concern for their children.

Social service to families in day care includes practices to ensure that the parent is involved in planning; day care is seen as an extension of the home; the child is informed of the parent's activities; the anxious child or parent is identified; parental criticism is understood; appropriate responses are made to parental threats toward the child and toward parental approval of aggression; parent-staff conflicts are resolved; parental strengths are supported; parents who are threatened by staff are given reassurance; there is understanding and help given to parents who are unable to cooperate with the program; and parents are praised when children show healthful development.

Special Annotated Bibliography

Belsky, J., and Steinberg, L. D. "The Effects of Day Care: A Critical Review." *Child Development,* 1978, *49* (4), 929-949. A clear and detailed statement about numerous studies on the effects of day care on children.

Galinsky, E., and Hooks, W. *The New Extended Family.* Boston: Houghton Mifflin, 1977. An examination of selected day care programs, demonstrating diversity in policy, program, funding, and staffing.

Hill-Scott, K. "Child Care in the Black Community." *Journal of Black Studies,* 1979, *10,* 78-97. A discussion of the problems of minorities in a Southern California low-income community, showing family needs and expressed values in a day care program.

Kamerman, S., and Kahn, A. "The Day-Care Debate: A Wider View." *Public Interest,* 1979, *54* (4), 76-93; and Woolsey, S. "Pied Piper Politics and the Child-Care Debate." *Daedalus,* 1977, *106,* 127-145. These two articles demonstrate the intensity of the debate over the benefits of publicly supported day care.

CHAPTER FIVE

Foster Care: Managing Successful Placement of Children

From the ancient Jewish custom of providing care for orphan children, through the boarding of destitute children under church auspices and the indenture of dependent children until age twenty-one under provisions of the Elizabethan Poor Laws, societies have addressed the need for children without parental supervision to have adequate provision for survival. The first system of organized foster care was developed by the New York Children's Aid Society in 1853 as a means of "rescuing" the child from his family; the intent was to get permanent surrender even though parents needed only temporary help. It was not until the late nineteenth century that the Children's Aid Society in Boston began to consider different children's needs by individualizing services.

Foster family care—the care of children in licensed foster homes, usually on a temporary basis—has now become a sophisticated and well-organized service: "The emphasis on foster family care for young children has been increasingly emulated by countries around the world as a preferred form of care" (Fanshel and Shinn, 1978, p, 496).

Many aspects of the parental role are taken over by foster parents. If biological parents or relatives cannot provide minimally adequate physical care and if social and emotional development is being delayed to the jeopardy of the child, then foster care is one possible service plan. The Child Welfare League of America (1959, p. 5) defines foster care as "substitute family care for a planned period for a child when his own family cannot care for him for a temporary or extended period and when adoption is neither desirable nor possible."

A specific crisis usually brings children into foster care: a major illness, a new baby, the loss of employment, separation of parents, or an eviction. The behavior of the parents in the following case illustrates the chronic upheaval of some families and their intent to use placement only at moments of overwhelming stress. With the sudden appearance of the parents when their children are in care and the threats of placement when the children are at home, there is no opportunity for agency staff to develop a service plan aimed at reducing family chaos or focusing on growth for children. Because of their extreme anxiety about alternating rejection and demands for loyalty, the children cannot develop a commitment to a new family living situation.

The five children of Mr. and Mrs. Young were put into foster homes, since the parents had nowhere to live, no money, and no family or friends in the community who would help them at that time. Three days later, the parents began demanding the return of the children. Mrs. Young now had a job, and her sister had found them a place to live. The living arrangements were found to be unsuitable and somewhat questionable; consequently, the Youngs made needed repairs for the children's safety and cleaned up their living quarters. The agency then agreed that the children would be returned the end of the month. In the meantime, the Youngs asked to see the three youngest children. When the visit took place, in the agency's office, Mrs. Young picked up her youngest daughter and ran hysterically from the building. The upshot was that those three children were returned to her that day. The other two children were returned at the end of the month, as promised. The whole family returned to therapy with a psychologist.

The living arrangements continued to be shaky, but the family managed all right for about a month. Then Mr. Young began having back problems and missing work. He also was in a car accident and sustained a skull concussion. The car was wrecked, and they had no money to repair it. In addition, Mrs. Young found that the living arrangements were not working out as she had expected and she felt that they should move. However, they were not eligible for welfare in this county, so they could get no financial help. Mrs. Young began putting pressure on the worker to "find" them a place to live. Although the worker gave advice and referred Mrs. Young to many places, she refused to "find" another living arrangement for the family.

Whenever Mrs. Young feels under stress, she phones the worker and threatens to place the children and to sign surrenders. She says she feels it is not fair that they be subjected to all this instability. The worker does not believe that she will follow through on the surrenders; in fact, once the children are placed, she will immediately want them back.

The caseworker foresees another cycle of moving, applying for welfare, placing the children, and demanding their return again in the very near future. Case goal is to short-circuit these events or change their direction. The Youngs are receiving therapy, day care, casework services, and Medicaid. In the past they have received the following services: day care, homemaker, rental assistance, emergency funds, food, welfare, counseling, foster care, and family therapy. The children are suffering emotionally and socially from the frequent upheavals in the family's living arrangements, changes in school systems, and separations when placed in foster care.

Not all parents are as unable as the Youngs to support their children in foster care. In most instances the biological parents can supply at least a portion of the total parenting role. At the very least, they can send greetings to their children twice a year and make one or two supervised visits a year. Some parents may be able to make regular visits or even to participate in decisions about school, to review report cards, and to attend periodic school conferences. Whatever percentage of care the parent cannot supply must be provided by agency and foster parent as an auxiliary to parenting but not as a substitute for it. This model for the role of foster care may diminish the loyalty conflicts that children experience. They have the opportunity to perceive the system as a supplement to the parents' adequacy rather than as a disapproval and replacement of inadequate parents. Thus, it may reduce the child's need to defend his parents and free some of his energy to deal with stresses of growth, relationships, and schooling.

The child who can best profit from foster care service is one who can take part in family activities and relationships and contribute to the tasks of running the household. The problem then is to find the best possible foster parents for such a child.

Finding Appropriate Foster Homes

In response to an agency's current and projected foster home needs, a homefinder must develop a recruitment plan—possibly including media advertisement and direct speaking engagements in community groups such as churches and service clubs. Many agencies recruit their best foster parents through referrals from successful foster parents. Some agencies screen applications during an initial meeting with several applicants. At such a meeting, an agency worker gives a detailed description of the tasks of foster parenting, the licensing standards, and the rights and responsibilities of the agency and foster parents. The worker also asks the applicants how they became interested in being foster parents, how they heard about the agency, and what they think foster care can accomplish for them. The answers are instructive.

Some persons believe that having foster children would be much the same as having adopted children; in other words, they openly or tacitly expect their relationship with the children to be permanent. Such applicants, if they are to be accepted, must give up any notions of permanence. They must be informed of agency policy and of the kinds of children that are served. If they still harbor a desire for permanence at the time of placement, the contract between agency and foster parent again emphasizes that foster care is a temporary service plan for some children when other services do not meet the need for care and nurture.

Other applicants believe that a foster child might replace their deceased child or be a companion to their own child or to the parents. Given the fact that there are heavy burdens on any child who must socialize himself to new family expectations, deal with the trauma of separation, and cope with conflicting loyalties to all the people who care for him, it is certainly too much to expect that he will also be a companion to anyone. He may have different interests or be so needy that outreach of any kind would be impossible to achieve.

Some parents have had solid experiences in parenting and wish to repeat the happy relationships they have had with children. However, successful parenting with one's own children wil not necessarily ensure successful parenting of foster children. The agency must find out what experience the applicants have had in parenting other people's children. Have they cared for nieces or nephews or the children of friends? Are they the oldest siblings and therefore experienced at holding many parental roles without having full rights and responsibilities?

Other applicants might wish to share or extend compassion to a needy child. Perhaps they received substitute care themselves as children. They may want to repeat a happy childhood relationship or wish to compensate for difficult relationships. If there are applicants who have any desire to save children from miserable living, their applications will probably have to be disqualified. When people see themselves as saviors, they usually expect gratitude from the recipient. It is unrealistic to expect any foster child to experience or express gratitude.

One worker made the mistake of placing an eight-year-old boy with a middle-aged, childless couple one early December. The new foster parents prepared for Christmas with great excitement and devotion. On Christmas morning their anticipation peaked as they looked forward to seeing the boy's face when he came downstairs and found a magnificent tree with a two-wheel bike sitting under it. This child was spared only the Polaroid camera poised to capture the moment. Unable to believe that the tree or the day or the gift belonged to him, the boy walked past the display and remained in the kitchen until bedtime. This foster child was right—the material things could become his possessions only if he were willing to demonstrate gratitude. The next morning the worker received the familiar call: "Get the damned ungrateful kid out of my house."

Some persons wish to engage in foster parenting to augment their family income. In most systems the payment is so small that we do not encourage this motivation—even though it can be a very healthy one. If a woman finds her best success and delight with homemaking, and if her husband supports this interest, she might well say, "I must make a little money. I don't want to go out to industry or to another household; I want to do what I know how to do in my own home—care for children." The agency must be assured that the family already has sufficient income so that a child will not be exploited with low nutrition or inappropriate clothing or recreation in order to help the foster family survive financially.

Initial sessions with applicants must include discussion of the major psychological task of foster parents: to act for but not replace the biological parents. That is, the foster parents temporarily provide the care that the parents cannot provide, but the child cannot be or become theirs. The agency, courts, and natural parents retain the rights, so foster parents must be willing to carry out and share the parenting with an institution that represents a reliable authority.

When discussing developmental needs of children and possible behavior patterns of children, workers should ascertain whether the applicants believe that a child's behavior is always under conscious control. Does the prospective foster parent think that behavior is willful and deliberate and therefore can be changed by children or parents if they wish? Or does he realize that foster parents cannot remake or reshape children and that children cannot control all their behavior at will?

One agency mistakenly selected as a foster parent a minister who could not tolerate obscene language. This mistake was compounded when a four-year-old with a street vocabulary was placed in the home. "Oh," replied the minister when informed of the fact, "no four-year-old could possibly have *that* much foul language. In any case, we can certainly retrain the speaking habits." The foster father tried all his usual disciplinary methods—rewards and restrictions—and insisted that the child take control of his speaking habits. One night at the dinner table, the foster father forced pepper down the boy's throat to silence a string of expletives. The child died at the table. The behavior did not change, but it was certainly stopped.

Applicants who appear to be concerned mainly with the effects of a child's behavior on themselves—"Do it for me" or "I can't take it any more" or "Stop and think what this means to me"—are probably too self-centered to be able to give sufficient affection and care to foster children. On the other hand, applicants who exclude any needs of their own may not have the sustenance to self that permits and enhances recovery from crises or prolonged stress.

An important question to pose to all applicants is "What changes in your family living will foster care impose?" A mother may have thought this through for herself, but a father may deny that there will be any change that affects him: "If she wants to do this extra work, that's OK with me. We have plenty, what's another plate on the table." He needs to be told specifically how his routine may be changed: "Some children do not sleep well and have bad dreams and keep foster parents up most of the night. Some children wet the bed and need help in the morning with changing beds and bathing. Some children cause so much confusion at meals that there is no peace to digest food. Some children sit in all the favorite chairs of family members. Some children demand attention during favorite TV programs. Some children do not want to share anything or even communicate with anyone for many weeks or months." The important fact for each family member to recognize is that there will be changes in day-to-day living when a foster child is added to the household.

Foster parents also must be able to understand and manage their own feelings about biological parents. All children have a multitude of feelings about their own family members, and these will cause confict in the child if he is placed in foster care. Foster parents may be inclined to react to the child's expressed or demonstrated feelings. For example, a child may tell about his father's very important job and express positive feelings about his family. Or, less often, he may make a critical remark about a family member. In either case, the foster parent must accept the feelings and the relationships. He must not say, "Come now, it is all in the past. Let's forget all about it, because now you will be fine." To accept these multiple feelings in any child requires a strong emotional capacity plus a willingness to increase understanding with agency support.

Every foster parent experiences conflicts when agreeing to work collaboratively with an agency. When should a foster parent be able to make a decision independently, and when must he use help and take a less important role in the decision making? Some agencies are reducing the conflict inherent in this shared responsibility of child care by developing policies that require written contracts at several points in the relationship. Responsibilities and rights of each party are spelled out first, in a general way, when a home is accepted, and later, quite specifically, when each child is placed. These contracts are useful only if foster parents understand and accept the content and if agency staff devote time to reviewing performance of all parties involved. If a foster parent values the relationship he seeks or has accomplished, then he may be so eager to please the agency that he will agree to anything. He may or may not perform as he has agreed. The foster parent is in a bind because he is accountable to the agency in specific areas. His performance will be measured, and an agency can decide to remove a child.

Foster parents must have the capacity, in addition to the willingness, to accept and implement the structure of visits between children and natural parents. Visits are most useful if the goals of the placement are accepted by foster parents and natural parents. Otherwise, either can sabotage any chance of the child's adjustment away from home.

Having collaborated on the arrangements, foster parents must be able to understand and accept the great variety of reactions that children have. When children exhibit difficult behavior—such as renewed bedwetting, sulking, or defiance (You're not my mother, I don't have to listen to you")—after visits with their natural parents, many foster parents insist that the visits are damaging and ask to have them limited or stopped. These parents should have been informed in the initial interviews at the agency that children succeed better in foster care if they do see their natural parents. As Fanshel and Shinn (1978, p. 487) demonstrated in their longitudinal study of foster children, frequently visited children gained in verbal and nonverbal IQ scores and made significant gains in emotional adjustment. "A higher level of parental visiting was a significant predictor of an overall positive assessment by the child's classroom teacher."

If prospective foster parents are unwilling to participate in parental visiting, their home should not be approved. An agency's eagerness to have a resource often promotes agreements to have visits away from the foster home. If the applicant cannot enable the child to cope with divided loyalty feelings and cannot accept the importance of natural parents for the child's growth, this person interferes with the agency's purpose or function. Therefore, the agency worker must elicit and evaluate the attitudes that applicants express and demonstrate regarding a child's feelings about parents, the visits by parents, the eventual departure of the child, and cooperation with the agency. Some of the assessment will include a developmental (physical, social, sexual, and psychological) history, a history of the marriage and current family interaction (unless the applicant is a single person), and a review of the applicant's experience in parenting. The qualities sought include good health or constructive adaptations to health problems, solidity in personal and family life, respect for human dignity, the capacity to respond in child-centered terms rather than in self-centered terms, and a desire to share in parenting temporarily with natural parents and the authority of an agency. To tolerate this type of partnership, the foster parents must have satisfaction in their own relationships and a conviction about the importance of foster parenting.

It is difficult to identify a good foster parent as a separate entity because parenthood is best observed in an interaction with childhood. Some foster parents nurture one child but reject another. Workers can increase the chances of parental success by selecting a child who evokes a positive response and then by giving supportive casework service to parents and children, so that behavior is thoroughly observed, understood, and interpreted. History has validated this concept since the policy statement of the Massachusetts Board of Charities in 1867: "A child of passionate temper must not be placed with a master or mistress of similar disposition. If this should occur, there is apt to be trouble" (quoted in Kadushin, 1974, p. 416).

Even the most thorough selection process cannot assure an

agency staff that foster parents will, in fact, act in a healthy manner toward children, since it is always risky to predict human behavior. Nonetheless, a careful, thorough process of screening and assessment—where a body of knowledge about selection of foster parents is put into practice—can help agencies reduce the number of inappropriate and harmful placements for children.

Working with Foster Parents During Placement

When the agency is ready to discuss a specific child or children for an approved home, information about all persons affected by this placement has to be obtained and analyzed in order to determine whether the match will be suitable. Prospective foster parents should be given all the information available about the child, so that they can help evaluate the possibility of their doing an adequate job. Foster parents frequently complain that they received insufficient information from the agency and therefore did not realize what they were getting into.

Foster parents should again be reminded that they will be acting in behalf of the child's natural parents, not replacing the parents. Finally, they should be assured that a certain amount of trepidation and anxiety on their part, as they confront their tasks, is acceptable and normal and does not mean that they are inadequate persons. However, all parties involved are expected to discuss these feelings and work them through, so they will not be translated into negative behavior to the child, the natural parents, or the agency.

Even though foster parents are thoroughly prepared, the actual encounter with any child now requires a change in the household balance. The necessary adjustments should bring satisfactions, but unanticipated problems also may crop up. For instance, a child placed in a home with household pets may prove to have a serious allergy to cat hair; this allergy may be a new piece of information because the child has never had prior exposure to cats. If he becomes ill, what adjustments should be made? Should the agency move the child, or get a series of inoculations for the child, or ask the foster family to dispose of their cats? The following case illustrates another adjustment problem.

One social worker was unprepared for the difficulty of obtaining school admission for a family of three young brothers placed in foster family care in a rural area. The school administrator insisted that the children were retarded and that he had no service for them. (This incident occurred before the passage of legislation requiring public educational services.) The social worker reviewed all developmental and medical information on the children and found no diagnosis of retardation. Before requesting a psychological workup, she asked for a meeting with the school administrator. She learned that he was basing his judgment on cultural retardation evidenced in the reading readiness test. "These boys do not even know what an apple is." "Of course not," the practitioner replied; "they've never seen an apple." This was an inconceivable notion for a rural school staff. After many weeks of patient teaching by the foster parents and with their continued support and help with schoolwork throughout the school years, these children were able to meet the required standards of the local school.

As mentioned, a major adjustment involves the child's continued relations with his natural parents. If children express affection for their natural parents, foster parents may feel that they are being rejected. Agency staff must establish a structure that is mutually acceptable and have the purpose of a visit by natural parents clearly defined—especially since everyone's feelings are aroused when visits are being arranged. The foster parents must deal with the inconvenience of the timing and the likelihood of increased difficulty in dealing with the child before and after the visit. They may be threatened by the competition for a child's loyalty or feel guilty that they have not done enough for the child. They may dislike the natural parents because of former harm or neglect to the child. The natural parents, in turn, may feel jealous and resentful of the foster parents; they also may feel guilty over their "failure" to care for their children, so that someone else is now in charge. The social worker should enunciate all these possible feelings to the foster parents, both before and after each visit by a natural parent. She should also point out that children might capitalize on the guilt by extracting promises the natural parent cannot keep. Foster parents should be asked not to exercise authority over the natural parents in front of the children. They should give no instructions such as "Be sure to have John back by five o'clock." Finally, the children, who already feel that they have been rejected by the parents who placed them in a foster home, may feel especially rejected after a visit. Foster parents must be alert to these feelings and accept and help children through the resulting adjustment problems.

Agency staff are responsible for providing ongoing advice, education, counseling, and psychological support to all foster parents. However, although foster parents often want support, they seldom want instruction or advice and will maintain that they know the child better than anyone else does. Therefore, they must repeatedly be assured that the agency is merely providing knowledge about general needs and reactions within the foster care process and adding this knowledge to the foster parents' direct experience with the child.

Working with Children in Placement

As indicated in Chapter Three, separation from the known and placement in the unknown is confusing for any child. Each child should be given a clear description of life in the foster family selected and should be told what will be expected of him in this household: "This family expects each child who lives here to help prepare one meal each day and to help clean up after each meal. You will be expected to come directly home on the regular school bus each day and to call home immediately if you are on a different schedule. This family sits down together for breakfast and dinner. I know this may seem strange to you, but this is how this family operates."

The purpose of the placement and the plans for the child's future should be clearly explained: "We have planned for you to live here while your parents are finding a new apartment, getting some vocational counseling, and getting started with new jobs. I will be seeing them every month to help with their tasks, and they will come here to see you once a month. We think you can return home in about ten months, but I will be letting you know each month how the tasks are being accomplished." In the following case, the boys being placed are told why and for approximately how long. The expectations in the foster home also are explained to the boys, and the parent demonstrates his approval of the plan and says goodbye.

Mr. B. indicated to the worker that he was having nervous problems and could no longer provide a place for his two sons— Jim, age fifteen, and Joey, age thirteen—because they were causing too much trouble for him. They were not going to school and were getting into trouble wherever they were staying. If he could be free of them for a while, so that his nerves could get better, he was sure that he could provide a place for them permanently in a couple of months. The worker said that her agency would try to provide a foster home for the boys for a specific length of time while he sought treatment. The boys indicated that they did not want to go to a foster home but agreed with their father that there was really no alternative, since they would not go to their mother's; they could no longer stay with their aunt, who was physically ill; and there were no other friends or relatives who could take them. The boys reluctantly agreed to placement on the basis that they would be returning to live with their father in a short time.

When an appropriate home was selected, Mr. B. came to the office with the boys, and an agreement covering a four-week placement was signed. Mr. B. also agreed to begin a program to work on his alcohol problems and his general emotional health. He also agreed to cooperate with whatever treatment plan was proposed for the boys. Mr. B. and the boys then transferred the boys' belongings from their uncle's car to the worker's car, so that the boys could be brought to their foster home. During the parting Mr. B. and the boys expressed emotions ranging from anger to apparent sorrow. Both boys continued to ask their father if they really had to go and if there might be some way that they could continue to stay with him.

During the initial part of the ride to the foster home, both boys were very quiet, but they began to talk and ask questions when the worker neared the foster home itself. The worker explained to the boys that the foster parent who would be providing for them could not tolerate cigarette smoking in the house; since both boys smoked, the worker asked them to do so only when they were outside. All seemed to go well during the

initial introduction, and the worker left the boys with Mrs. J.,
the foster parent.

When parents give their approval of a placement, children
are freed to use the living situation in a more positive way, but
whenever there is clear and strong loyalty to a parent—as there
was in this case—the children still may feel that they must defy
new expectations and even reject placement.

On December 22, two weeks after placement, the worker
received a telephone call from Mrs. J. about Jim and Joey. She
complained that both boys would stay in bed until they were
late for their school bus, so that they would not have to go to
school. She said also that the boys had stayed out until mid-
night the previous night. Someone from the Howard Johnson's
restaurant had called her after 11:00 P.M., saying that the boys
were there and needed a ride home. Mrs. J. informed the person
that she did not travel at night and that the boys would have to
find their own way home.

In general, according to Mrs. J., Jim was totally uncooperative. Although Joey did help with chores, particularly those
involving the horses, both boys simply took off each day without any explanation, and she could not keep the boys on that
basis.

On the following day, the worker spoke with Mr. B., the
father, and told him that the foster parent was no longer able to
take responsibility for the boys because of their behavior. The
worker indicated to Mr. B. that an effort would be made to locate another foster home but that he would have to consider
the contract terminated if another placement could not be
found.

The next day, the worker again spoke with Mr. B. and
told him that a foster home had been located. But Mr. B. became angry at the distance the boys would be from him and
stated that he would pick up the boys that day. Arrangements
were made for the boys to be brought to the office and for Mr.
B. to pick them up there. The boys arrived at the agreed-upon
time, but Mr. B. was about an hour and a half late. During this
time the worker asked the boys how they felt about their experience and their return home. Both seemed happy at the prospect
of being back with their father. During the wait Jim became extremely restless and at one point left the office to walk around
the building. Although it was a cold, winter day, he did so with-

out wearing a coat. The worker continued to talk with Joey and was impressed with his realistic approach and understanding of his father's difficulties.

When Mr. B. arrived, he seemed to be in a very defiant mood. The smell of alcohol was on his breath. He said that he had tried to get help for his boys, that no agencies wanted to help Indians, and that he would just have to take care of his own boys. He added that he had bought Christmas presents for them and that they were all going to go out and smoke marijuana that night. He did not know where they would be staying and said that they would probably just roam around. Both boys expressed embarrassment at their father's talk and asked him to cut it out. Since this interview took place on the day before Christmas, the office was in the process of celebrating. The worker invited the boys and Mr. B. to share food that had been brought in by the staff—hot food as well as a special punch. Jim spotted the punch and commented to his father that perhaps he would want a drink. The worker said to Jim that the punch did not contain alcohol, but Jim went to get punch for his father anyway. Mr. B. then made a big joke about the punch because it did not contain alcohol. It seemed to the worker that Jim had to perform some kind of defiant act in order to impress and please his father.

Apparently, neither the foster parent nor the children were ready to use this placement beneficially. In other cases, however, children can accept the plans and use the new living situation more easily if the worker visits them regularly and assures them that the agency supports their parents' efforts to improve parenting. A visit to talk only with foster parents is not sufficient for making accurate assessments of growth and of the child's needs. Because of divided or conflicting loyalties, the children should always be given an opportunity to talk privately, just as practitioners and foster parents talk privately. The worker can explain that every participant in foster care has the right to talk alone with a staff member and that private talks are more useful because the staff member then can listen without interruption.

Sometimes foster parents may use silence to control a child's behavior: "If you promise never to run off again, I won't tell the worker." These conspiracies only serve to undermine the placement process. It is useful to anticipate such agreements and to discuss the fact that they can be harmful: "Sometimes children try to deal with me by offering information if I won't tell anyone. I find that these deals do not really help anyone. It is better if we discuss problems and relationships and work together on any changes that should be made."

Sometimes a worker may visit a foster home and notice a change in a living arrangement or in the behavior of a foster parent or child. Since there are always enough problems to fill interview time and energy, the worker may be tempted not to rock the boat if no one mentions the change. She might even ignore a problem when it is mentioned. For instance, one foster care worker reported that a foster child alluded to sexual approaches by the foster father. The worker left quickly and ignored the remark, saying, "Boy, I didn't want to hear that. I have enough to do." However, avoiding an issue or not remarking on an observation, such as another child living in the household, or another sleeping arrangement, invariably leads to later problems. If assessments are made early and intervention can be initiated early and appropriately, then all clients receive better service. Foster parents should be told that it is in their own best interests for the agency to know of changes. If a very serious problem develops with the foster child, because of a situation that was withheld from the worker, the parents may be legally liable for not adequately providing for the child. The agency may then be their accuser rather than their advocate.

Working with Natural Parents for Placement

From the initial assessment of family need through to termination of placement and follow-up supervision and service, the goal is not to exert control over a family but to strengthen the family and involve all family members in the planning process. When a child is placed in foster care, the remaining family members have additional family stress to compound whatever original stress caused the dysfunction of parenting and the removal of a child. It is important to offer service to help the natural parents resolve their conflicted feelings regarding placement—feelings such as anger, guilt, and inadequacy—and rebuild their families.

What roles can natural parents take in the continued childrearing? First of all, they might participate in drawing up a written contract that spells out agency, foster parents', and natural parents' responsibilities for meeting the child's needs— needs that must be redefined as the child grows older. The natural parents also can be encouraged to visit the child regularly, at times convenient to them; if they need help in finding transportation or in confronting the foster parents, that help should be provided. Natural parents also should be asked to participate when their children are selecting school courses or sports or other extracurricular activities or when the agency is making decisions about the children.

During the initial assessment process, workers should try to establish and maintain a working relationship with the natural parents, so that they realize that their role is crucial to the continued rearing of the child. If contact with the parents is lost —and many agency records state "whereabouts unknown" after parents' names—a child's opportunity for successful adjustment both during placement and in adulthood may be destroyed. Parents who have been ignored by agencies can appear at inopportune times and spirit children away. Then there is no resolution of the child's conflicted loyalties, and he is left to deal with feelings of confusion and guilt.

Jessie, age fourteen, had been in a residential program for neglected and abused children for eleven years, and agency staff had worked sporadically with the mother for about two years following the placement. She subsequently moved, and no attempt to locate her was made. Jessie became pregnant and requested permission to marry the father. The request of the agency director was made on a Friday afternoon. He denied permission and planned for casework discussion the following week. On Monday morning the child presented signed permission for the marriage from her mother.

At long last, Jessie's mother, who had been ignored by the agency for so many years, could take charge of her child and could discharge her rights of guardianship. Because no one

had worked with this mother, the agency contributed to the neglect of a child. The mother lived within walking distance of the
institution, and Jessie had seen her regularly. Neither Jessie nor
her mother believed that their situations would be improved by
disclosing the information. When an issue such as marriage
arose, the mother was not about to enter into a collaborative
planning relationship for the child's best interests. She had
strong feelings of hatred for staff members who had ignored her
and who had long ago identified her as an inadequate parent.
Jessie was later battered in the marriage, as was the infant. Both
needed care, and there were many problems, partly because the
agency did not value the importance of all parents to all children. The physical separation of parents and children does not
automatically break the long, enduring emotional ties that exist
between them.

Permanency Planning: An Alternative to Foster Care

Calhoun (1980a, p. 4) notes that "in attempting to protect and nurture children who were not or could not be adequately cared for in their own homes, society took on a most
complex task. And the evidence is that almost as much harm as
good has resulted from our past efforts." He also notes that a
1930 White House conference on children set one of the rights
of children as "the right to a permanent home." In the 1980s
we are actually further from that goal than we were in 1930, as
evidenced by the tripling of the number of children in foster
care. Because of this increase, practitioners are concerned that
too many children are being reared in an "undefined" and sec-
ond-class status, belonging to no one. Out of this concern has
developed the concept of permanency planning and the very important Adoption Assistance and Child Welfare Act of 1980.

Permanency Planning. Permanency planning, one of the
most significant new concepts in foster care services, developed
out of the recognition that the numbers of foster children have
been increasing and that more children remain in care for longer
periods. Although permanency planning is a function of the foster care system, it is an effort to remove children from the temporary foster care placement, either by facilitating the child's

return to his own home or by developing a permanent placement—through adoption; placement with relatives, friends, or
godparents; formal, long-term foster care; or guardianship—
when it is clear that the child cannot return home.

According to Pike and his associates (1977, pp. 1-7), permanency planning involves the following steps:

1. *Early Planning with Parents.* Practitioners should involve
   the parents immediately in starting plans for the child's return, if feasible. If parents have deserted, it is easier to locate them soon after placement—before the child has settled
   into the foster home. If it is clear that the parents cannot
   have the child return home, then plans can be initiated for
   adoption or for other permanent arrangements.
2. *Casework Planning.* Many people—such as physicians, psy-
   chiatrists, psychologists, attorneys, judges, and foster parents—will have to be included in the plan. The central role,
   however, is taken by the practitioner, who sets planning activities in motion, coordinates activities, and keeps activities focused on permanency.
3. *Shared Decision Making.* The many people working together must make decisions about the plan.
4. *Internal Monitoring Devices*—often a case-planning mecha-
   nism that becomes part of an automated system.

Maluccio and his colleagues (1980, p. 519) suggest the
following guidelines to permanency planning:

1. Early intervention and early consideration of long-term
   plans for each child.
2. Examination of different long-term alternatives.
3. Delineation of a time-limited casework plan to achieve the
   best placement.
4. Organization of legal evidence for a plan.
5. Periodic case review—either internal, external, or a combination of the two.

In a study of permanency planning projects, Jones and
Biesecker (1980) indicate that four elements are present in suc-

cessful programs: leadership, regular review of children in care, goal-oriented casework, and consultation and technical assistance.

Child Welfare Act of 1980. The Adoption Assistance and Child Welfare Act of 1980 represents federal policy to keep families together. Specifically, the act encourages states to help children remain with their families or, if that is not possible, to place them in permanent homes. The emphasis of the act is on reducing the drift of children in foster care, developing a strict accounting of children's status, initiating permanent living arrangements, and eventually cutting the cost of foster care. Calhoun (1980b, p. 2) lists the major features of the act:

1. Federal aid will be available for the adoption of children with special needs, such as older, handicapped, and minority children.
2. By October 1, 1982, all states must have established an adoption assistance program.
3. Federal assistance for foster care mandates the provision of emergency and crisis-type services to prevent the placement of children in foster care.
4. Federal aid for foster care mandates increased services and procedures to reach the goal of permanent planning for children.
5. Financial incentives will be established to emphasize family-oriented programs rather than placement programs.
6. States will be required to conduct an inventory of all children in foster care under their supervision for six months or longer.
7. States will be required to develop a service program designed to help children return to their families or be placed for adoption or legal guardianship.
8. Federal funds can be used to pay for the foster placement of children through a voluntary agreement with the parents, rather than through a judicial decision. After six months of care, the case must go to court.
9. Federal funds available for public facilities holding no more than twenty-five children encourage placing children in

smaller facilities where a more personal and home-like atmosphere exists.

Practice Dilemmas

The urgency of planning for permanence, so that children
can avoid long years in limbo, sometimes results in abrupt rather than thoughtful decision making. If the worker does not
carefully evaluate the parents' willingness to nurture, even
though the parents may not demonstrate the ability or knowledge, court action may be initiated in error. If a child no longer
feels wanted by his parents, this situation may point to the appropriateness of permanent placement, but only if the parental
behavior demonstrates rejection and an unwillingness to change
behavior.

Some plans for permanence are disrupted. Maluccio and
colleagues (1980) examined the results of two projects where
such plans were instituted. In the Oregon Project, 91 percent of
the children remained in the same placement after eighteen
months. In the second project, which mainly served children
who were emotionally disturbed, only 66 percent remained in
the same placement. These results are inconclusive, and the attempt here is not to deny the important contribution of permanency planning for children. It is only to caution agencies not
to move too fast in the direction of permanent placements
when such placements might not produce an accompanying
feeling of permanence. That is, for children in permanent placement, just as for those in temporary care, the child's and parents' sense of permanence, rather than legal status, is the key to
the child's well-being.

Christine, age eleven, David, age seven, and Robert, age
five, were placed in foster care eight months ago because, according to their mother, she was unable to control them and
also was low in funds. She now is out of work and faces eviction
from the rooming house where she has lived for several months.

There had been complaints of neglect against this mother
in the past, but they were not substantiated and there was no
proof that the children were ever at risk. However, when the

Child Placement Review Board reviewed the case record, its recommendation was to terminate parental rights. The caseworker,
who did not feel that termination was justified, obtained a
court order to have an evaluation of the family by the mental
health service.

According to the worker, "The purpose of this evaluation
would be to determine what, if any, bonding exists between
mother and children, and between children. We need to know if
this mother is capable of parenting any of these children before
action can be taken on any course. Mother is vague about her
past, so I have only limited information. She was very close to
her mother, who recently died. A split was made with the rest
of the family on an issue around the death. Mother has been
married four times and had a child by each of three husbands.
She states that she had a nervous breakdown sometime around
her mother's death, but I am not certain of the time frame.
Mother is proud of the fact that she was able to provide the
children with a father, but she also states the children drove
each of her husbands away. She has tried to work and provide
to the best of her ability for her children, but I feel she expects
too much of herself and the children."

Description of the children's behavior by the foster parents includes dumping bleach, burning dolls, and biting each
other on the legs and feet. The foster parents reported that the
children resisted mothering and appeared to be very angry.

It appears that the needs of these children are in conflict
with the needs of all the adults. They are demonstrating unmet
emotional needs by their destructive behavior and inability to
accept nurture. On the other hand, the biological mother needs
to be free of their care when her life is stressful. In addition,
foster parents have difficulty controlling and receive no pleasure
from the child care.

The solution for this situation is not necessarily to terminate parental rights. The mother has not demonstrated any intent of neglecting. She has not abandoned the children psychologically; in fact, she is proud of providing each of the children
with a father. More information is needed regarding the source
of the children's disturbed behavior, so that an appropriate service plan can be developed. Reducing both environmental stress
and internal stress that overwhelms the mother may increase her
capacity to parent. There are no data to indicate that the family

was given any other community services prior to the recent placement. At this point, the children are not able to establish new relationships and use foster care. The important issue here is that the agency not rush to a termination of parental rights when there is insufficient information about the mother.

Before a recommendation is made to the court for termination of parental rights, several community professionals must assess the family's need, make every effort to provide resources, and then determine, based on their use of services, the capacity and the willingness of parents to meet children's needs.

A separated mother receiving Aid to Families with Dependent Children for herself and her two children—a boy, five, and a girl, two—was referred by the Parkland Child Care Center because of suspicious bruises and black eyes on the five-year-old, who attended the center. In this case the social worker concluded that serious jeopardy existed and that termination of parental rights was justified. She based her conclusion on the following findings:

1. The five-year-old boy was described by mother as "all bad," "monster, Jr.," "out of control," sick like his father and paternal grandfather, and as possibly having double Y chromosomes.

2. The boy was diagnosed by four accredited testing services in the community as being developmentally, socially, and emotionally retarded because of lack of stimulation and parental emotional neglect and unavailability.

3. The two-year-old girl appeared to be emotionally detached and was treated by the mother as something like a piece of furniture. The girl is "God's reward for having such a bad child as Jerry."

4. The mother had no recognition that a problem existed: "I like teenagers; when he'll be a teenager, we'll get along." Two years of intensive community treatment by six different agencies had produced no change.

This worker did enlist community services, did obtain full diagnostic information from several sources, and did arrange for intensive treatment. In this case she was forced to conclude that the mother would not be able to nurture and provide for her children.

Summary

The care of children in foster family homes is an important component of child welfare service to both parents and children. It includes care for a child when his own family cannot care for him for a temporary or extended period. Foster care has become a specialized and skilled service during this century.

Children who can make the best use of foster family care are those who can take part in family activities and relationships and cooperate with family expectations. Good foster parents are those who can cooperate with an agency and social worker, be nurturing and caring with children without expecting too much in return, be able to understand and manage their own feelings in relation to natural parents, participate in activities to enhance their parenting skills, participate with the social worker in analyzing children's development and behavior, and be willing to have natural parents visit the children. Children have many difficulties in adjusting to foster care: they must be counseled and given age-appropriate information about the reasons for their placement. Natural parents should help their children make use of the foster home, but not all parents can do so. Agency staff, in collaboration with foster parents, must also help children adapt. Contacts should be maintained with natural parents, and they may need encouragement to continue to participate in both decisions about, and activities with, their children.

There are many dilemmas in serving families; only two are presented: practitioners must not be too fast in terminating parental rights, and they must also recognize that a few parents may never be able to nurture their children.

Efforts should be made to keep parents engaged in relationships with their children.

There have been questions raised about the increasing number of children who have remained in a temporary status for long periods. Permanency planning, a recently implemented concept, has the intent of providing more permanent placements for children by either assuring a reunion with the natural

parents or by providing for other permanent living arrangements. The Adoption Assistance and Child Welfare Act of 1980
is expected to prevent family breakdown, help to keep more
families together, return more children to their own homes, and
increase permanent arrangements for children.

Special Annotated Bibliography

Emlen, A., and others. *Overcoming Barriers to Planning for
Children in Foster Care.* DHEW Publication No. (OHDS) 78-
30138. Washington, D.C.: U.S. Department of Health, Education and Welfare, 1978. Essential reading for those concerned
with implementing the concept of permanence for children.

Fox, R., and Whelley, J. "Preventing Placement: Goal Attainment in Short-Term Family Treatment." *Child Welfare,*
1982, *61* (4), 231-238. Describes a preventive program—using
communication theory, setting of clear goals and objectives,
and a high ratio of staff to consumers with intensive initial
services—that can avert the placement of many children.

Jacobs, M. "Foster Parent Training: An Opportunity for Skills
Enrichment and Empowerment." *Child Welfare,* 1980, *59*
(10), 615-624. Points to one of the constructive directions
for strengthening foster parents.

Maluccio, A., and Sinanoglu, P. A. (Eds.). *The Challenge of
Partnership: Working with Parents of Children in Foster Care.*
New York: Child Welfare League of America, 1981. A collection of far-sighted and practical articles pointing the direction
of improved services for both children and parents.

Maluccio, A., and others. "Beyond Permanency Planning."
Child Welfare, 1980, *59* (9), 515-530. Examines the current
status of permanency planning and discusses some of its
problems and prospects.

CHAPTER SIX

Residential Care: Matching Children and Treatment Programs

Residential programs are another form of care for children who must live away from their parents for any length of time. Whittaker (1977, p. 169) notes the various, sometimes overlapping, types of residential services for children: "residential treatment centers, therapeutic group homes, day treatment programs, crisis shelter services, and small 'treatment-oriented' institutional programs, many of which are offered in combination under the auspices of a single agency." These programs are designed for the physically handicapped, for blind and deaf children or those with a combination of handicapping conditions, for the mentally ill and the developmentally disabled, for dependent and neglected children, for those with a range of behavioral problems and characteristics that make residential care either a choice or a necessity, and for status offenders and other more serious law offenders.

It is often difficult for the practitioner to know which service can best help a particular child, since centers have many ways to describe and define what they do and whom they can best serve. They also may differ according to which type of child is currently being served. Even one or two children in a cottage can change the complexion of services received. Some programs also may stress benefits for the group rather than for the individual. Whittaker (1977) believes that residential programs will tend, in the future, to focus less on curing emotional disturbances and will increasingly emphasize teaching various skills for adequate social functioning.

History

Residential institutions for children were first established in the nineteenth century, so that children could be removed from the almshouses, prisons, and asylums. From 1900 to 1940, such institutions slowly disappeared as foster care became the preferable type of nurturing. But in the 1940s institutions became favored again, and the numbers of children in care slowly rose. Between 1960 and 1970, the number of institutionalized children in the United States continued to increase, but the rate of children admitted to these programs declined slightly and the number of dependent and neglected children declined: "Related to the decline was the added development of alternative-care facilities, as well as wholesale changes in social attitudes toward single-parent families and adoptions. The change was of such magnitude that leading facilities terminated residential programs and moved toward outpatient counseling, health and sex education, academic and vocational education, teaching of parenting, and other nonresidential programs" (Matsushima, 1977, p. 146).

These activities culminated in the "deinstitutionalization movement" of the 1970s, which was accelerated by at least four events: (1) Parents of mentally retarded children, appalled at findings of gross neglect and abuse of children in congregate quarters, began to band together and to seek improved services. (2) Federal funds were allocated to establish mental health programs in the community for the treatment and prevention of emotional problems and for services to the developmentally disabled. (3) The civil rights movement discovered and took action against enforced commitments to facilities and the detention of children and adults without proper legal protections, the commitment of persons to treatment facilities that failed to provide treatment, and other discriminatory practices. (4) Federal and state monies, through Title XX of the Social Security Act, were appropriated for extensive community services.

Another result of the change in philosophy and attitude toward institutional services was the advent of group homes (Adams and Baumbach, 1980). The group home is always located in a community, so that residents have easy access to school, work, and other parts of the community. These programs can obviously serve the youth who has achieved a fair amount of independence, cannot adapt to a foster home, requires help with maturation, and whose behavior is acceptable in the larger community. Specialized foster family care for the emotionally disturbed is another program available in many communities; in these programs treatment specialists often serve as consultants to the foster parents. The child may also be engaged in a therapeutic program with the local mental health center.

Benefits of Residential Care

Although there has been a decrease in the number of institutions, there has been an increase in the quality and professional preparation of the staffs employed in residential treatment programs. The therapeutic component of a program was formerly attributed to the therapeutically trained staff, and all others were considered auxiliary or supplementary personnel. Today much recognition is given to all the staff in the program, particularly the child care staff, also called cottage parents or by other titles, who provide the day-to-day care of the children. As diagnostic, treatment, communication, and relationship skills have improved, residential programs have been able to provide clearer statements of the children whom they can best serve. Just as the institutions must be explicit about the children their organizations can help, child welfare referring staff must provide the necessary information for the selection of children who will most likely fit into the programs.

According to Klein (1975, p. 16), a residential treatment

program is often the least detrimental alternative for the child. As evidence he cites a study by Wolins (1969), who found no differences in intellectual or psychosocial abilities between children in group care and those reared at home. Klein believes that if group living proves comparable to home living, then "it would seem incontrovertible that residential care is preferable to living in a noxious, disorganized, or rejecting family." He also believes that a stable residential placement with one facility for several or many years may be far more secure for the child than the foster placement and replacement of children in numerous homes, sometimes as many as a dozen. When a child is not able to use foster care, then it may be wise to consider the residential placement, even though the child may not demonstrate all the behavioral characteristics deemed as prerequisites for placement in a residential program. Klein also reasons that there is a dearth of good-quality foster family homes and that the residential program "is preferable to placement in foster homes of dubious quality" (p. 19).

Klein (pp. 239, 240) emphasizes that the child's return to healthy family living is the goal of residential treatment. Consequently, "intensive involvement of the total family as active participants in the therapeutic process is necessary. . . . Children come to treatment institutions as emissaries of malfunctioning family systems; it is imperative that the family change functionally or organizationally if the child is to return to the family and maintain the gains he has made in the treatment setting. If the family system does not change, the child will be seduced back to his old behavior shortly after he returns home." Finklestein (1981) and Whittaker (1981) propose a number of changes in residential programs to make them responsive to the entire family. Whittaker views the residential center as a "family support system," with activities such as family support groups; parent education; home visiting by child care staff; and parents' participation in school programs, child care tasks, birthdays, field trips, and other events. Finklestein reports on small-scale efforts to involve whole families in residential programs, and she sees these as more effective service to families than the traditional services. The implications of these adaptations are clear: all members in the family have to change. These innovations show promise to improve relationships and to decrease the time a youth spends in a residential program.

Characteristics of Residential Programs

Kadushin (1974, pp. 622-624) and Costin (1972, pp. 346-350) list some of the characteristics that differentiate a residential program from a foster family home:

1. There is a less intense relationship with parental figures. The child shares houseparents, cottage parents, or child care staff with other children who live in the same group. Child care staff, because they are employees of an organization and are busy with many children and with cottage, program, and administrative details, may have less need than foster parents for psychic and emotional responses from children. Their gratification is gained from their professional role and does not primarily depend on gratitude from, or achievement by, the children. Consequently, children who are unable to accept a close nurturing relationship and who have never developed the capacity to trust are much better able to handle a residential program, since they can keep at a safe emotional distance from the staff. Lester, in the following case, is clearly this kind of child.

Lester, age eleven, had been casually treated by his parents since he was three years old. The parents had gone to a mental health center when he was four, complaining that he was a daydreamer, did not want to be with other children, and had never wanted to be held much as a child. The parents separated twice for periods of about one year, and Lester had lived for short periods with his father. He also lived with an uncle and aunt for two years, from age eight through ten. They found him aloof, somewhat isolated from others, often a "loner"; he was caught twice for shoplifting. School reports showed that he was working below his ability, was not spontaneous, and did not seek out friends or engage in group activities.

2. The child has a choice of parent figures. Although he will have many working relationships with the child care staff in his cottage or unit, he also can relate to recreation personnel,

bus drivers, maintenance staff, social workers, and others. A well-operated institution will include all staff in the purposes and treatment concepts, since children can be helped by a variety of people. Programs with strong behavior modification regimes must involve all staff in the therapeutic program, and all staff must be aware of the specific treatment program for each child.

An extremely important person at one institution was the cook in the administrative building. Although she prepared no meals for the separate cottages, she was available most of the day for staff and visitor needs, and she was always around in the late afternoon when children came in from school. She was a natural, giving person, and many children stopped at her kitchen immediately after they dumped their belongings in the cottage. They went there not just to get some snacks but to be surrounded by her warm and caring attitude toward them.

Although staff such as cooks and maintenance personnel are often considered outside of "professional staff," they are often as integral to children's well-being as the staff trained in therapeutic procedures. Auxiliary staff can also serve as the "relief valve" for the stress of expected behavioral change.

3. Institutional programs may permit a wide range of individual behaviors that would not be understood or tolerated in the foster home or the wider community. For instance, losses to property—rug spills, mattress deterioration from urination, broken laundry equipment, jammed plumbing, missing utensils, broken dishes, damaged heating units, defaced walls, broken windows, slashed tires—are more easily absorbed by an institution than by a foster family home. Similarly, children who make distorted facial grimaces, store food under their mattress, smell all food or ask whether it has poison in it, or put their clothes and shoes under the sheets at night are more readily tolerated by the residential program staff than by foster parents. No aspect of this behavior needs to be viewed as a personal attack on the caretakers, or as a rejection of emotional investment in the child.

The executive director walked into the room used by the board of directors for their monthly meeting. The room has easy access from the hallway, which leads to one of the eight dorms on the campus. The room is often locked, but it had been open all day because of the board meeting scheduled for the evening. The director, in checking the room, found to his horror that the glass-enclosed breakfront had been smashed with a piece of heavy wood, left over from some renovations in the adjacent dorm. The child care staff determined later that the damage had been done by one or several youth who had been disruptive recently and who were known to be angry at the entire institution. The mess was cleaned up, and the board meeting proceeded without further incident.

4. Institutions usually have rules and regulations and a routine that can substitute for internal controls, which some children have not yet achieved. Because the rules apply to everyone, they are not as readily viewed by the child as being capricious or selective, and the child can recognize that he has company in the uniformity of the expectations. The rules provide a reliability that children may not have experienced before, if they have lived with parents who provided nothing consistent or stable. Some of the rules are written, so that children can read them or be reminded of them through bulletin board announcements, whereas in foster families rules are rarely formalized and seldom written down.

William, age fourteen, was very tired from an afternoon ball game, and the weather made everyone extra hot. The other boys had taken their showers, which was a requirement prior to evening snacks, but William kept delaying his shower. Jerry, the child care worker, reminded him gently of the house rules on this. William growled that they didn't apply to him tonight, but Jerry said they always applied. William suddenly dashed toward the table, breaking three large bottles of soda, saying that if he couldn't have his, the others wouldn't get theirs. Jerry quietly announced that another house rule was that behavior like this results in no treat, and William would still have to take his shower. Two of the boys yelled at him that rules were rules and he would get none tonight. Jerry talked quietly with William for a few minutes, since he was temporarily out of control. Two days later William admitted that he shouldn't have broken the bottles, but he "gets tired of rules."

5. The child is a member of a peer group, and that group,

in addition to child care staff, has some power to control a child's behavior. If the child is able to identify with this group as a member, then the group can exert pressure over his behavior, and child care staff can use the group for behavioral change of individual members. Residents who have been in the program can be helpful to newcomers.

When Lisa was admitted to the program, one of the oldest members of the dorm, Janet, was assigned to help orient her to the program and introduce her to other residents. When told about the work that residents were expected to do, Lisa protested that she was not going to serve and clean up after meals. Janet reminded her that everyone took a turn at this and would count on her to take her turn, so that the work—which was not really hard—was kept to a minimum. When Lisa continued to complain, Janet finally said, "If you don't do it, the rest of us will have to do your work for you for a couple of turns, and no one's willing to do that, so we expect you to do it. Karen and Laura [child care staff] aren't the only ones that make you do this; we expect it also."

6. Institutions often have a number of choices to help children. A foster family home has essentially one living arrangement, whereas institutions have many. A child can be transferred from one program to another, from one cottage to another, moved to live with or near a sibling, changed to a cottage of a child care staff member whom the child likes, moved to another cottage to change a child's behavior, or removed from the negative influence of a certain child. As noted earlier, the child has a number of adults to whom she can relate, and the institution can make many alternate arrangements to increase the choices for improving the child's opportunities and behavior. A child's social and emotional level may require that she live with children who are younger than she, until she has matured sufficiently to live with older children, although she still can associate with older children during the day.

Nancy was an angry child when admitted to the Leavitt Center at age nine. She came with her older sister, Leah, who was admitted to one of the adolescent girls' cottages. Nancy was given to many emotional outbursts, lied to cottage staff constantly about what she did, was short tempered, and would give up quickly on any task assigned to her. In spite of her emotional outbursts, she never assaulted anyone. She was more like a four- or five-year-old in her limited ability to share or cooperate in an activity or game. Other cottage members disliked her, because they saw her as rude and as a little baby. Nancy was transferred to a cottage containing seven- and eight-year-olds, and this was initially a blow to her. She was ridiculed by some of the members of the first cottage, but the younger girls liked the status of having an older child living with them. She became popular, and her outbursts ceased as she acquired a new status with the group. Nancy had never experienced anything like this at home or in the previous cottage. She stayed with the younger girls for about one year and then moved back to the original cottage of children closer to her age. She had become more mature and was now far more acceptable to her peers.

7. Institutions usually have specially trained staff who can meet the child's needs. Because many different types of staff can report on a child's behavior under varying conditions, assessments for further treatment planning or other service arrangements, including discharge, can be expedited.

Behavioral Characteristics of Children in Residential Care

According to Whittaker (1977), the following behaviors are typical of many of the children referred to residential settings:

1. *Poorly Developed Impulse Control.* Children referred to residential settings tend to have a low tolerance for frustration and find it difficult to delay gratification to a later time. They attack objects, others, and themselves out of frustration, tension, and anxiety and sometimes are not fully aware of the extent of their disruptive behavior. Many of these children are easily stimulated by others; consequently, residential programs often have clearly designated "quiet times" for relaxation and the reduction of stimulation, especially prior to bed.

Kenneth, age sixteen, jumps from one activity to another. The gym teacher at school reports that he is unable to follow the rules of games such as baseball or basketball and becomes very upset if he cannot always be a starter in a game, even though there is a clear policy that all players have a turn to start. During the last game, when he was told he could not start, he threw his towel on the floor and went storming back to his locker. He was told the day before and just prior to the game that he would not be on the starting team. He kicked the metal locker door and bent it slightly, injuring his toe in the process. Two other teachers report that he has to be kept separate from two other buddies, who "keep him wound up."

2. *Low Self-Image.* The child often considers himself bad, different, "a dope," and unable to change—perhaps because others have seen or defined him this way. A youth may be accused of looking and behaving "exactly like your mother" or just "like your old man" and then reminded that the adult "hasn't changed in twenty years; in fact, he's worse now than he was before!" Some of the other characteristics and behaviors of children in this listing would logically lead to a poor self-image, especially if a child compared himself to others and also accepted stereotyping images.

Lucinda, age fifteen, was having difficulties in her school-work and had failed to attend many of her classes last term. Her parents requested her placement. On the psychological examination administered at the center, she achieved a verbal IQ of 97 and a performance IQ of 90. The examiner noted, however, that Lucinda's depression during the exam may have contributed to the lowered IQ scores. She was tense during the session, giving the examiner the feeling that she was trying to keep her painful feelings in control. She maintained a serious, perturbed, and unhappy look on her face, often partially laying her head down on the desk. She has negative feelings toward both parents, identifies mostly with her father, and sees herself "as a loser," just as he is considered to be. She entertains feelings of hopelessness about her future. Because of her weak commonsense reasoning and judgment in everyday situations, she may need very close adult supervision. She is an emotionally distraught girl, experiencing a deep sense of loss and confusion regarding self.

3. *Poorly Developed Modulation of Emotion.* Many children admitted to programs have difficulty in understanding and handling their emotions. They may have marked mood swings

and also have trouble in defining what they are feeling. The presence of feelings that may be strong as well as rapidly changing makes it imperative for the referring social worker and the treatment center social worker to assist the youth in the transition to the program.

Nora, age sixteen, was known to have strong mood swings and erratic behavior. The parents had described her alternating hostile and cooperative behavior with her peers, which meant that she did not keep friends very long. They also described times when she would sit and cry quietly to herself. When asked what was upsetting her, she stated that she did not know. When admitted to the center, she was extremely protective of her own belongings and would accuse someone of planning to steal her possessions if that person even looked at them. She would agree to a social activity and then refuse to take part.

4. *Deficiencies in Forming Relationships.* Children might isolate themselves from others or attempt to overinvolve others in a relationship. As a result of their inability to pursue a middle course, such children have few friends or satisfying relationships. They may also lack the basic social skills essential to starting a relationship, and they often relate to adults in stereotyped ways.

Amita, age twelve, was recognized by the staff as a very needy child emotionally. She always sought friends who were willing to be close to her physically. She wanted to hold hands all the time and would squeeze a person's hand very tightly. During the summer people's hands became soaked with sweat, but this never discouraged Amita. When an acquaintance of a child care worker visited, Amita came up to him, quickly grabbed his hand, and asked, "Could you be my daddy for the whole day?" This behavior increased shortly after she came to the center, but it began to diminish after about eight months.

5. *Family Pain and Strain.* The families from which the children come have usually been out of balance for some time. In some cases parental behavior may have caused and contributed to the child's problem; but even the most stable of parents can become worn out and shattered by, for example, a hyper-

kinetic child with a short attention span and unpredictable behavior. The source of the problem is not the issue. The impact
of the problem is felt by the entire family, and both the child
and the family have been frustrated by failures to resolve the
problems.

Both parents admitted that they were absolutely exhausted
from caring for Linda. They had lost many of their adult friends
because few could tolerate her provocative behavior and because she required the full attention of the parents. Linda's irri-
tability, restlessness, and short sleep requirements had worn out
the parents as well as the two younger siblings. The father had
been so preoccupied by her behavior and his inability to help
her that he could not give full attention to their small business;
as a result, sales had fallen off. The mother begged for Linda's
placement "not because we don't love her but because we're no
good to her the way we are."

6. *Special Learning Disabilities.* The children may suffer
from dyslexia, which leads to a developmental lag in the ability
to understand written language; or from "minimum cerebral
dysfunction," also called hyperkinesis, manifested by a "short
attention span, marked distractibility, hyperkinesis ('organic
drivenness'), lability of mood and reduced frustration tolerance,
'catastrophic' anxiety, and certain specific intellectual deficits
such as a poor ability to distinguish between figure and background, perceptuo-motor difficulties, and some impairment of
the capacity for abstraction" (Lewis, 1971, p. 130). Both of
these conditions lead to a reduced rate of learning and are not
always recognized by educators. The child cannot meet the expectations set for his age. Intense frustration often follows, and
there is a lowered self-image, especially if adults use repressive
methods or criticism to try to correct a problem that the child
cannot help. Consequently, inept responses to a child with these
problems can create a secondary emotional problem, which is
superimposed on the original deficit.

If adequate screening has not been done, practitioners
may assume that the child's poor school performance is caused
primarily by emotional problems, and the child's physical problems may be ignored. When complete diagnostic procedures

have defined the probable genesis of the child's problems, and dyslexia is one of the causes, then the practitioner is able to plan more carefully for application to a residential program that has specialists available who treat dyslexics, if a choice of services exists. The percentage of children who suffer from hyperkinesis is not known, but it is estimated to be somewhere between 3 and 20 percent (Huessey and Cohen, 1978). Chemotherapy is one form of treatment, and if that treatment can reduce the child's symptoms to a manageable point, he may not need to live away from home. However, when the problem has not been detected until early adolescence, it is unlikely that behavioral change will be rapid.

Leonard, age fourteen, was born prematurely and weighed slightly over four pounds at birth. He did not leave the hospital for seven weeks, and his mother described him as a cranky child. She stated that he is currently uncooperative, destructive, and unpredictable. Unlike his two siblings, he resists any type of discipline. He gets up and down at the table and may take an hour or more to finish his meal, since he thinks of other things to do. Leonard was pushed through school, and elementary school teachers considered him immature, moody, and distractible. Current school records show that he is often truant, does not complete schoolwork, irritates others, is easily discouraged, and has difficulty following directions. A psychological examination revealed that he is slightly below average, with a verbal IQ of 94 and a performance IQ of 82. His reading level is 4.3; arithmetic, 3.6. During the examination he was very restless and could not concentrate on one subject for much more than eight minutes.

7. *Limited Play Skills.* Whittaker (1977, p. 172) observes that "many children have a limited repertoire of skills for playing and tend to overload one or two activities in the same way that relationships get overloaded. Some children not only have difficulty in joining and participating in group activities, they are also unable to play alone."

Amy brought a well-worn deck of cards with her when she came to the center. She asked others to play poker with her, and a few were interested. She could also play solitaire but always wanted someone to watch as she played. She was desperate to have others play with her, but her peers began to refuse because Amy insisted on a few of her own rules and would not follow the accepted game rules. When the child care staff played with her, they began to set limits on the amount of time used for cards and slowly introduced the usual game rules. The game seemed to serve primarily as a way for Amy to recall the pleasant part of her past with her father.

Services to Child and Family

Social workers have several obligations in the referral, admission, and discharge of youth to residential programs. Their first task is to explain to the parents and the child that there is a connection between the child's dysfunctional behavior and the parents' responses to the child, which may also be dysfunctional. The second is to assure that the parents participate in suitable service programs to stimulate their changed perceptions of the problems and changed behaviors in preparation for the child's return home. The third is to assist in the transition to the center, and the last is to assist the child and the family in the child's reentry to the family. Service does not end on the day the child returns home.

The idea that the family must change or the child will only revert to the previous pathological family pattern has major ramifications for the referring social worker and the social service staff who admit the child. Strengthening of the child and changed behavior on his part may enable the parents to respond differently to him when he returns home. This does not justify a do-nothing approach with the parents, since their response is crucial for the child. If a family has not grasped some of the reasons for the child's problems, then in all likelihood the child will be treated the same as before. The child who returns home has the added problem of finding his place in a family that has dynamically closed ranks around him. The household has adjusted to his absence for a long time, and the members may be relieved by his absence. Reentry requires the family system to readjust to his presence; members can find the change difficult. The parents must be helped to see that the problem did not arise spontaneously and cannot be blamed solely on the school, the child's peers, his Aunt Mary, or anyone else. It also must be clarified that, with few exceptions, the problem did not originate last week or even last month but has been developing for a fair length of time. Only when both the child and the parents make changes is it likely that the child's return home can result in the assurance of a satisfactory family adjustment. When parents are not helped to change and do not see their role in contributing to or reinforcing the problem, then they may continue to see the child as the sole cause of the behavior, blaming and stereotyping him, and then demanding his removal when the difficult behavior emerges again.

We first consider two cases where family support for the child was negligible. Placement occurred because the school and families could no longer accept the disruptive behavior.

Dan, age twelve, evidences seriously dysfunctional behavior at home and at school. The school counselor reports that he slumps frequently in his chair, teases other students, calls them obscene names, calls out loudly in class, giggles, doodles on the pages of books, and writes his name on each corner of every page. He can give occasional attention to schoolwork and responds correctly to some subjects. He has no friends, and he occasionally weeps without any provocation. He walks out of the classroom for no apparent reason and is returned with some resistance. In the lunchroom, he thinks it is very funny to take food from other students and to pour milk or water on their trays. According to the school psychologist, "these behaviors are of such severity that they inhibit learning to an extreme degree as well as impair the emotional well-being of the child." The psychologist adds that Dan's provocative behavior toward other students is "unremitting and has shaped his social environment so that nearly all persons interact with Dan in response to his negative behaviors."

Both his father and his primary caretaker, the paternal grandmother, say that Dan is a very difficult child whom they are unable to control. The grandmother states that Dan has temper outbursts every five to six weeks when he seems to go "wild"; she says that Dan is "sick." The mother left two years ago, lives with a sister, and is described as a "very inadequate person." The grandmother, who is in poor health, has been little more than a custodian.

The psychologist recommends family and group counseling, but the parents are unwilling and/or unable to provide this treatment. Therefore, Dan's emotional and mental well-being remains in jeopardy. When confronted with Dan's emotional and medical needs, the father said that he could not afford to take the time off from work to participate in family counseling. Under the threat of possible court action, however, he did take the family for one session and also conferred with the school about Dan's most recent suspension. A family friend, Lily, drove the grandmother and Dan to one other counseling session, but after that the father told Lily, and later the counselor, that they did not think counseling would help Dan.

The counselor feels that the parents blame Dan for everything and "are unwilling to look at themselves and their problems in relation to Dan." Since none of the local services can meet the boy's needs and there is no extended family or friends in a position to help, the counselor believes that Dan needs placement outside the home. The grandmother agrees and says that the father suspects that Dan will be taken by the state sooner or later.

Youth should not move by default into residential care, but that is what happened to Dan. The father did not like the plan, but he did not know what else to do, since Dan clearly needed an environment where he would not create so much hostility toward himself.

Mr. and Mrs. J. were divorced in 1978, and their children chose to remain with their father at his army post in Italy. Three years later, Mr. J. made a sudden decision to send his fourteen-year-old daughter, Maria, to her mother in the United States. Maria was already on a plane before the mother was notified. The mother and stepfather extended much care and nurture to Maria to facilitate her adjustment to the abrupt change in family, living arrangement, and environment. They provided her with her own telephone and television and bought her many new clothes.

In spite of the efforts of her mother and stepfather, Maria's adjustment was poor. Her behavior in school was "rude and obnoxious and interfered with classmate learning"; consequently, she was repeatedly suspended and then placed on home instruction. She ran away from home several times and had several short placements in a juvenile shelter. She is described as a habitual liar, and the school classifies her as emotionally disturbed. As Maria's behavior worsened at school and at home, the parents attempted to discipline her by restricting certain privileges, as stipulated in a behavioral contract established at the shelter and concluded at a family development center. However, they were inconsistent in their implementation of restrictions. According to the social worker at the center, "If Maria's privileges of going out on a specific night have been taken away, more likely it has been easier to give it back to Maria than cope with her nagging behavior at home." The social worker further noted: "This is a family with many internal problems, involving finances, marital strains, and Maria's emotional problems. Maria's difficulties stem from her past background, feelings of being abandoned at times by both mother and father. We have little knowledge about the abuse or neglect she suffered in Italy. Maria needs a structured environment where she can also obtain intensive psychotherapy. She is a bright child who has to learn to work within limits and experience trusting, secure relationships."

Maria's troubled behavior in school almost automatically excluded her from the option of foster family care. Without appropriate help she would probably become delinquent and placed in a correctional program. The mother and stepfather made it clear that they did not know "how we could ever" absorb Maria into their family again unless she made remarkable changes. Maria should have had further screening tests before planning for residential care, but the pressures for placement were strong. She was admitted with no prior psychological or psychiatric exams; interviews were held only with the parents and Maria.

A factor favoring early placement is the increasingly negative and desperate behaviors of community and parents alike toward a disruptive child. Furthermore, residential programs can provide "structure, consistency, and protection for the child"; and their "greatest strength," perhaps, is their diagnostic potential (Goldberg and Dooner, 1981, pp. 356-357). We may decry speedy admission, but the placement may provide a stable environment where an accurate assessment can be made. Maria also represents a number of youth who will probably never return to their families. With this type of admission, the parents will not engage in a treatment program.

The following case provides more detail of the family, and it includes the characteristics of the institution that will probably be a help to Lawrence.

Mr. and Mrs. A., in their mid-fifties, have been married for seventeen years. There are five children, three by the parents, one from the mother's previous marriage, and one from an illegitimate birth. The two oldest children, ages nineteen and twenty-two, had many difficulties in school and in general life adjustment. The family was referred to Social and Rehabilitation Services because of extensive problems with Lawrence, age fifteen, who came to the attention of police when he broke into a house three weeks ago. The mother is physically handicapped from arthritis and on the border of hysteria. She says she can no longer cope with Lawrence or with the two younger children, Hazel, age fourteen, and Jessie, age twelve. Hazel is described as verbally abusive toward the mother, headstrong, boy crazy, and doing poorly as a freshman in high school. Jessie is in a special education class, although she seems to be capable of higher-level work. She is apathetic and withdrawn at home and does nothing for herself.

According to the school counselor, Lawrence is of average intelligence, although he is in special education class; emotionally disturbed; and very upset about the break-in. The house owner did not press charges, but Lawrence was expelled from school for the remainder of the term (six weeks) because of his disruptive behavior in class. He had thrown books, destroyed property, and hit younger children. Some of the disruptive behavior followed a court hearing in which his being "sent away" was discussed.

The father admitted himself to the Veterans Hospital two months ago because he was afraid he was going to kill some of his family. A history of family violence was reported by Mrs. A. He has abused Lawrence and Jessie, and the mother frequently defended the children. However, her own arthritic condition, which has become worse in recent years, has prevented her from trying to stop him. He has often hit her but found more pleasure in striking the children. He laughs when she tells him to stop.

The father has been alcoholic for many years, although he always worked. He controlled the money and often deprived the family of food so that he could drink. He has never taken Mrs. A. anywhere except to a bar. He has been suicidal since age twelve; two relatives committed suicide, and three others have been in mental hospitals.

Mrs. A. got the courage to file for a divorce on the day he came out of the hospital. She had been wanting to dissolve the marriage for at least ten years. Mr. A. now lives with his mother but visits every day. His family never approved of the marriage, and he continues to criticize her. When Hazel recently told mother to "go to Hell," she said, "Ray, you could stop that," and he replied, "No, you stopped me from hitting them, and I won't stop them now."

When an agency psychiatrist met with Lawrence alone, he at first refused to talk. He was sullen and, when he answered queries, spoke in very few words. Comments were relevant but hostile. When the psychiatrist told him that she could not make a recommendation without his viewpoint, he said defiantly that he wanted to live away from home. He then asked whether he would ever see his parents again. He detested his father's many beatings and said that his mother called him a "dope," which he knows he is not, although sometimes he "acts that way." He stated that he knows what is right and what is wrong but would not elaborate further. Did he think his parents could ever change? Never. Would he want them to? No. He said he had three good friends, and he can find other friends.

The psychiatrist reported the following findings: "Diagnostic impression is behavior disorder of childhood. He is probably chronically depressed and may distort reality quite often. The family dynamics are clear, but treatment of this family would be almost impossible, especially with the limited services here. The school has done remarkably well for Lawrence, but he needs more services than are available. In view of the types of behavioral problems he has shown, a therapeutic foster home cannot offer the behavior control necessary for him. Residential treatment is the best choice."

The social worker had one brief contact with the father, who expressed no interest in Lawrence. He left the entire decision about him up to the agency and the mother. Mr. A. appeared tired and expressed little feeling for his son, stating only that he needed something to help him, "just like I need help." He became more animated as he discussed his own needs, indicating that they took priority over his son's problems.

The social worker met with Lawrence at home. She talked with him alone and with the mother present: "He was full of hostility and very saucy toward Mrs. A. in my presence. His understanding of being sent away is obviously one of rejection and punishment. I talked about his home situation and school. Lawrence blamed much of the problem at home on his mother, accused her of indifference toward him and always crying about herself. He was very angry at her for not telling him that he would be seeing a 'shrink.' He said he would be better off in a home, where 'you don't have to wonder what's going to happen.' He described his father as an 'old drunk' who had stopped beating him a couple of years ago, because 'I was getting too big.' Lawrence said he was never sure whether there would be food or not, and he blamed this on both parents. I believe that this youth is more capable than his class placement would indicate. He said it was too bad what happened at school, but 'it won't happen again, once I leave here.' He did, however, express some sadness at leaving home, especially for his sister, Jessie."

Two weeks later, in a discussion of plans for Lawrence's move to a residential program, Mrs. A. wondered how long he would have to be there. The worker encouraged the family to visit when Lawrence went for his first interview, but the mother was not highly motivated. She wanted to get her own family situation settled and hoped that she could arrange to have him come home in the future. She began to cry and asked Lawrence whether he wanted to return home, and he just shrugged his shoulders. The worker tried to involve them in a discussion of this separation. Lawrence commented that he had nothing to say, and Mrs. A. hoped he would miss them. She agreed to help Lawrence get his things together and go with him to the center, as long as she could get transportation home. The worker told them they would be hearing from the center in about three weeks.

This young man had had inadequate rearing—a passive, fearful mother who tolerated abuse; a sadistic, narcissistic father. Lawrence believes that his mother is indifferent to him, although she continues to express feeling for him. Her attempts to protect him and Jessie were well intentioned but ineffective. It is not surprising that he seeks friends outside the home; his parents failed him. The father's departure from the home for hospitalization may have contributed to Lawrence's delinquency. Lawrence shows promise of change; by his admission he knows what is right, but he does not know how to control some of his impulses at present.

Several of the features of residential programs are useful and appropriate for Lawrence:

1. Trained staff are available. The psychiatrist reported

that a group therapy program should be the first treatment effort with Lawrence, adding that individual psychotherapy at a later time might supplement the group effort. The questions of a learning disability could not be ruled out by Lawrence's school. An extensive psychological examination is also needed. His placement away from home, with only one consultant judgment to support the agency plan, can be criticized. However, community pressure, as well as family rejection, resulted in this decision.

2. At present Lawrence has inadequate self-control, and the institution can provide the external controls he needs. His behavior may not be a dominant problem, since the outbursts only recently became severe, following the father's departure and the court action. However, the disruptive behavior may still have emerged without precipitation, so he needs the external control until it is determined how well he can manage himself.

3. Peer group relationships and controls are readily available. Lawrence had friends at school and in the neighborhood, and he counted these important because of the deficits in his parents.

4. His delinquent and disruptive behavior can be more tolerated in the facility than in the larger community.

5. Lawrence would have difficulty handling a foster family relationship at age fifteen. He is moving toward independence, and he would probably be very suspicious of, and resistant to, close relationships. With exposure to many therapeutically trained staff, he may be able to change his perceptions of adults.

The last case reveals a youth's transition to a residential program and his return home to family. The mother has participated in several programs to modify her own behavior.

Jack L., age fifteen, was referred to Social and Rehabilitation Services because of his problems in school, at home, and with some of his peers. The staff of a local boys' club, where he had been involved in several programs over the past year, described him as highly impulsive, alternately suspicious and friendly toward staff, and often apprehensive of activities in which staff had a major role. He was usually willing to try a program but would also give up quickly. He was failing four of his five courses in tenth grade, cut classes frequently, and was described as "insolent" to teachers. Older youth sometimes picked a fight with him.

Mrs. L., age thirty-seven, was very negative in her comments about him, calling him uncooperative, sneaky, ungrateful, and verbally abusive to her. He shows no respect for the apartment and will never help out, although she works full time at a job that she considers far below her abilities. Mr. L. left shortly after Jack's birth. She has had two boyfriends, but none for the last ten years. She considers men "worthless" and said "It looks like Jack is going to be another typical male." He was a difficult infant with many feeding problems. When he would spit up after a meal, she would "scoop it up and make him eat it." He was an unhappy preschool child, and the day care center he attended had a hard time with him, since "he stayed a baby for such a long time." He does not know how to use things properly. She gave him a portable radio/tape deck for Christmas, and he played it so loudly that she took it away and hid it while he was at school. She was surprised when he screamed at her for disturbing a personal part of his closet. When he bought "weird-looking clothes" with his allowance, she forced him to take them back and has threatened to stop or reduce his allowance.

Mrs. L. accepted, with indifference, a referral to the mental health center, where she was seen by a male worker for two months. She also was included in a group of mothers with teenagers displaying problem behavior. In her sessions with the worker, she proved to be demanding and possessive. She demanded more of his time and wanted to know all about his personal life. The worker used her behavior toward him to illustrate that Jack has a right to his personal life, that she should not stay up at night when he is out late for the express purpose of asking whether "he had any sex," and that he cannot mature properly if he is asked too many questions which invade his privacy. She found it hard to see how she gives and takes away.

Jack was seen by an agency social worker, who described him as being "presentably dressed, slightly overweight, and cautiously friendly. He wasn't sure why he had problems at school and stated that he likes the boys' club and would rather be there. He was very angry that his mother had taken his radio away, since a number of his friends enjoyed it with him. They bought tapes to be played on it. He doesn't like to be in the apartment, since his mother is always criticizing him. He admitted that he sometimes messes up the place just to see her reaction. His friends call her a tyrant."

Both the psychiatric and psychological examinations revealed a young man with a very poor image of himself and of men and with marked hostile feelings toward women. He feels ineffective and lost in a confused environment. He is fearful and insecure in dealing with adults, especially females. Jack feels that his anger is uncontrollable, and he does not know what he might do. Intelligence is average, and his academic performance is much below his native ability. The psychiatrist made a diagnosis of adjustment reaction of adolescence and recommended treatment away from home. Jack has no reason to trust his mother, and at this time she seems unable to change her inconsistent and destructive behavior. Recommendation was for residential placement, with his mother also participating in some programs.

Mrs. L. was angry at the male psychologist for his recommendations, but she seemed able to accept the findings from the female psychiatrist. She said that she "might have had something to do with Jack's problems," and she was determined to help him improve. The staff supported her determination as a favorable sign, but pointed out that her current methods were only undermining and encouraging his behavior. The social worker emphasized the importance of her becoming acquainted with adults in her own age group. She agreed to participate in a treatment program while Jack was in residential care, to meet with a group of single parents of teenagers, to enroll for at least two months in a singles' group so as to socialize with her peers, and to seek other employment through either a training program or an educational program.

Jack had a stable experience in the center. He was lonely at first, missed the friends he had, but found it easy to transfer some of his interests at the boys' club to the campus activities. He liked baseball and often argued with whoever was acting as umpire. His schoolwork slowly improved, and he began to appreciate praise from staff.

Mrs. L. cooperated with the treatment program initially but did not attend as many sessions as she had agreed to. She joined the program for single parents of teenagers. She argued strongly with other parents, to the point that some were offended. She was, in spite of this, accepted by the group. Her overreactions to Jack caused some members to laugh at her, and she became incensed. But two persuasive members slowly helped her to see that she was "too uptight" about Jack, and she began to be able to laugh at herself. She made friends with two members of the group, and the three began socializing. This was the first time in many years that Mrs. L. had gone out with friends. She began meeting more people and after a year started to keep company with a man her own age. She visited Jack every other month, and she also started to investigate new employment.

After eighteen months, plans were initiated for Jack's return home. Mrs. L. became anxious just prior to his release, worrying about all that he would need when he first arrived home. She began some frantic activity, and the social worker reminded her of the reasons for his entry into care and the fact that he was now almost two years older and more capable of doing things for himself. Mrs. L. had to begin to accept choices that he made about his clothes and room. He, in turn, began to feel more at ease about her relationship with the man, which he had initially resented. Mrs. L. continued in the mental health program for a short time, and Jack's progress was followed by the Social and Rehabilitation Services. There were a few arguments between Jack and his mother over evening schedules and his search for part-time work, but otherwise there were no major difficulties. Both mother and son had learned to be more reasonable in working out problems.

Jack had been exposed to extremely inconsistent parenting by his mother for many years. It is surprising that he did not have major problems much sooner. His mother's hostility to men probably carried over to her feelings toward Jack. It was surprising that she could begin to relate to a man again, but her new friend simply overlooked some of her excessive comments. This case is a good illustration that environmental factors affect behavior. Exposure to other people in a group, beginning social experiences with some adults, a tentative relationship with a man, and a beginning search for a better job all contributed to Mrs. L.'s different perceptions of Jack and her altered behavior toward him. There is no doubt that her ideas about childrearing and men were extremely distorted, almost bizarre. But concentrating on psychopathology alone would not have brought about the needed changes. Mrs. L. probably retains many of her early ideas and feelings, as noted when Jack was about to return home, but most of them can now be diverted through her different interests.

Summary

Residential treatment programs are another form of care for a child who must live away from home for reasons usually related to the parents' inability to manage him and the community's inability to accept disruptive behavior. The child is often one who cannot adapt to foster family care or one whom foster parents would be unlikely to accept or handle.

There is a reasonable match between residential programs and the children who need a structured living arrangement. Children placed in residential care often have insufficient control over their feelings, an inability to understand some of their feelings, incomplete personality development, and a poor self-image. They have inadequate interpersonal relationships with both peers and adults, and they have difficulty in benefiting from school and other structured community programs. Older youths often have minimum manual or vocational skills. The residential programs permit a less intense relationship with parental figures than do other kinds of placement, offer a wider choice of parental figures, accept a wider range of disruptive and unusual behavior, have rules and regulations that can substitute for the child's undeveloped inner controls, enable peers to exert pressure for more acceptable behavior, have many living and program arrangements within the institutional framework to modify and enhance children's behavior and social and vocational skills, and have a variety of staff to assess and meet the child's needs.

Many children who enter residential programs will not be returning to their families; for those who will return, it is essential that the parents be involved in programs to modify their own behaviors.

Special Annotated Bibliography

Many of the readings on social work service in relation to the use of residential treatment would be similar to articles on family assessment, separation, termination, and reunion. For the services provided in the residential program, including services to families while the youth is in care, the following are suggested.

Kadushin, A. *Child Welfare Services.* (2nd ed.) New York: Macmillan, 1974. See the chapter on the Child Caring Institution.

Klein, A. F. *The Professional Child Care Worker.* New York: Association Press, 1975. The chapter on "The Place of Families in Treatment" is especially useful.

Treischman, A. E., Whittaker, J. K., and Brendtro, L. K. *The Other 23 Hours.* Chicago: Aldine, 1969.

Whittaker, J. K. *Caring for Troubled Children: Residential Treatment in a Community Context.* San Francisco: Jossey-Bass, 1979.

Whittaker, J. K. "Family Involvement in Residential Treatment: A Support System for Parents." In A. Maluccio and P. A. Sinanoglu (Eds.), *The Challenge of Partnership: Working with Parents of Children in Foster Care.* New York: Child Welfare League of America, 1981.

CHAPTER SEVEN

Protective Services: Helping Abused and Neglected Children

Child abuse or neglect refers to "the physical or mental injury, sexual abuse, negligent treatment, or maltreatment of a child under the age of eighteen by a person who is responsible for the child's welfare under circumstances which indicate that the child's health or welfare is harmed or threatened thereby." Child abuse is classified as physical, psychological/emotional, sexual, and verbal; child neglect is classified as educational, medical, moral, physical, and psychological/emotional (Midwest Parent-Child Welfare Resource Center, 1978, pp. 8-10). Each state defines abuse and neglect according to its own statutes and policies.

Polansky (1981, p. 15) defines neglect as a "condition in which a caretaker responsible for the child either deliberately or by extraordinary inattentiveness permits the child to experience avoidable present suffering and/or fails to provide one or more of the ingredients generally deemed essential for developing a person's physical, intellectual, and emotional capacities." Child sexual abuse is defined in the amended 1974 federal law as "the obscene or pornographic photographing, filming, or depiction of children for commercial purposes, or the rape, molestation, incest, prostitution, or other such forms of sexual exploitation of children under circumstances which indicate that the child's health or welfare is harmed or threatened thereby." The National Center on Child Abuse and Neglect (1978, pp. 1-2), in order to include all forms of abuse and exploitation, has adopted the following definition: "Contacts or interactions between a child and an adult when the child is being used for sexual stimulation of the perpetrator or another person. Sexual abuse may also be committed by a person under the age of eighteen when that person is either significantly older than the victim or when the perpetrator is in a position of power or control over another child."

Background and Legislation

The protection of children dates back a little over one hundred years to the famous case of Mary Ellen, in 1874. Henry Bergh, founder of the Society for the Prevention of Cruelty to Animals, intervened in her behalf as a concerned citizen and a recognized humanitarian. The child was removed from the home by the court, and Mary Ellen's stepmother was found guilty of assault and battery. The Society to Prevent Cruelty to Children was established that year. In 1877 the American Humane Association was formed, and by the early 1900s there were over 150 humane societies in the nation. Beginning in the 1930s, the police authority to intervene in order to protect abused or neglected children was gradually transferred to the public child welfare agencies where it logically belonged. Practitioners also began to ask whether the home, rather than just the child, could be rescued. The policy was gradually accepted that the family as a functioning unit should be helped, not just the child victim through removal (Williams, 1980).

During the 1940s physicians began to discover abuse to children through the X-ray study of bone breaks and healing which could not be adequately explained by parents. During the 1950s an increasing number of medical articles about physical abuse appeared in journals. In spite of the articles, many physicians denied that abuse existed. In 1962 C.H. Kempe, a physician, and several colleagues coined the term "battered child syndrome" and called for recognition of the problem. Many professional articles followed that definition, and abuse was rediscovered almost ninety years after the first cases were found (Williams, 1980). Articles began to appear in the popular press, and both child abuse and child neglect became well known.

National attention was focused on the child welfare field through the 1962 amendments to the Social Security Act, which required each state to develop a plan to extend child welfare services to every political subdivision of the state. In 1963 the U.S. Children's Bureau proposed a model reporting statute, and by 1966 forty-nine states had passed legislation to protect children. Today all fifty states plus U.S. Protectorates have reporting laws. In 1974 a National Center of Child Abuse and Neglect was formed to provide demonstration and educational programs, to develop new methods for diagnosing and treating abuse and neglect, and to help states increase and improve child protection services.

Key parts of state laws include "the purpose of the . . . laws, reportable circumstances, the definition of abuse and neglect, age limits of children, the required state of mind of the reporter, and who must and who may report." The major purpose of any statute is to identify the child as quickly as possible and to designate an agency that will investigate suspected abuse and offer services and treatment. In addition, the statutes are designed to encourage increased reporting, so that more children can be protected; provide for services to prevent further abuse; and assure that the unity and welfare of the family will be preserved. Situations to be reported include "physical injury, emotional harm, sexual abuse and exploitation, and neglect." A reporter does not have to *know* that abuse has occurred but must have "reason to believe" or suspect that abuse or neglect is occurring (National Center on Child Abuse and Neglect, 1978, pp. 2-3). It is the responsibility of the child protection agency to determine the presence of abuse or neglect.

Statutory definitions of abuse and neglect vary from state

to state. Many states have a general statement of abuse and neglect; they also have policy statements that define and specify
conditions. Definitions of abuse and neglect in the statutes include words and clauses such as "battering; dependency; deprivation; abandonment; exploitation; overwork; emotional maltreatment; failure to provide necessities, proper supervision, or
care; and excessive corporal punishment." Many statutes refer
to "harm or threatened harm to a child's welfare by the acts or
omissions of his parent or other person responsible for his welfare." Some states "specify a variety of manifestations of abuse,
such as "skin bruising, bleeding, malnutrition, failure to thrive,
burns, fractures of any bone, subdural hematoma, or soft tissue
swelling." Sexual abuse may also be included, with a statement
such as "any act or acts involving sexual molestation or exploitation, including, but not limited to, incest, rape, or sexual of-
fense in any degree, sodomy or unnatural or perverted sexual
practices" (National Center on Child Abuse and Neglect, 1978,
pp. 2-3).

Florida has a broader definition of sexual abuse than
most states, and it specifically includes exploitation: "aiding,
abetting, counseling, hiring, or procuring of a child to perform
or participate in any photograph, motion picture, exhibition,
show, representation, or other presentation which, in whole or
in part, depicts sexual conduct, sexual excitement, or sadomaso-
chistic abuse involving a child." More than half the states include the concept of mental or emotional injury. Wyoming defines "mental injury as . . . an injury to the psychological stability
of a child, as evidenced by an observable or substantial impairment in his ability to function within a normal range of performance and behavior with due regard to his culture" (National
Center on Child Abuse and Neglect, 1978, p. 5).

The lack of specificity of some of the statutes and the
state's implementation of policies have led to problems for practitioners in accurately interpreting and applying the laws and
regulations. For example, how is corporal punishment defined?
It can be described as inflicted nonaccidental physical injury,
and it is, therefore, abuse. However, attention must be given to
the age of the child, the frequency and duration of the punish-

ment, and the presence of such physical changes as skin bruising, bleeding, soft tissue damage, and bone breaks. No state prohibits a parent from using reasonable punishment in rearing children. Kneeling on thumb tacks, kneeling for a long period, or holding one's arms outstretched for a long period are all unreasonable. An issue that is still not settled is the right of parents to deny medical treatment to their children because of their religious beliefs. Almost all states recognize the right of a parent or guardian to deny certain medical treatments, and the child is not thereby to be considered either abused or neglected. However, a number of states have compensated for this exclusion by providing that medical treatment must be provided if denial would result in death.

It is difficult to estimate the exact incidence of abuse and neglect. The numbers of substantiated reports have continued to increase throughout the United States, and it is clear that the cause of the increase is primarily related to improved reporting laws, procedures, and investigations, although the rate of increase is leveling off. One example of improved reporting will suffice: In 1970 Florida recorded seventeen cases of abuse and neglect. The next year, after installation of a statewide hotline, 19,120 reports were received. Some observers believe that the actual incidence of abuse and neglect is increasing, and it is probably related to the breakdown of family life and to economic and social stresses.

In 1981 the National Center on Child Abuse and Neglect reported on a study of abuse and neglect. Based on a sampling of twenty-six counties, it was projected that over one million children (1,101,500) were reported to child protective service agencies as abused or neglected during the period from May 1, 1979, to April 30, 1980. The national reported incidence of alleged victims per one thousand was 17.8, and the incidence of substantiated victims (470,600) was 7.6 per one thousand children. Using other sources of data within those same communities, the study staff projected a national estimate of 652,000 substantiated children, establishing a national incidence rate of 10.5 per one thousand children. Girls suffer slightly more physical, sexual, and emotional abuse, and boys suffer more physical, educational, and emotional neglect. An increase in abuse for girls begins about age ten, and neglect among boys begins to increase at age seven (National Center on Child Abuse and Neglect, 1981, pp. 11-26).

Unique Characteristics of Protective Services

The Child Welfare League of America (1960, pp. 1-2) defines child protective services (CPS) as "a specialized child welfare service which carries a delegated responsibility to offer help in behalf of any child considered, or found to be, neglected." The practice of protective services involves a number of unique aspects, stemming from the nature of child abuse and the role of laws which dictate its treatment.

Protective service workers represent the authority of the state itself, and they must be prepared to encounter a number of forces particular to this specialized type of practice. The nature of child abuse and its treatment from the legal and casework standpoints often create an unusually hostile reaction to intervention and treatment on the part of the client. The client rarely seeks help himself; more often than not, he is the subject of a report from a concerned professional or neighbor. Workers should, therefore, be prepared to deal with client fear, hostility, anxiety, and distrust.

Whereas many casework techniques and situations allow for the time to reflect on and discuss at length a particular problem, time is often at a premium in cases of serious abuse. The worker must be able to analyze a situation in which a child is at risk and to make accurate recommendations that will serve the best interests of the child within the framework of the law. And often he is not given enough time to evaluate the situation as fully as he might believe necessary. The skill of foresight is often of greater importance than the skill of insight.

Another characteristic of protective services is that all assessment work must be accomplished in accordance with the possibility of presenting the findings in court. After employing fact-finding techniques, the practitioner decides when legal action will persuade the parents to agree to a treatment program or will discourage and restrain their abusive behavior. He uses knowledge to consult with agency attorneys and to prepare specific cases for presentation in court.

Finally, this practice demands a skillful interpretation of the community mandate to all clients—a specialized ability to send a clear message that the protective service worker represents a force to relieve burdens, to meet needs, and to intervene in behalf of children. Since protective services deal with the involuntary client, it is the unique task of the worker to raise doubts in the client's mind about the propriety of *some* of the parenting behavior. When abuse behavior has been a way of life, rather than a one-time incident of inflicted injury, it takes specialized skill to represent the community standard of parenting behavior and to insist on a change in the behavior pattern. At the same time, individual initiative, rights, and freedom must be preserved as much as possible.

Assessment

One of the frequent pitfalls of this phase is making generalizations about abusing and neglecting characteristics and treating everyone in a similar manner. The worker must not characterize too rapidly. For instance, a classification "head of single-parent family" may not be useful, since some young women do not have an image of themselves as a parent or a head but, rather, as a daughter with a child.

The worker goes initially to a family to share something that it has a right to know—that a report has been made. There may be some relief when a worker arrives. The worker's presence, interest, and activities may make the family members feel that they are important and worth something. These feelings can be reinforced further by the worker's stated intention to stay with them—not to reject or desert them.

Assessment of the family situation begins at intake and grows more extensive as case plans are made, adjusted, and reviewed throughout the period of service delivery. It remains dynamic until case closure. The purposes of assessment include gathering information about current and past problems; the physical, intellectual, social, and emotional functioning of each family member; the self-concept and problem-solving competence of each family member; and the available resources within the family and friendship networks. In addition, information regarding family functioning must be gathered and should include patterns of interactions and communication, power (authority and decision making), division of labor, expectations, balance (emotional climate), and relationships to the community.

The primary source of information is usually the family itself, but inferences are drawn from the situation and environment and the interactional processes within the family. A severely abused child may be withdrawn and passive or might make noticeable efforts to do the correct thing, thus being sure to please adults. A less abused child might be aggressive or misbehave in provocative ways. Communication between family members may be unspoken but inferred from eye contacts or body language. Protective service challenges practitioners to become equally alert to eating, sleeping, working, playing, the comings and goings of the family, and the environment in which all of these take place. Amidai (1977, p. 19) confirms the necessity to obtain complete information. She defines a "new morbidity for children," observing that children seen in protective services may have faulty vision, hearing, speech impairment, chronic respiratory illness, orthopedic impairment, reading problems, and paint-based lead poisoning.

Information may be gathered from other members of the household and from extended family members, particularly if they have any authority or take part in decision making for the family. Since information also may be available from other professionals, practitioners should review the previous problem-solving efforts of the family as well as concurrent problems, such as medical and legal issues, in order to determine availability of other professional information. Assessment frequently reveals deficits of all resources: money, housing, reliable family or friends.

To obtain the necessary information requires purposeful conversation directed by a patient, positive, accepting practitioner. We are taught to enhance a client's motivation by establishing a relationship—to relate to the ego. Unfortunately, the protective service specialist carries out many tasks of assessment without the strength of relationship. Information must be sought even when there appears to be no remnant of an ego for relating. The practitioner must find something to indicate that the client is functioning at least minimally, even feeding himself and staying alive from one day to the next.

The following is a brief summary of a telephone report of sexual abuse in the Taylor family and the first visit by the CPS practitioner.

A grandparent called the child protective services to report that Mr. Taylor has been sexually involved with his two daughters for several years. The oldest daughter was married recently and left the home. Because of her distress over her experiences, she gave information to the caller, who, in turn, reported the abuse.

The mother receives Supplemental Security Income because of a physical incapacity caused by a stroke. She does not groom herself and is unattractive and often malodorous. She complains constantly, and all family members claim that they cannot get along with her.

The initial and continuing response from the father and Laurie, age fourteen, is denial of the incest. The mother suspects that the allegation is true, and she has threatened suicide. In a classic pattern, the father says that he loves his daughter and wants only to protect her, kisses her on the mouth, and is very controlling regarding the daughter's involvement with friends. Laurie has not attended school for the past five months, and she has had no contacts outside the family. The school's efforts over her truancy have produced no parental cooperation.

Father and daughter are often observed sitting close to each other in the family car, and the mother has observed them lying close to each other on the bed. There are frequent recreational outings without the mother. Nonetheless, they all refuse to cooperate with any protective service intervention, indicating that there is no problem except that caused by agency interference. They believe that they are disliked because they manage by themselves and drive an expensive car.

Assessment to this point indicates the following: Although the agency-identified problem is the sexual abuse of a fourteen-year-old daughter, the family members do not agree with this statement. They have handled school problems by withdrawing; similarly, they have no outside contacts and perceive others as disliking them. These social-functioning problems are further compounded by the mother's disability and her low self-image, as evidenced by uncleanliness and poor grooming. Mr. Taylor is currently unemployed.

Although this is an intact family in adequate living conditions, each member is very isolated from any community resource except for SSI service, which provides only financial support. Although the mother's hygiene and personal care are poor, the other family members have adequate grooming.

The parents do not support each other, do not communicate effectively with each other, and appear to have little affection for each other. The family operates by excluding the mother, and this daughter appears to have assumed the companionship and sexual role of the mother.

Continuing assessment must include at least the following:

1. The school's role in requiring the daughter's attendance.
2. The married daughter's willingness to discuss the abuse and to encourage the family to accept agency help.
3. The possible role of the reporter to encourage the family to use agency services.
4. Each family member's level of intellectual functioning and ability to relate to other family members differently.
5. The father's capacity to respond to reality-based treatment.
6. The mother's capacity to resume the role of wife.

Case Planning

While gathering information and after reviewing it, the practitioner must consider the meaning of the data and reach some conclusions or prognosis. Specifically, he must decide whether the current problem is likely to become worse or better or to remain the same and whether the family members are likely to change—and, if so, whether the change will constitute an improvement or a deterioration. When reviewing the material, he may become very pessimistic and find it difficult not to communicate this feeling to the family members. This may inhibit service efforts and those of the family for improved functioning.

As service delivery plans are developed, treatment goals should be arranged according to a priority list. The resources to effect necessary changes must be located and the frequency of family contacts determined. Since family members are expected to achieve the goals, they must first have the benefit of the social worker's or the multidisciplinary group's thinking and then be involved in the negotiation for specific measurable and realistic goals—for example, "Mrs. B. will take Tim for a medical checkup each month."

Other specific goals might be:

"Mrs. B. will admit the public health nurse each week and will follow the nurse's instructions for care of head lice."

"Mrs. B. will take Tim to the day care provider each weekday and will follow the requirements regarding his clothing and pick up Tim on time. Mrs. B. will attend the weekly meetings for parents at the day care center."

Unattainable goals—goals that a particular family cannot possibly achieve and that merely reflect a worker's personal value system—should never be formulated. Such goals act as a roadblock to change and thus prevent the reunification of the family:

"Family will sit down together at the table for at least one meal a day."

"Mother will be able to discuss sex with her daughters using appropriate genital terminology."

"Mother will fold laundry regularly and place it in appropriate cabinets."

"Father will spend one hour each day in recreational activity with children."

Although the agency is the prime mover in the contract, the objective is to obtain the best contract under the circumstances and the strongest commitment from everyone. Clients must never be surprised by the case plan; so the practitioner must tell them what problems were identified, what steps must be taken, what the practitioner is expected to do, what family members are expected to do, and how they can meet expectations in relationship with all identified and selected resources.

Confirming our knowledge of the importance of this period of initial case planning, Maluccio (1979, p. 181) states, in relation to unplanned terminations, "Often there was evidence of lack of openness between client and worker and lack of clarity or agreement in respect to their roles, goals, and expectations. These were cases in which problems in client-worker interaction were evident as early as the initial session. . . . Clients and workers . . . had a vague sense of what would be happening in treatment, were unable to establish an emotional connection between them, did not actively engage in contract negotiation, and ended the first session with marked vagueness and uncertainty about future plans." The following case shows the need for rapid assessment and the difficulty in planning with a neglectful parent.

In response to a call that two young children had been abandoned, a worker went to 88 South Street on November 11 and found the children, a girl, age two, and an infant boy, in the care of a Mrs. Jones. Allegedly, the mother had asked Mrs. Jones to care for the boy for a few minutes on November 10, at about 5 P.M., had given Mrs. Jones the key to her apartment, and then had left and failed to return.

At about 5 A.M. the next morning, Mrs. Jones heard a child crying in the mother's apartment and entered, finding the daughter, Marge, alone, hungry, wet, and dressed in very tattered pajamas. Marge was removed from the apartment, fed, clothed, and cleaned up by Mrs. Jones, who then called the police. She was advised by them to call the welfare department. The mother, Mrs. Valdez, was located later by the police.

When the worker interviewed Mrs. Valdez, she denied that Mrs. Jones was unaware of Marge's being in the apartment alone, and she steadfastly maintained that Mrs. Jones was very much aware that she was to have the care of both children for a prolonged period. She claimed she had been moving furniture and cleaning her previous apartment all night, preparatory to moving to South Street.

Although Mrs. Valdez reportedly had lived at South Street for two weeks, there was no furniture in the apartment other than a refrigerator, a stove, and a crib mattress on the floor. Also, the gas company had not turned on the gas.

A decision was made to return the children to Mrs. Valdez's care and to provide protective services. The children were taken to a clinic first and found to have mild ear and throat infections. The prescriptions were filled, and Mrs. Valdez and the children were dropped off at a friend's house.

It was made very clear to the mother that any further incidents such as the one described could not be tolerated. Also, since she had physically threatened a caseworker who was investigating an earlier report that the children had been left alone, Mrs. Valdez was informed that her cooperation was expected and that a protective services worker would be calling on her.

Mrs. Valdez was seen by a worker twice during the next week. The children's colds had not noticeably improved, although they did not appear ill. The electric company was still refusing to turn on the gas, but there was now a double bed, a crib, and a youth bed in the apartment. There were also blankets for the beds. Two windows in the apartment were broken, but the mother said they would be fixed by the landlord. They were supposedly broken while she was moving in.

Three days after the worker's last visit, Mrs. Valdez again left her children without making adequate provisions for them. Consequently, the worker concluded that "these children are at serious risk, and physical and legal custody is requested."

In this case the original plan was to return the children, even though the living arrangements included very little furniture and a history of neglect and abandonment. Protective service treatment included medical examination, procurement of medication, transportation, and interpretation of the protective service mandate and role. The case was opened in a firm and nonjudgmental manner, even though there had been physical threats to a prior worker. When the children were abandoned again, it was determined that risk was increasing, and the plan shifted to a request for custody.

Interviewing Abused or Neglected Children

When interviewing a child who has been harmed by adults, and therefore has little reason to trust an adult stranger, practitioners must establish their own credibility and, at the same time, try to reduce the child's pain and feelings of aloneness: "Sometimes it helps to talk about what has happened." "I often talk to children who have had these things happen in their families and to their bodies—it is all right to talk about it. It doesn't sound strange to me. Perhaps you have felt very alone."

Workers should express concern and caring without being judgmental. Whenever they appear distressed or shattered by information, or avoid discussing some activity, they convey to the child that it is frightening to talk about that behavior. For example, the following information about a young child might make it difficult for a practitioner to keep an even tone and to be comfortable during the child's interview:

During her infancy a girl was hospitalized due to lack of weight gain. When she was one and a half years old, there were reports of her being in the street unattended and being severely spanked by her mother. The child was often struck by her father, and he denied her food. A subsequent report was made by the landlord, who heard repeated screaming. The mother is blind, and the father has a prior charge of sexual assault on his seven-year-old daughter.

A community-based team developed a service plan, including part-time day care for the child, monthly pediatric review and homemaker, as well as counseling services for the mother. When the child was three years old, the day care worker reported that she behaved in an infantile manner, was never clean, and was now asking the worker to rub her genitals.

It will be a long time before this child can be expected to behave appropriately, so the worker should not focus on that goal. If the child asks the worker to rub her genitals, suitable responses include: "It probably feels good to you to be rubbed, and I'm glad you have some good feelings. Does it make you feel very special? We can do some other things together that are also special, such as drawing, or playing with dolls, or setting up a doll house, or playing with animal toys."

Whenever a practitioner is seeking information, he must pause and wait for responses, so that feelings and concerns emerge at the child's pace. It is not good practice to be so involved with direct questions for form completion that the child's story and pace are interrupted. Since young children may not have an accurate perception of time, the practitioner must determine how each child perceives and relates events. When the time sequence of the story does not make sense, such questions as "When did you say it was?" "Does he always come to your room?" can confuse the child and lose the vital information. Details can be filled in during subsequent interviews.

Sometimes there is no information from the family members or outside sources, and all data gathered regarding abuse and its effects may have to come directly from the child. Very frequently children who have been extensively abused are withdrawn and unable or unwilling to relate. They may be passive, quiet, and reluctant to reveal what has been occurring, especially when they feel shame. Alternately, some bubbly little children chatter along very happily about what is going on, causing doubt about how much of the shared information is true and how much is fantasy. To be helpful, the practitioner must be aware of these differences and of the child's personal reactions to the differences.

The fact that a person says very little or nothing does not mean that the person feels little or nothing. Everyone develops some way of expressing emotions when he does not feel like talking about them. To discover ways that a nonverbal child can express emotions, practitioners can try to find an activity during which the child can produce something such as a drawing, or a painting, or a pasted picture. There is nothing wrong or right about a personal creation, so a child cannot fail. When the worker accepts what the child has produced, the child may begin to feel accepted.

When interviewing children from whom the only information is "My daddy plays with me," the practitioner must seek all social information available about the family, such as changes in the child's behavior or in eating or sleeping habits. Then the conversations with the child focus on "Your teacher is concerned because . . ." or "Your mother tells me that you haven't been very interested in playing with your friends lately." The goal is to convey to children an interest in them specifically and a desire to learn about their lives, their feelings, and their concerns.

When children divulge information, guilt usually commences. Even if no adult has given the instruction not to tell, the child has now initiated an unknown set of consequences. Fear of the unknown is difficult to handle at any age; so the worker must reassure the child that it is correct to be discussing the matter but must not give false assurance that everything will be all right. It is good practice to anticipate the child's probable concern by saying: "Some children are afraid they will be punished or that their parents will be harmed. Some children are afraid their parents will hate them. Some children think they should have kept the secret; so the next time I talk to them, they change their story or tell me they made it all up."

If the initial interviews are handled with a display of caring and concern, plus anticipation of probable guilt feelings and pressures, the later interviews can be dealt with more easily. If there is a denial or a change of story, an appropriate comment might be: "Yes, remember I said that sometimes children grow so afraid about the trouble they have caused that they change their story, but I want you to know that it was correct to tell me, and it is still right for you to be talking with me."

A ten-year-old boy reported sexual molestation by a foster father. His older brother also reported he had been molested. The agency moved promptly to a court hearing, during which the ten-year-old withdrew his statement, saying, "I never thought it would go this far." The adult claimed that he never meant to hurt the children. The brothers were in this foster home originally because of their own parents' fighting and neglect. When the agency separated them to close the foster home, the boys' loyalties were very mixed. They were guilty about harming an adult, liked most things about living there, and could not easily go back to biological parents. They had provoked an unknown new living situation for themselves.

Appropriate comments to the ten-year-old include: "When children see the results of talking with us, they often wish they had not said so much." "It is always scary to find out all the trouble it causes to talk with a social worker." "It was right for you to tell us. Sometimes adults get mixed up and do the wrong things." "You may think that you can get everything back to

normal or protect the foster father by changing this information." "What do you wish I could do for you now?"

If a child sends signals or gives verbal information that he
has been frightened by an adult's activity, the worker should
ask "What frightened you the most?" and then remark that it
isn't easy to feel so frightened. Knowing what the child perceives as frightening enables the worker to reassure and calm the
child. Responses must deal openly with a child's possible fears:
"Sometimes when adults don't know how to change a child's
behavior, they threaten him." "Sometimes when people want
exact information and when they must have it to do their jobs,
they push a child very hard about how important it is to be correct. That upsets many children."

If children are encouraged to share ambivalent feelings as
well as any pain they experience, workers can assist with the
necessary healing process. Enabling children to deal with the
psychological effects of abusive behavior requires such responses as "I know it is important for you to talk with someone. It often helps to talk. First, I want to listen to you as you
tell me what has been happening to you. Then we'll talk about
what happens next. It is my job to talk to other people who
know you, including your parents. Otherwise, I can't really
help."

Treatment

Treatment is frequently provided directly by the child
protective services practitioner. Additional counseling may be
provided by selected community resources that have specific
functions, such as mental health, medical services, or legal advice. Treatment will be directed at the behavior that results in
abuse or neglect to children. In addition, treatment must be designed to reduce the stresses of any negative life circumstance;
economic, social, and environmental. It includes, therefore, all
activities and resources used to help clients manage their lives in
such a way that children's safety and well-being are ensured.

Treatment is initiated with the first agency contact and
proceeds if abuse or neglect is suspected or probable. There may

be no recognition on the part of adults that behavior is unacceptable, but this does not preclude the initiation of a working alliance to focus on behavior change.

All activity is based on the understanding of each client and on the outcome needed and expected. Working with families whose activities and behavior may be disorganized demands precise planning for the accomplishment of each established goal. If crises occur frequently, it is possible to be trapped into reactive behavior, rather than holding to a responsive, selective treatment approach.

The DeGama parents have given birth to twelve children, and eight are still living. The oldest is twenty-six and is known to the welfare department in another state. The parents and seven children have moved in and out of six states during the last twenty years. The mother has no work history; the father periodically is a very productive farm worker. Most family support comes from stealing and begging. The four youngest children were removed from parental care because they suffered severe neglect and were frequently exploited by the parents to steal and beg. On removal, medical examination revealed lice, impetigo, and malnutrition. They were without sufficient clothing and had been educationally deprived.

During a subsequent period, children in foster care made some physical and educational gains, but each child displayed a multitude of relationship problems, as well as repetition of the survival tactics of stealing and begging. This has produced repeated replacements.

Parents move constantly and are not accessible for regular interviews. When they do appear, they make demands for their children and give false information regarding living arrangements and sources of income.

In order to improve this family's functioning, community resources would have to be utilized for the basics, such as food, shelter, and medical care. This may require the use of an advocacy group from the Chicano community. Discrimination, both intentional and unintentional, is well documented (Gibson, 1980). Assistance may require an advocacy stance in behalf of the family members to assure that they receive the basic services to which they are entitled. Agency service to the family includes help to the parents so that they provide accurate information, assuring eligibility for services. When the parents realize that the practitioner can help them negotiate through the service system, they may begin to trust the worker. A selective treatment approach for the children in care might include discussions of different modes of survival without stealing and begging. The father's strength is that he can be a productive worker, and the mother's strength includes her loyalty to her husband and to the children.

However, it is likely that change will be slow, and much of the treatment for this family is probably reactive to each crisis of family demands, children's behavior, and foster family replacement. Much worker tenacity and persistence will be required to remain goal focused and not spend all activity on settling crises.

Since many abusing and neglecting parents distort or deny reality and have distorted perceptions regarding their behavior and its results, treatment must often focus on the conscious levels of the client's functioning.

The Taylor family, discussed in the section on assessment, illustrates a denial of reality. Each family member denies that a problem exists. Treatment will include discussion with the father about the constant attention he pays to his daughter: "You spend much of your time alone with your daughter, riding around in the car, having picnics on the beach. This is not usual for most families. Let's talk about your time together and the excursions you take." And "Your wife tells me that she never has any time with you and that no one likes her. Is she perceiving this accurately? What time do you spend with her. Does anyone like her? Why do you think she feels that way?" Treatment will thus be focused on the marked imbalance of family roles, since this father totally excludes any role for his wife.

The worker also should determine whether the father demonstrates any comprehension that his activity causes others to question his relationship with his daughter and that his activity prevents her from developing normal peer relationships: "Many parents do not realize that sexual interaction causes psychological damage. You have told me how much you love your daughter and you know that you are not hurting Laurie physically. Perhaps you think that, therefore, everything is all right. Let me tell you about some feelings that children have when they are having intercourse or are sexually involved with family members. . . ."

If it is possible to involve Mr. Taylor in these discussions, it might be appropriate to gather more information about the marriage: What attracted the parents to each other initially? Is the marriage what each expected it to be? How does Mr. Taylor perceive his wife at this time?

Obviously, treatment must include focus on the reality that Laurie is not attending school and therefore is not acquiring an education or making friends. Work with Laurie will focus on how she perceives the family situation. Perhaps she fears becoming disabled and repulsive. Perhaps she is trying to hold the family together and protect both parents. Since she is not protected by either of them, she may be very angry or afraid. Being angry at a disabled mother produces immense guilt, and these feelings must be addressed during treatment interviews.

Initial work with Mrs. Taylor must include more knowledge about her self-image. How long has she been disabled and excluded? Are her perceptions about being disliked of immense proportions, and should there be a mental health evaluation? What strengths can be identified so that self-esteem might be improved?

Many cases of reported abuse involve parental use of force as a means of discipline. Treatment with these families must raise doubt in the parents' minds regarding the correctness of their behavior in relation to the goals of the discipline or punishment. The following questions are an excellent guide to the childrearing practices of the parents (Holder and Mohr, 1980, p. 151):

1. What form of discipline is used on the children?
2. Is the type or severity of discipline or punishment appropriate for the situation?
3. Do the parents lose control of themselves when disciplining?

4. What is the parents' intent when disciplining?
   a. Do they intend to punish?
   b. Do they wish to teach a lesson?
   c. Is there no conscious intent to their punishment?
5. Do the parents involve themselves or disengage themselves appropriately from participating in the children's activities?
6. To what extent do the parents understand developmental stages of children—the children's physical and intellectual abilities at different ages?
7. Are the parents' expectations for children appropriate for their level of development?
8. Are the parents aware of and accepting of the children's feelings?
9. Are the parents consistent in their approach to parenting (do they work together or disagree on how children should be raised)?
10. Do the parents perceive children as independent beings with their own personalities or as small carbon copies of themselves?
11. Do the parents individualize children?
12. Do the parents enjoy their children or do they see them as a necessity or a burden?
13. Were the children planned or unplanned?
14. Are the children praised, encouraged, criticized, ignored, comforted, valued, and/or intimidated?

In the following case, inappropriate discipline is being enforced, with moderate to severe physical punishment inflicted in an attempt to reduce the child's unacceptable behavior.

Arthur, age eleven, was reported to the child protective services by the school because of his frequent absences from school, his failing schoolwork, his restlessness in class, occasional theft, and evidence of physical beatings. Confirmation of excessive beating was confirmed by a medical examination at the Darlington Hospital and by the child's own admission. The inflicted bruises were substantial, showing a belt buckle mark, and two of the cuts were infected, requiring antibiotics.

The worker visited the parents in the late afternoon of the day following the report and advised them of the report and the medical findings. The mother was very apprehensive at first, saying almost nothing, but did admit that Arthur was hit by his father when he misbehaved. The father was less hesitant about his discipline, stating that the boy had gotten out of hand, and "The only way to control him is to beat him." There are three younger boys in the family, ages eight, nine, and ten. The father stated that these boys caused no trouble, "because they know what they'll get if they step out of line." The father was firm, almost belligerent at times, as he described his disciplining of Arthur. It started when Arthur was seven and began to talk back. After a while, Arthur stopped talking back, but he began to refuse to help with dishes and other chores. If Arthur cried too much after a punishment, the father would hit him still harder. Arthur then started to steal small items from stores. The father discovered that this was going on, since the boy arrived with things that he could not have purchased. Arthur denied the theft, which made the father furious. Both parents said they had never done anything wrong in their lives and were very worried that Arthur would soon be caught by the police.

The father denied, however, that he had inflicted bruises on Arthur. The mother then said, "You do beat him kinda hard sometimes."

Treatment in this case should be addressed to the form of discipline, its severity, and its usefulness in trying to stimulate Arthur to change his behavior. The father has obviously lost control of his own behavior in beating Arthur; therefore, the punishment is not suited to the child's needs but is primarily related to the father's frustration. The punishment is also used to show the younger children that they will receive the same beatings for any misbehavior. Consequently, Arthur receives a disproportionate beating to carry a message to siblings. He serves almost as the sacrificial lamb. The parents also expect excessive responsibility from Arthur, wanting him, and him alone, to serve as a "mother's helper." The parents also do not appear to agree on the type or extent of discipline. The mother takes no part in any discipline, and she recognizes that the father has lost control. Last, there is little praise given in this family; minimum individuality; and Arthur is criticized, ignored, and intimidated.

The selection of a treatment method is based on the cli-

ent's needs, the goals to be accomplished, and the available resources. A parenting class is an inappropriate method if the
adults are filled with rage, engage in physical fighting, are severely disorganized, or have never experienced sufficient formal
education to develop an awareness of group exchange. It may
be a very appropriate method for an articulate and self-controlled
adult, but the community may not have parenting classes available. In that case the goal of education remains the same, but
the method to achieve the goal may be the use of individual or
group counseling.

Much parenting education is being delivered by parent
aide programs developed under the supervision of protective
service departments. Volunteers, who are carefully screened and
trained, provide consistent, nonthreatening social experiences;
meet very time-consuming dependency needs; give nurture and
serve as models for appropriate parenting; provide companionship; and give direct instruction on the tasks of housekeeping
and parenting.

It is painful and frustrating to work with families who
physically or sexually abuse their children, and the characteristics of such families present one of the more difficult treatment
dilemmas. Some families are unable, through their own lack of
ability and limited intelligence, to care for children adequately.
Some parents have no knowledge of how to rear children, and
some are unwilling to invest energy in raising children. Dealing
with apathy, passivity, and hopelessness drains the practitioner,
so that his enthusiasm and efforts to initiate change are reduced. Not all families who neglect their children have the
"apathy-futility syndrome," as defined by Polansky (1981, pp.
39-40), but most of the families have one or more of those characteristics:

1. A pervasive conviction that nothing is worth doing. The
    feeling of futility predominates, as in the schizoid personal-
    ity. As one patient used to say, "What's the use of eating
    supper; you'll only be hungry before breakfast."
2. Emotional numbness, sometimes mistaken for depression.
    It is beyond depression; it represents massive affect inhibi-
    tion from early splitting in the ego.

3. Interpersonal relationships typified by desperate clinging; they are superficial, essentially lacking in pleasure, and accompanied by intense loneliness.
4. Lack of competence in many areas of living, partially caused by the unwillingness to risk failure in acquiring skills.
5. Expression of anger passive-aggressively and through hostile compliance.
6. Noncommitment to positive stands; even the stubborn negativism is a last-ditch assertion that one exists.
7. Verbal inaccessibility to others, and a related crippling in problem solving because of the absence of internal dialogue.
8. An uncanny skill in bringing to consciousness the same feelings of futility in others; this is used as a major interpersonal defense against efforts to bring about change.

The message from Polansky is clear that the apathetic-futile parents have great difficulty in using help or resources. The practitioner must do concrete things for these families. For instance, he must arrange to have leaking roofs fixed; intercede with landlords and utility companies; provide transportation for medical services or day care; and even go to the home, get children out of bed, and take them to the day care center. Parents are so needy and lonely that treatment frequently includes companionship visits. When parent aides, students, or volunteers can make friendly, supportive visits, the parents may begin to believe that change can occur. Because the feelings of detachment are so pronounced, and because verbal accessibility may be low, many visits should be short in duration. If clients are visited frequently, they may begin to form attachments and relationships. For the severely deprived parent, the practitioner should attempt to connect to the family in any way possible, through a baseball game, a television soap opera, or the neighbor's pet dog. The neglectful family usually requires all the familiar community supports. In brief, the very neglectful family, unless the children must be removed, needs almost every supportive and enabling community service available, including the authoritative child protective service. If the family is to function at all, community services must make up for the numerous parental deficits. Work with these families is demanding, thankless, frustrating, costly, and often unsuccessful. Practitioners must never expect quick gratification for their efforts. They are often trying to save the next generation of parents, not this one.

Treatment is a search and a process for resolution of family problems. Therefore, it progresses through several stages. Change may be dramatic or easily visible, or it may be so slight and incremental that it is not even recognized as progress. The only improved functioning may be some reduction of the neglect or abuse. Other family relationship problems or life-style difficulties may remain constant. If the plan has been realistic in determining what can be accomplished, and if the practitioner can accept the family while not condoning neglectful or abusive behavior, parents will usually recognize that they cannot return to every aspect of their old life-style.

An initial treatment success is identified when parents admit to acts of inappropriate parenting (Zaphiris, 1975). As clients ventilate feelings of guilt because of their behavior toward children, it is important for the worker to accept these feelings and to review the behavior with such comments as "I'm glad you can talk about this." "You are right, it wasn't helpful to John." "Let's try to figure out what happened to trigger your anger." "It must not happen again, so we'll work on ways to anticipate your feelings of loneliness or worthlessness."

When a client is expressing guilt, it is a common reaction to provide comfort or absolution with such remarks as "Oh, I'm sure it's not as bad as you think." "Come on, there seems to be no major harm, and I'm sure you didn't mean it." These comments only serve to stifle the movement a client is making and will delay the treatment process. It communicates the practitioner's inability to deal with the seriousness of the situation as it affects the safety and well-being of children.

Once parents can recognize the need for behavior change, continued treatment should bring increased self-esteem and improved reality testing. Self-esteem may be demonstrated by improved homemaking skills or an improvement in self-grooming or health care. It may be much less visible in a small decision made independently. Recognition of every achievement must be given repeatedly to reinforce feelings of self-worth.

Since treatment may have focused on teaching cause and effect, the practitioner may now begin to hear his own words coming back, with such comments as "If I rock him for a while, he doesn't cry as much when I put him to bed." "If I talk to her in the morning, she goes off easily on the school bus." It is always gratifying to hear oneself quoted and to have growth so clearly indicated. Unfortunately, caseload size is often so high that much treatment has ceased once the parent agrees to shift behavior and to provide care. These families return often for additional service, because they have not accomplished a sense of worthwhileness and have not integrated cause and effect.

Further treatment success is possible to achieve with some protective service families. Some parents can grow sufficiently to provide psychological nurture to their children and to care about children's feelings. This is apparent when parents talk with pride about children's accomplishments and begin to display any schoolwork or report cards. It is shown when parents respond promptly to children's signals of discomfort with such remarks as "It must hurt, I'm sorry you fell." "I wish I could help you feel better." "It's OK to cry, I'll hold you until it's all better."

Whenever parents begin to offer psychological nurture, it is important that the frequency of treatment contacts be increased. When parents make all this effort, they must have consistent support from practitioners. Children also may not trust this nurture, and they will develop provoking and testing behavior. This can cause the parent to reject or even to reinjure the child. Increased casework effort is needed with the child, so that feelings of doubt or disbelief can be expressed and dealt with. An important treatment goal is to have the child accept the nurture.

Summary

Child abuse and neglect include the physical or mental injury, sexual abuse, or negligent treatment of a child by a person or persons responsible for the child's well-being. Abuse and neglect can be physical, psychological, moral, medical, emotional, and educational. Protection for children began about one hundred years ago, and within the past two decades abuse and neglect have been "rediscovered." All states have legislation for the prevention, reporting, and treatment of abuse and neglect. Child protective services is a specialized child welfare program to help the abused child and his family. It is unique from other services, since the worker represents the authority of the state, must reach out to unmotivated clients, must accurately assess situations to prevent further injury or neglect, may use parent-supplied information to testify against the parents, must recognize and maintain parental rights and initiatives, and must require the family to change and help parents improve parental performance.

Assessment includes an analysis of all relationships within the family, the extended family, and supporting networks; the potential of the caretakers to change their behavior; and the development of a treatment plan, including an agreement between the parents, the practitioner, and all services involved in the treatment. Children must be interviewed, and the practitioner must be sensitive to the emotional needs of the child and to the child's view of the abuse. Further, the practitioner must make it clear to the child that he knows about the hurts and troubles of children who are abused.

Treatment of parents and children is often provided by the child protection worker, but workers from other community programs, such as homemaker, day care, mental health, and parent aides are often utilized. The message must be conveyed from the very beginning that change is expected, is possible, and that service is designed not only to help the parents change but also to reduce the stresses of negative life circumstances. Services may continue to be offered even though the family members may not clearly agree that there is a problem; it is often necessary to provide parents with accurate information on child rearing and on the impact of their behavior on the child.

Much of the work with neglecting families is very slow and thankless; with those who physically and sexually abuse their children, workers may be angry and frustrated. However, practitioners do receive satisfaction when they see parents provide not only physical comfort but psychological nurture.

Special Annotated Bibliography

Eekelaar, J., and Katz, S. N. (Eds.). *Family Violence: An International and Interdisciplinary Study.* Toronto: Butterworth, 1978. A thorough and scholarly examination of all aspects of violence in families throughout the world. Includes many legal aspects of abuse.

Holder, W. M., and Mohr, C. (Eds.). *Helping in Child Protective Services.* Denver: American Humane Association, 1980. The major handbook used by the American Humane Association in training staff for practice. Comprehensive and specific.

Jones, M., Magura, S., and Shyne, A. "Effective Practice with Families in Protective and Preventive Services." *Child Welfare,* 1981, *60* (2), 67-80. A review and distillation of proven practice methods.

National Center on Child Abuse and Neglect. *Child Abuse and Neglect.* Vol. 2: *The Roles and Responsibilities of Professionals.* DHEW Publication No. 75-30074. Washington, D.C.: U.S. Department of Health, Education and Welfare, 1975. A concise overview of the protective service role.

Polansky, N. A. *Damaged Parents: An Anatomy of Neglect.* Chicago: University of Chicago Press, 1981. Gives practitioners a full understanding of the behavior of neglectful parents and the types of counsel and services that can help them.

CHAPTER EIGHT

Terminating
Service
Productively

Termination of service delivery is not a sudden event that is separate from the entire service provided to the consumer. Although it is the point at which the treatment process ends, the practitioner prepares for termination at intake and continues to prepare for this phase during the assessment and treatment phases of service. At termination, assessment of the success of the service is made, and clients are encouraged to continue to use the problem-solving experience of service. Shapiro (1980) indicates that termination is not a "moratorium" of the work but a significant episode in it.

When service plans are being developed, the practitioner and clients decide what they will accomplish together. In a similar way, when the proposed goals or modified goals are achieved, then the consumer and practitioner plan together to terminate the activities. Just as there is a discussion of what will be accomplished during service, there needs to be a final discussion of what changes occurred and what type of future can be anticipated.

In other words, termination should be a phase, not an event. When terminations are planned and carried through over a period of time, they can be a very productive period of learning and consolidation of experience for the consumer. Unfortunately, many terminations are simply events. Because many participants are involved in the child welfare services—children, parents, foster parents, residential program staff, courts, attorneys, advocates, and others—practitioners may have little or minimum control over the decision to terminate. Staff may anticipate that a child will be returning home to her parent or will be discharged as an emancipated minor, but the actual date of the severance of service may occur sooner than expected. When a child is a runaway and never returns to service, when a court decides abruptly to discharge a child, there is little or perhaps no time to discuss endings. However, in the discussion prior to any court hearing, the worker should introduce all the possible outcomes. The worker could address some of the feelings about termination if this is a likely outcome—although he may have to telescope his discussion into a ten-minute one in the courtroom. Where there is sufficient time, the responsible worker will develop a process to facilitate a constructive ending.

Terminations that are part of a planned process or part of the social fabric are more easily handled by people than unplanned and unexpected ones. The completion of elementary school or high school is a clearly structured event. Although students may feel ambivalence about leaving, there are many activities that lead up to and celebrate the event; and through these activities many of the emotions associated with termination can be expressed. Graduation is also a recognition of accomplishment. Terminations are also easier for individuals to handle if a group of persons is separating. A camper who has to leave camp before the end of a camping period will probably have more difficulties in leaving than if he left along with the entire group.

Most social service programs do not have clearly defined and socially sanctioned and celebrated program periods. Their very design and purposes are to provide assistance until certain goals—often set with a single person or family—are achieved. Service may begin and end at any time, and for children the service period may be eighteen years or longer. The young person may experience many separations during that period as practitioners leave the agency or as the child is moved from one facility or home to another. Even mutually contracted "brief goal-oriented" services may develop new contractual periods, and some services will continue longer than originally planned. In certain situations there may be many unanticipated and uncontrolled service disruptions. A case may be reopened after it has been terminated because new, unforeseen problems emerge. In short, with a few exceptions, time frames in the social services are unpredictable.

Tasks and Feelings During Termination

The tasks of the consumer and the practitioner include at least the following steps:

First, they must try to reach a mutual agreement on termination. For a number of reasons, a mutual plan may not be possible; a parent may withdraw, a child may be released from care, a court may terminate services. Nonetheless, the ending should be made as constructive and as smooth a process as possible within the various constraints of the situation. Since many terminations are a negative experience, practitioners should try to construct an ending plan or at least make a statement that establishes a positive completion.

Second, when termination is becoming evident, worker and client should discuss accomplishments. As Pincus and Minahan (1973) note, it is important to state accomplishments in terms of original goals. In some instances accomplishments related to original goals may be minimal, whereas the short-range change may appear substantial but in fact is rather small. Changes must never be negated, but it is desirable to recognize the original goal. It is also important to consider events that may have impeded additional accomplishments. Intended and unintended outcomes of the service should be included in the evaluation. It is also helpful to try to understand why a change took place.

Third, later client problems should be anticipated. Although problems may have been resolved, they may emerge again and cause the client difficulties. When the dysfunction is within range of the person's control, the consumer should be prepared to recognize when the problem may be emerging again, how to handle it if it occurs, and how to prevent it from getting worse.

Fourth, the worker should assure the client that community services are ready to serve him if he seeks help again. He should also be made aware of other helping services in the community. Although one agency service may be terminating, referral may be made elsewhere for another service that the family needs—a service that is not provided by the current agency. The client has a right to know what resources are available and how to go about connecting with them.

Fifth, the worker should focus on the client's feelings about the ending. Many authors agree on the four major stages that consumers may go through when they are informed about and work through the termination of service (Germaine and Gitterman, 1980; Pincus and Minahan, 1973; Shapiro, 1980). The stages and the behaviors expressed will vary according to the extent of the relationship developed during the service period and the reasons associated with the termination. An intense, satisfying experience probably will require movement through each of the stages; an unsatisfactory one may go through none of the stages, and the consumer will be glad to "get rid of the agency." Germaine and Gitterman (1980, p. 270) describe the stages:

1. *Denial.* The termination is forgotten, and the person believes it will not take place.
2. *Negative Feelings.* Denial is replaced with a recognition of termination, and negative feelings toward the worker and toward the self may occur.
3. *Sadness.* After a variety of feelings are expressed, the consumer and the worker may both go through a period of sadness over the ending.
4. *Release.* Feelings about the ending become resolved, and the person senses relief and freedom. Three separate events should occur here: "(1) recognition of gains and the speci-

fication of work yet to be done; (2) development of plans
for the future, such as transfer, referral, or self-directed
tasks; and (3) final goodbyes and disengagement."

The expression of feelings related to the steps may not
emerge in the same sequence as those listed. The first feeling
may be that of relief that the service is over and the family will
not have to wait around for the worker or plan to go into the
agency office. Later there may be an expression of sadness that
the family members will not see the practitioner. They have
found that they will miss the worker and realize that she was
helpful to them. Clients may form close attachments even in
brief services. The person may not be able to state the importance of the relationship and may not recognize the strength of
the relationship until a termination is about to begin.
    Anger, sadness, a sense of betrayal, and other feelings re-
lated to loss are not easy ones to discuss. Strong feelings may
be transferred into behavioral responses. Failures in a recently
learned activity may also be a covert appeal for continued assistance. The client may avoid any attempt to focus on the reality of the ending and may miss or cancel appointments so that
the plan cannot be reviewed or even fully presented. Later the
client may become more dependent and may reveal important
information or feelings just as an interview is ending. If the
practitioner can be made guilty, perhaps the service will continue. Through all these reactions, the client is saying that it is
frightening to have loss of service or support. Knowing this, the
practitioner should devise opportunities for the client to deny,
ventilate, or even to regress. She should discuss the client's
achievements—including his ability to express and deal with his
feelings—and repeat the belief that functioning can be maintained without direct agency service.
    Some clients revert to a behavior that proves the need for
continued service. Once employment has been obtained, the client fails to show up for work and is dismissed. Once housing is
suitable, some behavior on the part of a client causes eviction.
The worker must deal promptly with such regression: "We have
worked together for such a long time that it must seem strange

—even impossible—to think of getting things accomplished without our help." "It won't be easy, but we believe that you can manage. Let's talk about the things you've managed this month. I suppose you were scared when you contacted the school, but you did it, and I think you can do it again and make the plans yourself."

Categories of Case Termination

Reasons for case termination include the following:

1. The service goals have been reached. The agreements developed at the time of service initiation have been completed. Specific tasks have been achieved or accomplished, behavior has changed, and the family or consumer is able to continue independently of the agency. Goal completion includes separation from a day care program, with the child moving on to an elementary school; a young person achieving minority emancipation status; the reunion of a family following a child's stay in a residential treatment program; and a group's completion of a six-session series on understanding adolescence.

Few cases proceed in accordance with easily defined, general stages. Practitioners should nevertheless be aware of stages of work, even though they may not succeed in helping a person through each stage. The following case presents a planned termination, but it is complicated by the worker's departure. If two or more losses occur at the same time, the practitioner must be aware of the additional analysis and understanding required and the importance of clarifying the meanings of the terminations.

Mrs. Lanzer and her two children—Arie, age five, and Leonard, age eight—lived in a dilapidated, small house in an area scheduled for redevelopment. The mother had to be hospitalized for several weeks and treated for cancer; and the children were placed in a residential program for temporary care. During her hospitalization, the Lawrence County Redevelopment Authority initiated proceedings for the first phase of demolition. Since Mrs. Lanzer's home was in the first zone, she would have to move to an apartment when she got out of the hospital.

Mr. Osario, a social worker, maintained contact with the mother through her hospitalization and convalescence, arranging for public health nursing services and supporting her emotionally when she questioned whether she would survive to be able to care for the children again. She had many doubts about her own ability to be a parent, and the prognosis for recovery was doubtful; however, she recovered more quickly than expected.

Just as plans were being made for the boys' return home, the social worker sought and obtained employment with the Lawrence County Mental Health Service. He had to tell Mrs. Lanzer of his own plans, since it appeared that he would leave just before the children were discharged. When he told her of his departure, she wept openly, stating that his support was the one thing in her life she could count on. Her husband was "somewhere in another state," and her illness had "demolished me just like they're doing to my old house." The biggest upset for her was revealed in the statement "Lawrence County took my house away, and now they're taking you away." As pleased as she was to be getting ready for the children's return, she seemed overwhelmed at the loss of the practitioner.

After she began to recover from this upset, she wanted assurance from the social worker that he was going to work "at a good place." Even though he assured her that it was a good job, she seemed puzzled about his new employer. It then became clear that she felt betrayed because he was going to work for the same county that had put her out of her home. She could not admit anger, because he had helped her so much, but she still felt disappointment.

Three days before the children were discharged from care, the mother talked again about her hospitalization, including the fact, not revealed before, that she had had a long illness as a child of seven or eight. This illness had resulted in an extended dependence on her parents and difficulty in relating to her friends again. As she and Mr. Osario discussed the relationship between her earlier illness and the present illness, she began to see a connection between her slow recovery then and her recent feelings that she could not adequately take care of the children now. She also acquired some understanding that her illness now, and accompanying need for the social worker, was similar to her experience as a child and the special help from her parents. Mr. Osario repeatedly assured her, however, that the two illnesses were not similar in all respects: "You cared for the children before you got ill, and you haven't necessarily lost that ability just because you have had surgery and a slow recovery."

She volunteered eventually that she could probably get along now without agency assistance, especially since he was leaving. She understood that she could come back for further assistance, "but it wouldn't be the same." Eventually the discussion became somewhat lighthearted. He reminded her that the mental health agency had a district office near her home. She agreed to consider using it, stating that, even though she might not feel kindly toward the county right now, she could see that as a place to discuss childrearing.

There was great pleasure for everyone when the children returned home. Mr. Osario left the agency several days later.

This mother was very open in her feelings of distress over termination. She was suffering from several losses at one time. Her own internal strength and coping ability were probably greater than she thought, since she was able to handle and work through her feelings of loss and abandonment. It is unlikely that she would have had so much upset if the social worker had not been leaving at the same time and if she had not had to leave her house. However, she had known before the hospitalization that demolition would occur soon. Her capacity to be open about her feelings and the practitioner's accurate perceptions of her interrelated fears facilitated a resolution.

2. Original goals have not been reached, but progress toward the goals has been sufficient to warrant termination. This happens in many cases, and it is a sound reason for termination. A family that has achieved some or most of the goals set may do very well on its own and then return at a later time or seek help from another service in order to reach goals originally set or to set new ones.

Mr. and Mrs. Murta had four children, ages two, three, four, and six, and were expecting another child in three months. The family lived in an isolated rural area with almost no friends nearby, but Mrs. Murta's older sister lived about a mile away. The parents had numerous quarrels, with the father maintaining that she was a poor housekeeper, could not handle most family situations, and was indifferent to his needs. There was some truth to this, since she was overwhelmed by most things and often broke into tears with minimum provocation. He was verbally insulting to her. She followed her mother's pattern of seldom cooking. Family members dipped from a large pot of stew that was always on the stove. More food was added each day—although food was not always available because the father sometimes spent the grocery money on things for himself. They owned one car, and he did the shopping at his own convenience. During family crises the sister would step in and help.

The Murtas were referred to the child welfare service by the County Public Health Nursing Division. The social worker offered help initially to organize housekeeping and to set agreements between the parents about mutual responsibilities and getting health care for the children, who appeared to be in poor health. The mother especially had some recognition of this need, since they would have a fifth child soon and would have to meet that child's needs also. The father agreed that something had to be done, but he placed the responsibility for change on the mother. A homemaker was provided for one day a week, and the father welcomed this, but used it as proof that Mrs. Murta needed the help. He was unable to see that he contributed to the family's problems by failing to give his wife emotional support, by spending grocery money on himself, and by not encouraging Mrs. Murta to get out of the house periodically for a change of pace.

For two months there was a small measure of stability in the family, but then Mr. Murta's job was cut to thirty hours a week. He became frantic and less responsive to the family's needs, even though he had more time available. As Mrs. Murta approached delivery time, he became unaccepting of her increased needs and on the day of her delivery refused to take her to the hospital. Both the public health nurse and the social worker were there when she went into labor, and the nurse finally took her to the hospital. Emergency plans were made with the sister for the children's care. The father took no responsibility for child care during the two weeks following delivery, and the mother petitioned for placement of the two youngest children until she could make other plans.

The parents separated, and the mother went to live with her mother thirty miles away in a small town. This was a good arrangement for the children, and it helped meet some of the mother's dependency needs. The tentative goal set was to have the two children in care until the parents could make a new home together. As a start to rebuild the marriage, the parents agreed to attend an eight-week series on marital relationships. The father attended once and refused further contacts. After several other disappointing contacts with him, Mrs. Murta realized that she had to plan to live without him. After two years

Mrs. Murta had improved substantially in her care of the three children. She petitioned for the return of the two in care, and the agency agreed to the discharge.

This case had three different goals established during the course of service. The first was to attempt to strengthen the existing family unit before and after the delivery of the fifth child. At first it appeared that this might happen, because stability was established for a short time. The father's loss of some employment and the mother's increased needs at delivery placed too many demands on the father, and he was unable to respond. On the day of her delivery, he flatly refused to help and sped off in his car. The second goal was to begin a reconciliation of the parents and rebuild the family. The father was again unable to participate. The third goal was the return of the children when the mother was in a position to have them. The maternal grandmother provided the stability Mrs. Murta needed to enable her nurturing capacities to increase.

3. There is disagreement on service goals. The consumer and the agency cannot agree on either the problem or the methods to resolve the issue. If clients are attempting to make an independent decision to terminate service, the signals may come by missed appointments, less initiative for contact by the client, or reluctance to have discussions when practitioners initiate the contact. When staff reach out, the client may say, "I have no time," whereas prior contacts have been lengthy and involved. Other signs of withdrawal may be discussion that focuses on "I'm fine now" or "Remember when I first called you I was having trouble with Sally? Well, that all worked out fine so we probably don't need to see each other any more." Clients who attempt to terminate service before the plan can be based on a mutual agreement may be attempting to reject the agency before they endure a rejection themselves. It is important to identify the behavior and possible feelings with such remarks as "You are talking as if our work together is completed. I thought we had agreed that we would deal with the following issues." "Recently you have been talking about . . . and that really has nothing to do with the problems we have been working on." "I

see that you are making a plan to move, and I'm concerned that I have not been included in your planning." "Sometimes the people I work with think that we aren't getting much accomplished and that the agency will want to end the service. That can be very frightening for some people, and they decide that they might as well stop the work together before they have to be rejected."

If clients attempt to disengage from the service plan early in the working relationship, perhaps the client has no commitment to the plan. If this occurs, it is important to discuss the identified needs and to review the goals and tasks that were discussed initially. Perhaps the plan was the practitioner's alone and is not accepted by the client. Or perhaps the client has no capacity for change or expects the agency to cope with his problems.

The worker received a telephone call from Mrs. C. regarding her daughter Lucy, age fourteen and a half. Mrs. C. demanded that the worker remove Lucy from the home. Lucy had not come home for two days, and this morning the mother had found Lucy in bed with a boyfriend. The mother also stated that Lucy had broken windows in the house and gotten into a fight with other tenants. The landlord threatened to evict the mother, ostensibly because of Lucy's behavior and destruction of property. The worker had been attempting for three weeks to negotiate an agreement between mother and daughter. Lucy did not follow through on earlier agreements with the mother, and the mother admitted that she too had not kept to her part of the bargain.

In this case neither the mother nor the daughter has engaged in a service plan. The mother's goal is to have an incorrigible child removed from the home. At this point the worker's goal is apparently to negotiate rather than to accept the mother's goal of removal. There are strong signs, however, that neither the mother nor the daughter will adhere to an agreement. Lucy may perceive the problem as too tight restrictions by her mother, whereas the mother sees the daughter as the cause of all her difficulties, including the threat of eviction. Although the worker should probably focus on the mother's perception of the daughter, more data are needed in order to initiate the assessment.

It is always startling to the practitioner if a client begins to disengage when work together has appeared to be harmonious and when goals are being accomplished. If a working relationship is to continue, it is necessary to discuss the events and the feelings that may be prompting the withdrawal. Support should be articulated for the progress the child or family has been making up to this time.

Jane is seventeen and a half years old with two children, Mary, age two, and John, nine months. She is unmarried, has an eighth-grade education, and is currently receiving welfare. She has a young boyfriend who does not seem to have steady employment although he is at present working. Her mother lives nearby and works in a local nursing home, and Jane is involved voluntarily with the Work Incentive (WIN) program.

Jane is quiet, passive, and generally uncommunicative with the worker assigned to her case. The worker reported the following impressions: "She has occasionally surprised me by being actively receptive and following through on projects; but recently she has been less interested in discussing projects. Her interaction with her children is noticeably cold and harsh. I have not observed any spontaneous show of warmth or affection between them. Client mainly is a disciplinarian, and the children reflect this. Mary is fearful and withdrawn but over the time period she has warmed up to me. John is quiet and undemanding. The home consists of one room with a bathroom in a dilapidated old rooming house. This atmosphere is neither stimulating nor conducive to growth for the children. Client has resided there two and a half years, and just located a small, renovated apartment. I first met the family in November 1980 and with substantial effort located a day care provider for the children, thereby allowing client to be certified for WIN in December 1980."

Initially the mutually agreed-upon goals of this case included moving the family into an apartment and getting Jane involved in a productive daily activity. In addition, the worker felt that she needed information on basic parenting, health, and nutrition, in order to upgrade the quality of the children's care. The worker also attempted to bring in a parent aide to work more intensively with Jane. However, Jane's passivity and general unresponsiveness seemed to be signaling her desire to terminate her relationship with the worker and the agency. Consequently, the worker attempted to ward off a premature termination by reminding Jane of achievements reached so far and by focusing on feelings that might be prompting the disengagement:

When we began to work together, it was difficult for me to know what you were thinking, but then you began to follow through on some projects. When you are working with other people, remember how hard it has been for you to communicate. What did you learn by working with me that you might do again with someone else? We can practice it through again together when you are meeting residents at the new apartment building.

You lived in one place for two and a half years, and then I came along and said it is important to have a better living place. Now we have located another place, but I wonder if it will really feel better for you. Perhaps I am just a person who has uprooted you. Maybe that is why I sense that you don't want our help any more.

We have talked to many agencies, counselors, employers, and doctors. Do you remember anything in particular about these contacts we made together? Would you do anything different if you contacted people like this yourself? I am helping you with contacts now, but when our service is really completed, you will be able to do it by yourself.

4. Service is completed, and there are no further services available for the family. In such instances the case is terminated with the recognition that the family either needs or wants another service, but it simply is not available. The community may not have a full array of services; or the programs are too distant to be used on a regular basis or are available only at certain times; or the services that the family may need are unacceptable for religious, ethnic, language, or other reasons.

Mr. D. was required to participate in the WIN program because he was unemployed and receiving public assistance for himself and his family. The family consists of Mr. D.; his second wife; a son, David (from his first marriage), age fourteen; and a

daughter, Joy, age two and a half. David has been classified
trainable mentally retarded and also has emotional problems.

During Mr. D's participation in a WIN Intensive Employ-
ability Services Group, he mentioned to his counselor that his
wife was having difficulty handling David and he was afraid to
leave the two alone together for long periods of time.

A protective services worker visited the family at home to
discuss the situation. Mrs. D. was quite willing to verbalize her
frustration in caring for David. She has been responsible for his
care since he was two years old; his mother died of cancer when
he was an infant. Mrs. D. described David's behavior in the
home. He frequently wets his bed and soils himself. Mrs. D.
feels it is intentional. He also hits his mother and sister. She
also has observed David attempting sexual activity with Joy. Mr.
D. has more control over David than his wife does. Both Mr.
and Mrs. D. were enrolled in a child management group at a local mental health clinic. Mr. D. was not able to continue in the
group because he returned to work.

Mr. D. still needed a service, but he discontinued because
no group met at an hour that he could attend. The goal of employment was achieved.

Mrs. D. has become more frustrated with David since her
husband returned to work. She has most of the responsibility
for his care. She feels that David is manipulating her. She also
feels that David's behavior is having a harmful effect on Joy.
She would like to have David out of the home. If he remains in
the home, she is afraid that it will affect her marriage. She is
also afraid that she might become so frustrated that she will
abuse the children. Mr. D. has been reluctant to have David
placed, since he has two severely retarded sons in a state
school. Mrs. D. feels that he might be more willing to have
David placed now.

This case comes to termination because the agency procedure is to close when the goal is accomplished—the client has
employment. However, staff believe correctly that another service is necessary to improve family working relationships. Specific discussion with both parents might go as follows:

It is very hard to manage David. Mrs. D., you
believe that he may be purposefully causing trou-

ble, that perhaps he can control his behavior. We must have a thorough assessment about David's capacity to control his behavior.

Mr. D., you do not want to think about a special placement for this son, because two of your severely retarded sons are already in state schools. That is not easy. What kind of care are they getting? What concerns you most about a placement for David?

You say, Mrs. D., that David's behavior may affect your marriage. In what way do you see this happening?

If you grow very angry with David, what do you think you will do?

We must terminate our service in the WIN Program, but I think you need the service of a child welfare agency.

5. The agency decides that the client's situation shows almost no prospect of changing. The parent or parents may possess such limited adaptive abilities, intelligence, or self-awareness and ability to relate to others that change will probably never occur—although no neglect or abuse seems likely to occur. Or, even with environmental services and agency counseling supports, the parent may not be able to nurture a child adequately or even to live with much independence in the community. Included here would also be long-standing, bitter, rejecting, and indifferent relationships between adolescents and parents in which there is no effective mode of intervention and no willingness on the parents' part to attempt to change.

When the case is closed at the initiative of the agency because there is no apparent movement or because there seems little likelihood of any change, discussions of termination should focus on whatever advances have occurred in the situation, even though these may have taken place a long time before. The same process of evaluating change should occur, as well as a redefinition of the current problems and what should be done about them.

It is painful for every practitioner to count the hours spent on a case and to realize that no useful adaptive abilities have been engendered. There is a temptation to refer to the client as nonmotivated. However, every client is motivated—but not necessarily for the achievement of agency-defined goals. If clients miss more appointments than the worker manages to hold, the client's motivation to avoid the system is high. In fact, the client's motivation to avoid may be higher than the worker's motivation to involve him.

If it is possible to engage the client in some dialogue, expressions of concern such as the following can be made: "We have been seeing each other for several months, but I can't discover much change in the way you deal with your children. This is discouraging because we think that daily living could improve for each one of you. It did improve a little bit when we got the rent payments caught up and the landlord stopped hounding you. But right now we're not making any changes. I think it would make sense to stop seeing each other for now. Perhaps you will be able to talk more about how to give care to children as they get a little older. You know you can call us if you think we can help."

In some instances termination occurs because the practitioner believes it is impossible to work any further with the child or family. The goals may be unrealistic, and the client may not be able to achieve them; this produces worker frustration. Perhaps there are no positive signs of client motivation or participation. It may be such a time-consuming service that other caseload demands preclude continuing with a difficult family. Staff may not like the client or may actually be afraid of family members. The following is one worker's report on a "hopeless, untreatable" case:

This family—a white mother on AFDC; a black father; a four-year-old boy by a first marriage; and two racially mixed children, a girl, two, and a boy, seven months—was referred by City Welfare. The staff there felt that the children were in jeopardy because the mother and father kept separating and fighting over the children, literally breaking down doors to get the kids back from each other.

It was soon obvious that both parents were mentally ill. The mother had been diagnosed as chronic paranoid schizophrenic and refused all aftercare, especially medication. The father also had been diagnosed by several hospitals as a paranoid schizophrenic with a history of shock treatment and known problems of alcoholism and violence.

Both parents love their children—to the point of plotting to kill the other parent to get them. Basic physical needs of the children are met, with help from City Welfare, homemakers, and relatives. The children are constantly grabbed by each parent, with violent assaults frequent. Police say it's a domestic matter. A recent court decision gave custody to the mother; then the parents decided to return to live together the next day. The reconciliation lasted one week.

Long-term emotional trauma for the kids seems assured if these attacks continue. Neither parent is rational or able to recognize the problem. Neither wants any help.

The case seems hopeless, untreatable. Jeopardy here, however, is of a type rarely recognized by the court. I personally fear the father attacking me if I went to court. We have great difficulty gathering the necessary legally admissible evidence, because both parties refuse to cooperate.

I'm merely holding this case, hoping the children are not killed and that I'll also live through whatever happens. This case is a good example of the effects of mental health deinstitutionalization on the community's requirement to protect children.

Termination decisions based on impulse or feelings about clients are not acceptable. However, strong feelings about clients, especially when agreed to by several staff, may be useful in understanding both the severity of the problems and the treatment choices available to try to change family relationships.

The worker would certainly like to close this case. There is demonstrated assaultive behavior, so the worker's personal fears, plus beliefs about the children's jeopardy, are very realistic. With the absence of evidence for a return to court, the practitioner has limited service options. Termination is not the solution; so the same or additional community agencies must remain involved in order to document abuse or neglect. It is apparent that relatives have given help to the family, and a homemaker agency has given service. The practitioner may be able to work through these two sources for both monitoring and supportive help. One of the violent assaults may eventually produce the evidentiary material for a court decision for removal of one or both children. This staff member is also facing the problems of a community in which one of the systems does not support intervention in domestic violence. The police call the assaultive behavior a "domestic matter."

In the following case, minimum change has taken place, even though the social worker provided support and counsel for four years. Several services were used by the family.

Mrs. H., age thirty-one, and divorced from her husband, lives with her three children—a daughter eleven and two boys, ages five and four. They have been on AFDC for the past four years. The father left home when the youngest was born and now lives on the East Coast; he occasionally sends some money for the children. Mrs. H. has had two boyfriends, each of whom lived with her for less than six months. The mother was inadequately cared for when she was a child, and she has found it very difficult to fulfill a parenting role.

Mrs. H. became depressed when her husband left, and her care of the children bordered on being neglectful. She seldom prepared meals or washed the children's clothes. The children were frequently ill and received insufficient medical care. Mrs. H. often purchased items for herself at the expense of necessities for her children.

She requested foster care for the youngest child, and he remained in placement for six months. When she asked for his release from care, the agency staff doubted that she could manage the three children and encouraged her to accept both brief homemaker service and then a parent aide. She learned almost nothing from the homemaker, and although the parent aide came to the home three days a week for seven months, the mother made only a few behavioral gains in parenting. She was encouraged to take part in meetings for parents and to engage in social activities at the YWCA. She went to two meetings, but declined all others.

After four years of agency service, very little had changed in the family, except that Mrs. H. had not become totally immobilized or depressed by minor crises. Her care of the children had improved slightly; she prepared meals more often and would take the children to a health clinic if they were very ill. Nonetheless, she provided little, if any, psychological nurture for the children's social and emotional development. Agency staff agreed that the mother had minimum motivation and ability for further change at this time, and the case was closed.

6. The case is closed abruptly by legal action or by parental or child decisions. There may be minimum or no agreement on the goals to be achieved, and the natural family or foster family brings the case to court in order to reach a decision. Or the natural parents want a child released from residential care and the agency disagrees, but the court concurs. Or an agency recommends that a delinquent child stay at home and receive community mental health counseling, but the court places the child in a residential program in another state, discontinuing any further services by the agency. Or a parent decides to disavow any further responsibility for a delinquent child and further refuses to engage in any way with the agency. Or an adolescent runs away and does not return to care. Or a family moves to another community.

If the practitioner meets with hostile or indifferent clients and the termination process is a negative experience for all concerned, he should attempt to terminate in an amicable and constructive manner: "I know that you and I disagreed on many things during the time we worked together, and even though this did not end in the way I recommended, I do want you to realize that I am concerned about you and want good experiences for you." "I recall that you said that I did nothing but interfere with you and the children. You also said that another staff member had not treated you nearly as badly as I did. Please remember that if you do believe in the future that you would have to return to our agency, we will work with you to meet your needs at that time. We do not cease our service because we have been criticized." "Perhaps you don't even want to say goodbye, but I do very honestly hope that things go OK for you." "You were very angry at me today, because of what I said in court. That makes it difficult for you to believe that I am concerned for your well-being."

The following case cannot be described as typical of termination, but it is an example of some of the difficult endings that occur in child welfare practice. When an ending is as traumatic as this, it requires judgment on the part of the practitioner to decide how much effort, if any, can be expended on attempting to encourage any process of termination.

Mrs. Frank called to request placement for her seventeen-year-old adopted son, Allen, because he was "uncontrollable, belligerent, won't listen, and got into a wrestling match with his father." The social worker was able, with considerable difficulty, to locate an emergency foster home placement for the night. Mr. and Mrs. Frank, through their attorney, demanded immediate removal.

The police had been called to the house and reported the following: "Allen is a decent kid. Disrespectful to parents. Okay in school, was okay to police. Parents are outstanding people in community. They cannot deal with Allen. Want him to be grateful to them for adopting him. Last night Allen cursed at mother, father went to slap boy, and the kid protected himself. There will be a charge of assault going up to probation. Another sibling in the home, female, fourteen years old. Parents having problems with her lying and stealing. Adoption has not yet been finalized for her."

The attorney reported similar information. The family had been in counseling for one year but discontinued because the boy's behavior became worse. He was adopted at age fifteen and a half in another state. He had been in several foster homes but was adopted from an orphanage. The Franks were thought to be able to give him the love and stability he had been seeking.

The worker met with the parents to obtain additional information and to determine what ongoing relationships, if any, could be established with Allen. They agreed to hold this one interview but otherwise would have nothing to do with him. They both felt at first that Allen was a son whom they could love and who would love them back. The adoptive mother now feels he never showed them any love. They started having problems with him about a year ago, when he became aggressive and verbally abusive. The parents made some very bitter comments about Allen, including their belief that he was ungrateful. The worker did not contradict them but commented that she knew that youngsters adopted in their teens did not always express affection. The worker added that even though Allen did not express appreciation, he may have nevertheless appreciated what they had done for him.

In an attempt to establish something positive in what was to be the first and last interview, the practitioner asked if they had felt any satisfaction in things they had done with Allen. The father made a curt comment about some pleasure they had on a short vacation, just after he was adopted. The mother saw nothing that gratified her. She referred to him as "bad seed and good riddance" and began to weep. The father abruptly ended the interview.

These parents had no working relationship at all with the agency, but they did have a relationship with Allen, and he probably had given them some satisfaction. Because of the recent event and the deterioration of the relationships, Mrs. Frank was now unable to see anything positive in Allen. The father could mention only one time of satisfaction, and he would not dwell on that. It is unlikely that the worker felt much sympathy for these parents, but they were nevertheless entitled to some support in discussing any feelings they may have of abruptly terminating their relationship with him. They may have been afraid to say anything positive for fear that they would be asked to reconsider Allen's return to their home. There was insufficient time for any real discussion of ending, and the mother was too hurt to dwell on anything except her own feelings of trauma. To encourage any exploration of ambivalence in his departure or any sadness in not seeing him again would have been offensive to them. They were also only two days removed from a crisis and were still in a stage of disorganization, too soon to be concentrating seriously on the separation. If and when time heals the wounds of the fight and the verbal aggression, the parents may be able to recognize that they had some satisfactions from Allen and be able to work through feelings about the termination.

In marked contrast to the adoptive parents, Allen was able to reflect on the end of his relationship with them during several interviews.

He described his mother as a perfectionist, someone who never laughs and who does nothing wrong. He described his dad as more understanding, but as one who always supported the mother. He was able to express appreciation because they had removed him from the orphanage, and he felt he would not do anything to jeopardize the adoption. He admitted that he should not have cursed at her, but she would never let up on anything and insisted there was only one way to do things. He did not know how his father could put up with her. When he was first placed away from their home, he wanted to go back and work things out, but he later accepted the placement and felt that he was better off away from them. He admitted that he missed them for quite a while.

Allen did well in his foster home, worked part time, did satisfactorily in schoolwork, and participated in school activities.

Practitioner Feelings About Termination

Social workers who are well aware of the needs of consumers at the time of termination may still have difficulty introducing the subject because of the feelings that will be generated for both worker and client. The effect of termination on the practitioner may be a crucial factor in the way the case is handled. Germaine and Gitterman (1980) and others refer to the difficulty that practitioners often have in ending some cases. Practitioners experience guilt, inadequacy, depression, and anxiety (Shapiro, 1980). These feelings may lead to a range of behavioral responses in terminations, such as failure to introduce a discussion of the termination steps; doubt about what was accomplished and consequent failure to define improvements; avoidance and lack of responsiveness to the consumer, who needs help in ending the relationship; and precipitous and poorly timed movement to a closing. It is important for workers to have their own feelings well under control, since clients need a stable environment when they are about to assume additional responsibility and independence. Sometimes practitioners do not want to "hurt" people by informing them soon enough that service will end. Consequently, persons are hurt because information about termination is delayed and the person has insufficient time to adapt to the change. (Feelings generated by separation are addressed in Chapter Three.) Practitioners must be able to admit that they do not like to stop seeing some families, that they have enjoyed and profited from the relationship and would like to continue. It is perfectly understandable to feel pride and fulfillment in the accomplishments of a successful client. In a comparable way, workers must recognize that, even though they do not feel kindly toward someone or that few apparent changes have been made, the client may have profited considerably from the working relationship and needs a sufficient amount of time to work through feelings related to the termination.

Summary

Termination is the last phase in the provision of a social service to a family. It should not be considered an isolated event, but a significant episode in the treatment process. At the beginning of a service agreement, consumers and practitioner decide what they will accomplish together. Similarly, when the goals, or modified goals, are achieved, the persons involved again plan together for the ending of activities.

The tasks of termination include the following: (1) to reach a mutual agreement on termination, (2) to discuss explicit accomplishment in terms of original goals and why the changes occurred, (3) to anticipate later problems, (4) to offer the consumer continued agency services and to acquaint the person with other community resources, and (5) to focus on the person's feelings about the completion of work together. Depending on the length of the service, the types of services provided, and consumer satisfaction with the service, clients may demonstrate the following feelings toward ending: (1) a denial that the service will end; (2) negative feelings toward the agency, practitioner, and even toward the self; (3) sadness that the ending must take place; and (4) a feeling of relief and freedom that it has terminated. All persons will not necessarily experience or express these feelings, and the sequence may vary.

The reasons for case terminations in child welfare include the following: (1) Service goals have been reached. (2) Original goals have not been reached, but progress is sufficient to warrant termination. (3) There is a disagreement between consumer and agency on service goals. (4) No service is available or acceptable. (5) The agency defines a total lack of goal achievement. (6) Case closing is effected by legal authorities or by parental or child decisions.

Practitioners should be prepared to complete the tasks of termination and to help clients resolve conflicted feelings during the end of a service. Termination can be a very productive segment of the entire episode of service, since emphasis is placed on positive accomplishments and on the consumer's improved performance. Practitioners may have little control over the time and the circumstances of a case closing, and they consequently must be prepared to telescope a discussion of termination into a very short time. It should not be assumed that, because a service was brief or even somewhat negative, the consumer does not have some strong feelings related to the termination.

Practitioners must also face their own feelings about termination. Workers may feel guilt, inadequacy, depression, and anxiety; unless these feelings are understood and handled, they may produce behaviors that are not conducive to a constructive last phase of service.

Special Annotated Bibliography

Fox, E. F., Nelson, M. A., and Bolman, W. M. "The Termination Process: A Neglected Dimension in Social Work." In B. R. Compton and B. Galaway, *Social Work Processes.* Homewood, Ill.: Dorsey Press, 1975. Deals with termination following therapy and reveals the feelings that should be dealt with if behavioral changes are to be maintained.

Germaine, C. B., and Gitterman, A. *The Life Model of Social Work Practice.* New York: Columbia University Press, 1980. The chapter on "The Ending Phase: Termination" provides an analysis of client and worker activity in both group and case service.

Pincus, A., and Minahan, A. *Social Work Practice: Model and Method.* Itasca, Ill.: Peacock, 1973. The chapter on "Terminating the Change Effort" is a short and very clear description of the steps in case endings.

CHAPTER NINE

Serving as Advocates
for Children
and Families

Advocacy is the act of pleading a cause, speaking or writing in favor of, and being an intercessor or defender. When a practitioner acts as an advocate on behalf of a child or a group of children, he may be challenging and seeking changes in systems that he regards as unhelpful or injurious to children. Or he may be attempting to help consumers, whether parent or child, obtain services that they are entitled to but have difficulty in getting. Advocacy may require heroic efforts. Some would say that unless it has a high personal cost or risk—including loss of job, income, and friends—the activity cannot be called advocacy.

There are two types of advocacy: case and class. Both employ similar methods to achieve change, but class advocacy usually involves more formalized steps, more people, and more time and funds than case advocacy. Legislative lobbying is included in class advocacy, and it has the obvious goal of effecting legislative changes. Litigation is a form of advocacy that involves redress through the court systems.

Advocacy for families and children is concerned with

both rights and needs. Rights, or entitlements, are guaranteed under legislation, statutes, or administrative regulations, whereas the social-psychological needs of individuals and families are not necessarily enacted into law. If a *right* is not being implemented, or if it is being violated, there is a better chance of having that problem corrected than there is of having a *need* met. Our understanding of needs derives from social science knowledge or practice wisdom rather than from the law. Koocher (1979, p. 85) defines three kinds of rights: statutory rights, human rights, and enabling rights. Statutory rights are those guaranteed by law. Human rights, referred to above as needs, are those viewed from the perspectives of child development, family dynamics, and clinical psychology; as such they are not legal rights. Enabling rights are those that would ensure the development of programs or policies that enable children to ultimately attain their full potential. These also are not legal rights. Advocates must recognize whether they are seeking change to meet children's needs and interests, are seeking implementation of existing rights, or are attempting to transform children's needs and interests into entitlements or rights. Rights can be categorized in four areas: (1) rights in relation to the family, (2) rights of children without families, (3) rights in juvenile-oriented institutions, and (4) rights in relation to society.

Bases for Advocacy

A worker's sanction to engage in advocacy may derive from the law and from various regulations and administrative entitlements that carry the weight of law. Included here would be the agency's stated objectives, policies, and procedures. Professional ethical standards or codes also give sanction to the practitioner. Colleague support can be obtained from other professionals who adhere to the same values as those of the advocate. Client support and endorsement is a further form of sanction, especially when the advocacy involves only one person or family.

Advocacy against large, bureaucratic organizations places many practitioners in a double bind. Such organizations are a

major source of employment for human service staff, and workers may advocate for change in the very program in which they
seek or hold employment. Depending on the extent and severity
of an agency's denial of rights or services, the practitioner may
remain in continuing conflict with the administration, may have
to take a demotion, may risk loss of promotion, may have to re-
sign, or may be dismissed from employment. However, direct
service staff who do not advocate may sometimes engage in
what Polier (1975) calls the "professional abuse" of children.
Thus, a practitioner who does not reach out in a consumer's behalf becomes a functionary or a passive agent of the system.

Patti (1974, p. 543) states that it is often easier to advocate against another agency than to seek change in one's own.
The stress of internal advocacy is high because most staff, especially direct service staff, have neither the status nor the role to
initiate change in policy or practice. Yet internal advocacy can
be justified for four reasons:

1. One's knowledge of the situation. The direct service practi-
    tioner may have a greater knowledge of the problem than
    anyone else—especially when he has assignments not carried
    by other staff.
2. The necessity to preserve the organization. When an agency
    is not performing according to its own stated objectives,
    changes should be made. The agency should implement
    new policies and programs or else change existing ones.
3. The obligation to communicate to the administration.
    Staff are responsible to inform management of problems
    and practices, and this would include the idea of advocacy.
4. Political self-interest. An entire service unit or department
    could be held accountable for violating regulations or poli-
    cies. Staff would be acting in their own self-interest to ad-
    vocate, as well as serving consumer interests.

Job specifications should never limit a person's involvement in advocacy or social action. Agencies cannot restrict a
practitioner from engaging in advocacy on one's personal time,
although agencies may bring sanctions and restraints against the

activist practitioner. In some instances, advocacy work may result in a revision of the job specifications.

Daily work in an organization may dull the awareness of staff to injustices to clients in the agency or in the agencies to which clients are referred. Some staff may be inclined to let others take action for change, just as people in a crowd wait for someone else to respond to a crisis. Therefore, practitioners must make an effort to perceive if any procedures require correction, define the problem situation, and decide to be personally responsible to initiate change.

Steps and Behaviors in Advocacy

A number of steps, decisions, and analyses must be considered in the conduct of advocacy. The following items should not be considered mutually exclusive, and the sequence of steps may vary considerably, especially if class action, in contrast to a case effort, is taken.

1. The problem must be recognized. Practitioners need to be alert to the concerns of consumers. It is important to clarify whether service denials occurred, and the consumer may not always be able to identify them. The extent and the severity of the problem must be examined. Does the inequity affect one or two children or an entire group of children? Severe, capricious, and abusive injustices may take a high priority, especially when a high-risk group is affected.

A mother had to appear in court about the placement of her child, and she was told by a new attorney that he would not be able to meet with her prior to the hearing. However, he assured her that she did not need to worry, since the hearing was only a routine procedure. The practitioner told the mother that this was incorrect and described the purposes of the hearing; a plan was made to meet the attorney.

2. Facts must be obtained. *All* the facts should be sought. A practitioner's anger or distress over the alleged abuse must not color the collection or analysis of preliminary information. Inadequate data may only jeopardize and delay vital efforts;

false or poorly documented charges can also damage the advocate's reputation. Although practitioners may assume that other professionals know about discovered inequities and service problems, Polier (1975) found that practitioners were often unaware of the extent of local problems, even when studies in their own communities had documented abuses. Furthermore, staff may dismiss the existence of problems: a study of numerous service deficiencies with children was reported to a group of child welfare executives. They agreed the findings were shocking but no worse than elsewhere. Nothing was done. (In situations such as this, the advocate has more than sufficient reason to take action.)

3. Facts must be reconciled. After the data are obtained, can they be reconciled with what is already known about the agency? Is the information on the inequities markedly at variance with what is known about the staff or program? This step is crucial, since a decision for action—or inaction—may hinge on the analysis. Has a single worker made a simple error with one or more consumers? Has a policy been changed, with erratic implementation of new procedures? Was a division understaffed the week of the injustice? Was a supervisor or staff member on a short, personal "crusade" that has now ended? Even if agency services have deteriorated, are improvements being planned? Has the offending practitioner already been transferred or fired?

A community health agency received three complaints from parents who were in need of both social supports and complete medical information for their children. All three families had been referred to a diagnostic center well known for its high quality of service. The health agency contacted the social work administrator, who, when informed about the three families, admitted that one pediatrician had been quite abrupt and inconsiderate in team conferences with the families.

All three situations had been discussed with the pediatrician. In one case, she had been unable to make a diagnosis, and the family had gone to another hospital. When she learned that a competitor of hers at the other hospital was able to diagnose the problem, she became upset and angry and took out her frustration on the parents when they returned for a comprehensive review of all the findings. In two other cases, the physician stated that she was tired of "crying, dependent people" and had given insufficient and confusing medical information to the families. Following the official complaint and discussion with the pediatrician, no further problems occurred.

If the facts cannot be reconciled and if the injustices cannot be corrected by a straightforward telephone or written contact, staff should begin to draw attention to the problem. A memorandum to management or a supervisory conference is rarely sufficient to stimulate change, and the practitioner must often take more vigorous steps.

4. The object to be changed should be specified. A person, a policy, a procedure, a regulation, or even a building may need modification to eliminate the deficiency. Advocates may not know the precise cause or causes of the difficulty, but they should be able to determine where the problem is located.

The assistant director of the Asian Resettlement Program referred many families to the income maintenance program in a small city. It seemed apparent that families with three or more children did not receive their checks as quickly as smaller families or couples did. Telephone calls were made regarding two or three families to see whether checks could be released. When a call was made, social service staff always contacted the accounting office, which was quick to release the money. The assistant director collected data over an eight-week period and met with the intake division to request that checks be released more rapidly, believing that the problems originated in the accounting division. An internal investigation revealed that the accounting manager and one clerk, who were assigned to handle these checks, were in collusion in holding back checks for large families. Both staff had close relatives whose employment had been affected by the Asian immigrants, and they retaliated through a slowdown of check releases to large families. (They did not attempt to hold all checks back for fear of being detected.)

In this case staff of the resettlement program pinpointed the probable division that was not performing adequately. They did not know that a personal vendetta was causing the check delays but, perceiving a problem, collected sufficient data to demonstrate the deficiency. The case illustrates that an agency may not know that a problem exists until it is notified. The agency was grateful for the data and took immediate corrective steps.

5. After the facts are obtained and the problems defined, goals should be specified, including recommendations for changing the condition. This step may require the formation of a committee and discussion with colleagues. If the violation affects only one client, an agreement should be sought with the client about next steps. The change may be effected through a telephone call, a personal conference, a letter, or a formalized interagency procedure. Change may also require a grievance complaint, including appeals and administrative reviews. These procedures should be known prior to initiating action. If the violation affects many clients, group effort may be required to start class action.

The new Head Start director in a semirural area decided to make home visits to a number of families who had many difficulties. It was known that they had inadequate housing, and there appeared to be a connection between the housing and the children's poor health. The director found that several families lived in severely overcrowded conditions in the same small cluster of houses, most of them with no indoor plumbing. A check on municipal housing codes for the area revealed that overcrowding existed and that both the landlord and the families were in noncompliance with housing codes. A meeting with staff from the sanitation division of the health department revealed that they had become aware of many plumbing code violations a year ago and were ready to insist that the landlord make immediate changes. A discussion was held with the four families involved, and they were initially eager to demand improvements. However, within a week they all changed their minds, asking that nothing be done. They recognized that, as bad as the housing was, their rents were comparatively low. The landlord had stated he would make no improvements and threatened to evict them if he were forced to do anything. He had shown his capacity to carry out his threats by boarding up two houses over a year ago. In addition, the rental vacancy rate in the surrounding towns was only 1 percent, and families knew that there would be great difficulty in relocating. Advocacy efforts were not initiated, and families were slowly relocated over an eighteen-month period by the county housing authority.

The Head Start program had a strong advocacy component. The staff position was that Head Start is far more than service to a child within the center. The data from the municipality confirmed that overcrowding existed. The health department meeting confirmed plumbing code violations and stimulated the staff to take immediate action. The department was well known for its vigorous enforcement of codes. If the consumers were ignored by the advocates, they could have been the victims, rather than the beneficiaries, of efforts to improve their housing. Code enforcement would have caused their evictions.

6. All costs must be computed. This includes money, staff time, and material. Advocacy for one consumer may cost very little, but the cost may be substantial if many consumers are affected. It is also wise to make an estimate of the possible costs to the organization that should make the change. If the advocacy effort requires an entirely new program or a decentralized office with additional staff, then the feasibility of change must be weighed against the probable costs.

7. The timing of a proposal for change is crucial. If a proposal is submitted when an organization is facing other major crises, the proposal may be flatly rejected because other problems seem more important. On the other hand, if the agency is examining policies related to a proposal, it may be welcomed.

8. The simplest and most direct approach to change should be taken. Almost everyone likes an efficient, economical way of working. In a study of 150 child advocacy events, only about one quarter of them showed the use of adversarial strategies (McGowan, 1978a, p. 174). It is apparent that most problems can be resolved by direct and sincere suggestions for change; therefore, first efforts should be made in a friendly, collaborative manner.

9. Change must be monitored. Responsible advocacy includes follow-up to ensure that the changed policy or practice has been fully implemented, especially when class advocacy has been used. Neither written policy nor laws guarantee policy implementation. Rodham (1979, p. 30) reports that after the U.S.

Supreme Court "ordered juvenile judges to ensure the presence of counsel in cases with incarceration as a possible punishment, many judges resisted the directive, continued holding court without lawyers, and decided on their own what should be done with a juvenile. . . . Lawsuits were sometimes brought to enforce . . . the mandate." Cases may have to be followed on an individual basis to see that the advocated changes occur. Monitoring may not be as invigorating and challenging, but it is equally vital to other advocacy activities.

Advocacy Tactics

Most change efforts require a mix of different types of intervention. These basic types include (1) intercession—pleading in behalf of the consumer; (2) persuasion—convincing by reasonable argument; (3) negotiation—settling the issue by discussion and compromise; (4) pressure—exerting persistent and continuous influence; (5) coercion—compelling by force.

Once the decision has been made to conduct class advocacy in order to bring about changes, several strategies or forms of intervention can be selected. Since social action and community organization literature describe a variety of methods, this chapter will not attempt to cover those practices in detail. Specht (1969, p. 9) includes four strategies, each of which is called a mode of intervention: collaboration, campaign, contest or disruption, and violence. The final strategy would meet with marked disapproval, since it includes guerrilla warfare and deliberate attempts to harm, tactics that almost everyone deems to be outside the Social Work Code of Ethics and other professional-ethical standards. Brager and Holloway (1978) and McGowan (1978b) include only the first three in their range of tactics and discuss them as follows:

1. *Collaborative tactics* "are characterized by open communication. Problems tend to be stated as such rather than as solutions, information regarding the perspectives of both parties is widely shared, and a climate of tentativeness typifies the interaction. Collaborative tactics include problem solving, joint action, education, and mild persuasion, each involving a more or

less active attempt to influence another party" (Brager and Holloway, 1978, p. 131).

This strategy is used when there is little or no disagreement about the problem and when it appears that desired changes can be brought about by cooperative methods.

2. *Campaign tactics* fall at the midpoint of the "continuum between collaborative and conflict tactics and contain some elements of both. They include 'hard' persuasion, political maneuvering, bargaining and negotiation, and mild coercion" (Brager and Holloway, 1978, p. 132).

This strategy is used when there is some, but not total, disagreement about the particular situation, and the advocates hope to obtain a compromise through negotiation.

3. *Contest tactics* "carry coercion a considerable distance further, involving public conflict and pressure. They include virulent clashes of position (through 'no holds barred' debate and public manifestos), the violation of normative behavior (for example, moving out of the bounds of organizationally 'proper' behavior by means of protest activities such as demonstrations), and, in the extreme, the violation of legal norms (for example, halting operations by sitting in)" (Brager and Hollway, 1978, p. 133).

The contest tactics result in an adversarial strategy, which is used when there is serious disagreement about the basic values in the problem to be solved. Adversary does not necessarily mean *enemy,* although strong feelings of hostility may be invoked in this strategy. Disruptive tactics are increasingly used by middle-class people and are far more acceptable than many are willing to recognize. In 1979 farmers who were protesting federal agricultural policies traveled to Washington, D.C., attempting to clog traffic routes with their tractors. In 1980 farmers in Maine dumped potatoes on the interstate highway and closed traffic to Canada for two days. Only minute sanctions were brought against the Washington farmers. The Maine farmers clearly violated a number of laws, and yet not a single charge was brought against them. Instead, a task force headed by Vice-President Walter Mondale was formed to study farm policies regarding the potato crop.

Restraints to Advocacy

Two major restraints to changes in services occur in modern agencies: professional and bureaucratic. Bureaucracies are essential to the provision of many services and goods in a modern society. They require large numbers of people, all performing rather limited tasks, with minimum discretion beyond that which is prescribed. Bureaucracies are expected to show no favoritism, to be impartial, and to give equal and courteous service to all. Each person in the system is essential to enable others to carry out assigned tasks. Policies are clearly established, communication lines are set, and the favored employee is the one who follows the rules. Bureaucracies are known for their efforts to save themselves and to attempt expansion. It has even been suggested that a bureaucracy develops a life of its own. Bureaucratic characteristics and processes lead to reliability, consistency, and continuity, but they may not encourage spontaneity and imagination, even though most of them are undergoing continual change.

Unlike most profit-making organizations, social service bureaucracies are monopolies and are not directly accountable to consumers. Since their funding and policy direction does not derive primarily from consumer demand, agencies must be responsive to state, local, and federal legislators and officials and to private funding organizations such as United Funds and other charitable foundations. Some public agencies will have advisory boards designed to review and analyze programs and will thus have to respond to this group's direction as well. Bureaucratic restraints do not deny consumers' needs, since these needs are in fact filtered through both public and private officials and through consumer representatives on advisory boards.

Not only may there be bureaucratic resistance to an advocate's efforts, but professionals as well may object to attempts to make changes. Knitzer (1978, pp. 83-85) found that professionals have raised at least three specific types of objections concerning advocacy: (1) They are offended that other professionals raise questions about their judgments. They also resent the intrusion of nonprofessionals, such as parents and citizen advocates. Professionals view themselves as being above criticism or question. (2) Practitioners object that advocacy siphons off time and resources that are needed for direct services. They take the position that advocacy is acceptable while others engage in it, but they themselves do not wish to be personally involved. (3) They hold that advocates are needlessly monitoring programs to make sure that all children do in fact get served, that children are not endlessly left in foster care when they could return home or be adopted, and that every family gets all the services to which it is entitled. They see this continual follow-up as another threat to professional autonomy and integrity.

A third emerging restraint to service change is the employee labor union, which is found primarily in the larger bureaucracies. Contracts with the public agency will often preclude any work-force modifications until a new contract is negotiated, thus reducing or eliminating the possibility of speedy changes to benefit the consumer. If the agency is violating its own regulations, there may be some fiery interchanges between management and the union as the agency attempts to comply with the law.

All this resistance to change may cause the advocate to say, "Why bother?" However, it is important to recognize that the same features that make change difficult also ensure the delivery of improved services—once the change has been made and incorporated into practice.

Bureaucracies tend to wear people down. Staff who work in large organizations for many years tend to lose some of their professional values and to adopt organizational values. Policy manuals, countless procedures, and numerous forms interfere with personal contacts between practitioners and consumers. Those practitioners who frequently try but fail to change unjust rules and practices may soon give up their efforts. If subtle or overt sanctions have been brought against them for advocacy efforts, it is understandable that change-oriented staff may decide to keep a low profile, avoid conflict, "behave themselves," and do a maintenance job. We must recognize this human factor in

practice. Recent studies on "burnout" reveal the physical and
psychological distress that some practitioners face in public welfare work, especially in positions involving red tape and high-
stress relationships with consumers. Burnout does not justify in-
activity, but it must be recognized as another type of resistance
to change. The worker who says, "I tried it before, and it
doesn't work," may be perfectly accurate. There are many pitfalls in advocacy work, and the practitioner may or may not
have used known steps and skills. Even with a carefully conceived plan to attempt change, the tired practitioner may refuse
to participate.

Final Considerations and Implications of Advocacy

Is it realistic to insist that every practitioner be an advocate? For case advocacy every professional should be prepared,
in behalf of and with his client's agreement, to take steps to ensure the provision of all services. Class advocacy may be different; some staff are not good advocates, but they are good practitioners. Every staff member can be aware of injustices and
denials of rights, but it may not be practical for each person to
carry the advocate's role. And a nonadvocate can still report injustices or supply needed data to someone else. Class advocacy
invariably requires a united effort, and specific roles and assignments have to be delegated in a large scale effort.

The line between advocacy and substantial social change
is very thin. For example, many residual services do little more
than patch things up after social breakdown. Foster care is a
residual service, since it is offered after breakdown; it can inflict
considerable trauma on families, especially children. It would be
far better to prevent the breakdown in the first place. Although
reasons other than adequate income are given by parents for the
placement of children, the truth is that adequate income supports would cut placements by one third. Furthermore, it has
been adequately demonstrated that intensive services to families
at the point of breakdown do enable families to stay together.
Specialty crisis intervention services, such as the Homebuilders
in Tacoma, Washington, not only cost less than foster place-

ment but also eliminate the traumas of separation and placement (Kinney and others, 1977). We must ask ourselves whether
we should work to perfect a residual program such as foster care
or advocate for preventive programs that would substantially reduce the placement of children.

Changes advocated today to enhance and improve services may be viewed tomorrow as a policy or practice that is unjust. It is interesting that the very creation of some pioneer social workers, the juvenile court, is today one of the major tar-
gets of advocacy effort. This reality does not justify a do-nothing
attitude but should lead staff to recognize the difficulty of fully
understanding all the ramifications and implications of new
policies and programs.

Involving consumers in advocacy is important. Some clients conduct advocacy entirely on their own and handle it very
well. Consumers can often speak far more vividly to the injustices of policies and practice than professional staff advocates.
Nonetheless, practitioners should not press consumers to participate; for those who have suffered extensive abuse from an
agency, it may be cruel to ask them to expose themselves to further possible conflict and antagonism. Consideration must also
be given to the fact that administrators who receive too much
criticism or verbal abuse from angry consumers may become
more resistive to change efforts. Furthermore, advocates should
consider what effect case advocacy, if it is successful, will have
on clients who do not have advocates. Will services to other clients be reduced, since additional staff time may be used in responding to the advocacy efforts? Will *other* services to a client
be reduced or slowed because he obtained services as a result of
advocacy? Will other staff in the same division from which services were obtained be cool toward requests for normal services
to other clients? All such factors need to be considered in any
change strategy.

Successful advocacy can be measured by what services
have been obtained for consumers, but advocacy efforts also
need to be assessed realistically in terms of what impact they
have had on a particular agency. There is often a disparity between what advocates perceive as their impact and what the

agency itself perceives. Consider, for example, the experience of the Roxbury Multi-Service Center (RMSC) in Boston and its efforts to stimulate various public services to improve the quality and extent of services to client groups. The RMSC was advocating on behalf of its clients for services from many public welfare agencies; it directed considerable attention to the Boston Housing Authority (BHA), which had been denying units to black residents. Whereas the RMSC described its efforts to have black applicants admitted to public housing as "militant advocacy" and as using "conflict strategies," the housing authority described RMSC staff as "cooperative, improving coordination, supplying up-to-date information" and also called their behavior "highly positive." These descriptions hardly represent the reactions of an agency perceiving frontal attacks on its policies. The authority did admit blacks, and the RMSC staff was successful in its efforts. The important message is that the RMSC staff had a very different perception of their own behavior and tactics than did the BHA (Perlman, 1975, pp. 83-85).

Change is often slow. But slow, deliberate progress has one advantage: it allows for more perspective on all the implications of a given change.

Advocacy to a Child: A Case Example

Alex C., age five and a half, had been abused extensively by his father and, more recently, by his mother. The child had lived with his mother in the grandparents' home from birth until September 1980, when the family moved into an apartment with the paternal aunt and her son. The father, Lawrence K., age twenty-six, unmarried, was in prison for five years for armed robbery and was released in May 1980. The mother, Kim C., age twenty-three, also had a six-month-old child, conceived during a conjugal visit with Lawrence.

In July 1980 the maternal uncle referred the family because Alex had strap welts and bruises on his legs. Alex said that "Daddy whipped me," and he expressed fear of his father, who visited daily until August 20, when he was violent with Kim and was restrained by a court order.

When initially referred, both parents were belligerent, resistant, and uncooperative, blocking medical examination and pictures of the child. They stated they would discipline Alex as they pleased, describing Alex as a "sissy" who had to be hardened and had to behave more maturely—dress himself completely, comb his hair correctly, and not wet his bed at night. Agency visits continued until the family moved, leaving no address. In October Alex was referred again; he had been seriously bruised on the cheek and also had a cut lip and four-inch welt on the thigh. Alex told of four other serious beatings for not getting to the bathroom on time during the night, sniffling instead of blowing his nose, and not finishing the food on his plate. Alex was very fearful, cried, and begged not to be whipped. The mother said "So what" to the beatings, and the father said that he had the right to beat the child for sniffling. An emergency removal was made, which required police assistance. The mother fought the removal, refused to give Alex his coat, physically threatened the worker, and told Alex not to believe the worker's lies.

A show cause order was filed and signed by the judge, giving temporary custody to the agency. The mother was antagonistic in court to both the judge and the agency litigation specialist, and she refused to acknowledge what had occurred. The father looked angry but was quiet.

A series of terms were set at the hearing: temporary custody by the agency for six weeks until the parents had fulfilled certain obligations, placement in a foster home (parents objected to placement with grandparents), psychological examinations, parent enrollment in a six-week Parent Effectiveness Training course, parental visiting during the six weeks, and return of Alex to the parents under agency supervision at the end of the six-week period.

Information presented at a review hearing seven weeks later included the following: the mother had attended two sessions of PET, the father, none; the mother kept all appointments for the visits and the psychologicals, the father, none; the father claimed to have moved alone into another apartment and to be unable to keep any appointments during the day, since he was employed.

A verbal report of the psychologicals revealed that Alex related to the maternal grandparents as his own parents and viewed his mother as another adult available to meet his needs occasionally. The father was feared by the child and viewed as unpredictable.

The agency requested return of the child to the maternal grandparents, which upset the mother. As in the previous hearing, she became antagonistic. The father made little comment,

and his appearance and comments in court indicated cooperation. The judge gave little time for any discussion and stated,
after asking the father about his home situation, that Alex
would be placed with the father. Everyone was shocked and surprised. The judge further decreed that Alex would attend a day
care center near the father's home and that the social worker
would provide counseling in the evening to the father. The agency attorney protested, but the judge declared the case closed
and scheduled a rehearing in three months.

The social worker, a capable woman in her mid-thirties,
was appalled at what she believed was an irrational decision.
Later she was almost in a daze as she described to her supervisor
what had to be done. She stated her concern over the father's
known violence, adding that she could be held accountable in
the event of the child's injuries or even his death. After recover-
ing from the upset of thinking about danger to the child, she began to realize her own fear of working during the evening with a
very angry father who now lived in the most dangerous neighborhood in the city. Staff attempted to analyze the reasons for
this bizarre decision but could arrive at none except the judge's
displeasure with the mother. He had previously been equitable
in such cases, even though he had not always followed the agency's recommendations. Whatever the reason for the decision,
they believed that they would have to live with it for three
months.

The worker, although committed to helping families,
could not bring herself to begin meeting with the father. Several
days after the court hearing, the case consultant was informed
about the situation. She took the firm and absolute position
that a serious error had been made, that the judge had not let
himself be fully informed of the facts, that the child's life was
in danger, and that the agency could not be expected to provide
service to a violent man in such a dangerous location at night.
She proposed an immediate appeal. Staff reaction was reserved,
with concern over the effect this move would have on continued relationships with this judge. Would other cases be ad-
versely affected? If the appeal lost, the judge would appear to
have potentially greater power. Staff had disagreed with this
judge on occasion before, only to find that his decision was reasonable. The consultant was firm, adding that she did not believe the caseworker should set up appointments with the father.
Other staff blanched at this comment, since it meant defiance
of a court order. The implications of service refusal could be far
reaching; the child's injury or death would be blamed on the
agency. The case consultant asserted that the court had actually

placed both the child *and* the social worker in jeopardy. The agency could not participate in service plans that were life threatening to both child and staff. It was decided to discuss the case further with top administration and the agency attorney.

A conference was held the following day with the child welfare director. The agency attorney was available through telephone conference. The consultant and the worker presented the child's situation and stated that Alex's living arrangement was more precarious today than when the case was first reported. A discussion of evening visits centered on agency responsibility to the father and child and the physical dangers to the worker. Although worker safety was a critical issue, it was considered secondary to the child's safety and the inability of the agency to protect the child while he was in the father's custody. The consultant pushed for immediate appeal. The child welfare director explained that any move should first be cleared with the state's attorney, since a major conference had recently been held to discuss agency submission of information to the courts as well as related agency-court working relationships. The courts had become concerned about a number of agency cases in an adjacent area of the state where several appeals were made, thus tying up attorneys, social workers, and the courts in additional litigation. Rather than try to resolve case problems with appeals to a higher court, an attempt was being made to improve agency testimony and agency-court working relationships. The agency and courts had taken almost two years to reach a beginning working agreement. Therefore, this appeal was judged by the director to be untimely in spite of whatever case needs existed.

The consultant was adamant in her demand that the case be immediately appealed, reminding the director that organization problems may be important but that a child's rights to a fair hearing were apparently denied. Furthermore, the state's attorney had been known as a cautious person, legally competent but reluctant to push for change. He would have to be pushed by the director.

In view of this delay, the social worker asked for, but did not receive, a commitment from the director that the administration would accept responsibility for declining to set up appointments with the father. The worker gave additional details about the father's abuse and unpredictability, then made her point personal by suggesting that the director herself might not be inclined to work with this man. The director got the message, and it was agreed that a day would be found to relieve a male worker from some duties in order to accompany the regu-

lar worker on at least a single meeting. A substitute plan was
also made for the worker to meet the father twice a week in the
morning when Alex was dropped off at the day care center.
The director's weak support for the child left the worker both
angry and depressed and also placed her clearly in favor of appeal. The attorney agreed with appeal, leaving the director as
the one dragging her feet. Although the director indicated she
wanted only to notify the state's attorney of the planned action, it was apparent that she really wanted the attorney's approval. The consultant offered to discuss the case with the
state's attorney, so that the case could be moved rapidly. At
first the director stated that no appeal action was to be started
until the attorney could be reached, then agreed that work
could begin now. That afternoon the state's attorney agreed to
the appeal.

During the next two weeks, Alex's attendance at the day
care center was sporadic, and when he was not at the center, he
was left alone in the apartment or in the apartment of a neighbor. The center staff suspected beatings, and the child was fearful, but they could not document more serious physical abuse.
The father's behavior toward the social worker was not only uncooperative but hostile.

At the appeals hearing, held three weeks from the first,
the lower court's ruling was overturned, and Alex was returned
to the maternal grandparents.

This case illustrates a number of features about advocacy,
including the fact that those closest to the case, and in a position to define an injustice, may be captive to the circumstances.
It may fall to another person to be the prime spokesperson for a
victim of the system. The practitioner, who most clearly was
aware of the father's hostility, was primarily concerned with
helping the child and parent under almost any circumstance.
Only her immobilization to meet with the father in the evenings
enabled her to see clearly the dangers for Alex and to recognize
that the court decision was totally wrong. The supervisor, committed to monitoring the adequacy of services, was similarly
trapped. The attorney, most familiar with court procedure, was
slow in responding to this child's need and was not sensitive to
the worker's jeopardy. The attorney did not feel kindly to the
natural mother in view of her hostility toward him. The mother
had helped to create this decision by her courtroom behavior,

and few felt sorry for her. The consultant was completely separated from the circumstances, and she could see vividly the dangers to Alex and the inability of the agency to protect him. She
initiated the conference, as advocates often have to do, and she
had to convince those who best knew the case that the situation
was a crisis and that the agency would be negligent if it did not
act and act quickly. To do otherwise was to endorse the court
decision and confirm for the father that abusive treatment was
not only acceptable but sanctioned. It would also confirm for
the grandparents and the mother that violent acts against a five-
year-old were justified if a child sniffled instead of blowing his
nose.

The child welfare director had a strong connection with
the state's attorney, and, after finally establishing a better working relationship with the courts, she did not want any event to
jeopardize the agreement that had been reached. She knew that
the social worker gave competent testimony in Alex's case and
that the court decision was in error. But the bond to the state's
attorney and to the head of the court system was stronger, *at
this point,* than the agency's commitment and the administrator's own professional responsibility to the child and to the
safety of a staff member.

The consequences of winning the case in an appeal had to
be taken into account, but the consequences of a fatally injured
child were more serious than future strained relationships with a
judge. Furthermore, if the child died, the judge would also be
criticized. If his future decisions were unjust, then more appeals
would be made, including other more organized advocacy steps
to initiate change and assure adequate court reviews.

Summary

Advocacy in child welfare means to challenge and seek
changes in systems that are regarded as unhelpful or injurious to
children and to assist consumers in receiving services to which
they are entitled but have difficulty obtaining. Advocacy is concerned with both rights and needs, and needs are not necessarily
enacted into law. Advocacy to change one's own agency is justi-

fied for four reasons: one's knowledge of the situation, the necessity to preserve the organization, the obligation to inform the administration, and the self-interest of staff to abide by regulations.

Steps and behaviors in advocacy include: recognizing the problem, obtaining all the facts, reconciling the facts with what is already known, defining the object to be changed, specifying the goals and the recommendations for change, computing the total cost of advocacy, selecting the timing of the proposed change, using the simplest and most direct approach to achieve improvements, and monitoring the change to ensure the continuation of improved service. Change efforts usually require a mix of interventions, such as intercession, persuasion, negotiation, and pressure. Tactics for change primarily include collaboration, campaign, and contest. Although most agencies are in a constant process of change, there are two major sources of resistance to change: bureaucratic and professional. A third emerging source, especially in large public agencies, is the employee labor union. Worker burnout represents another barrier to the initiation of change. Interestingly, some of the same characteristics that restrict change will ensure that services are provided after program modification.

Every practitioner should be sensitive to injustices and prepared to advocate on behalf of consumers; a social worker may not be the prime mover in advocacy but may be involved in one or more phases of the effort. Consumers are often better spokespersons for injustices than staff members, and they should always be consulted in any change effort directly affecting them. Practitioners must also ask themselves whether any disadvantages will accrue to consumers from an advocacy effort.

Special Annotated Bibliography

Brager, G. A., and Holloway, S. *Changing Human Service Organizations: Politics and Practice.* New York: Free Press, 1978. Addresses the theories, problems, prospects, and steps for changing human service agencies.

Edelman, M. W. *Children: In Pursuit of Justice: On Mounting*

Effective Child Advocacy. New York: Rockefeller Foundation, 1977. Provides data on the problems of many children and youth, examines public neglect and oversight of their needs, and proposes solutions.

Fernandez, H. C. *The Child Advocacy Handbook.* New York: Pilgrim Press, 1980. Gives many of the "how to's" of effective advocacy.

Mearig, J. S., and Associates. *Working for Children: Ethical Issues Beyond Professional Guidelines.* San Francisco: Jossey-Bass, 1978. This book and the Vardin and Brody book cited next provide many chapters on the theory, practice, and necessity for improvement of services to children.

Vardin, P. A., and Brody, I. M. (Eds.). *Children's Rights: Contemporary Perspectives.* New York: Teachers College Press, 1979.

CHAPTER TEN

Summary: Working Effectively in Child Welfare

Numerous articles on instances of child abuse or neglect are increasingly appearing in the American press. Many of the articles shock and offend and give a sense of immediacy and urgency to child welfare practice. It sometimes appears that there are simple and easy answers to the problem—for instance, "Get rid of the parents." Even those with training and extensive experience sometimes long for the quick solution. However, there is no shortcut to serving others competently and compassionately, and the demands for quality service will increase as more knowledge accrues and as consumers demand and become legally entitled to effective help.

We must never deny the painful and traumatic effects of a child's separation from primary caretakers, even when the parents have been abusive or neglectful. Children develop within and adapt to the intimate, interpersonal relationships of the family configuration, and the bonds that develop are not readily severed by time or distance. Although the parental behavior may objectively be described as destructive, and although children may sense the hurt of this behavior, children do derive security from living in a family. Some of the pain of separation can be reduced, but never eliminated, by planned separations that include the support of the parents and other persons of significance to the child. Separation is also a component in case terminations, and again, whenever possible, terminations should be carefully planned so that the benefits and accomplishments achieved during the service phase can be reexamined and confirmed. Case termination also requires an assessment of the client's current strengths, personal limits, and vulnerable characteristics, so that future stress situations can be defined and handled as well as possible. Practitioners must also recognize their own personal reactions to the ending phase of service.

Day care is an increasingly important service for families who have diminished capacities to provide for children's care—that is, for families where the primary caretaker must be employed, where temporary or extended crises exist, or where major transitions are occurring. In day care service, a family orientation, rather than an individualistic orientation, is necessary and obvious, since parents are present and a constant reminder of their relationship and connection to the child. This family orientation must not be overlooked in other services, such as foster and residential care, where parents are more easily bypassed because of their absence or limited availability.

Foster family care is a service that provides temporary care for a child in a private home while the natural parents are unable to care for him. Children have many difficulties adjusting to foster care, and they need the support of parents and agency staff in adapting. Services to help the parents rebuild their families should be provided, so that children can return home as quickly as possible. Residential care offers a living arrangement for children and youth who may not be suited for living in a foster family home and who have behavioral problems that the community finds difficult to accept. Since the parents have probably contributed to the problems, they should be closely involved in any treatment program to modify the child's behavior. Since residential care is usually a more restrictive arrangement than foster care, it should be pursued with caution, but it is recognized that the problems presented by troubled youth are often of such a magnitude as to demand quick resolution by both parents and the community.

Child protective staff have a difficult role, since they are exposed to some of the most offensive and unthinkable acts that a caretaker can inflict on a child. All the education, understanding, and compassion that practitioners may have for helping can temporarily erode in the face of heinous abuse by a parent. Nevertheless, the commitment to sustaining and supporting the family unit requires that every dignity, right, and service be extended to the parents to help them develop into caring and nurturing persons. Child protective service is unique among child welfare services, since the worker represents the authority of the state, reaches out to unmotivated and sometimes hostile clients, assesses a situation rapidly to prevent further injury or neglect, testifies against the parent if the case goes to court, and with some highly neglectful parents carries the bulk of the initiative to effect change. Some abusing and neglecting parents may never be able to carry parental roles, and even additional children born to them may have to be removed. Such a situation is the exception, but staff must be alert to the possibility. With less than a generation of intensified public awareness and authoritative analysis of child abuse and neglect, there is still much to learn. The good news is that the skills of helping and the means of assessing and preventing abuse and neglect are improving.

In addition to the many activities that a practitioner engages in while assisting a client, advocacy efforts may also be required if clients are denied services to which they are entitled, if the help offered is inadequate, or if the policies and programs are unjust or inequitable. Sometimes the abuses are found in the very agency where the practitioner is employed. Case advocacy is taken on behalf of a single family or person, and class advocacy may be initiated for a large group of consumers. Each practitioner should be prepared to intervene for a single family or person, but class action may involve many staff and community participants. Practitioners should be sensitive to the failure of agencies or human service staff to respond to needs or to recognize legal rights and entitlements. Legal rights have increased significantly for consumers over the past decade and will continue to expand. The impact of the changes will affect both policy and program, including the skills, knowledge, and behaviors of practitioners.

A Look to the Future

Public day care programs are currently in marked decline because of drastic federal funding cutbacks during the past two years. Many centers have simply closed; others must serve a delineated and deprived population, such as children who have been abused or neglected. Although there were marked public funding increases over the prior two decades, they were accompanied by strong protests of conservative religious and political groups, such as the Moral Majority and organizations opposed to the proposed Equal Rights Amendment. These groups believe that day care threatens the family structure, interferes with parental obligations, and weakens the moral fiber of people. Unless there is very strong private foundation and state and local funding support for day care, it is likely that programs will be inadequately funded for many years. Day care, like most human services, is labor intensive. However, day care salaries and wages are extremely low, many below poverty levels, and if staff demand raises, then service rates will have to rise accordingly.

Foster family care will continue as a major component of child welfare programs, although there may be variations to the program, such as five-day care in which the child is with a foster parent most of the week and with a parent on the weekend. Both permanency planning efforts and the Adoption Assistance and Child Welfare Act of 1980 may reduce the number of children requiring traditional foster placement. If practitioners can fully support the idea of keeping a child in his own network, then children may be kept with family friends and neighbors, rather than being placed long distances from home. This concept may not overcome the need for placements, but may reduce the trauma of separations.

Residential care programs continue, although in slightly

lesser quantity, in spite of the strong deinstitutionalization movement of recent years. These programs are expensive, and their high cost may be the primary cause of their slow demise. The private therapeutic facility—for the families who can personally afford them, and for the states who must place a child in one of them—will be the major residential service available in the future. We may also see "brief residential" program service followed by intensive community service. Intensive and extensive community service is also expensive, however, when it requires a team of practitioners to live a short time with a family or to provide in-depth crisis intervention and counseling services to maintain a family in the community—especially when complicated legal, court, and medical costs are included. In short, top-quality, aggressive outreach service does not come cheaply, nor do broad comprehensive screening programs to prevent problem occurrence. The small group home in the community is an alternative to the more complex institution, but the small facility cannot provide the multitude of services available in the residential program.

Child protection programs are now provided throughout the United States, but quality and coverage are very irregular. They are still in a rapid stage of growth, and many lessons are yet to be learned. This is another service whose costs are rising, but the programs are popular with legislatures, receive substantial citizen support, and have continued to receive basic, although declining, funding support from Congress while other social programs have suffered cutbacks. Agencies continue to struggle with the precise definitions of abuse and neglect. However, as agencies gain experience with the programs, and as citizen groups, particularly minorities, negotiate, collaborate, and contest administrative and court decisions, more consistent policies and definitions will be established. Just as there is opposition to day care programs by those who believe that they disrupt family life, civil libertarians oppose child protection programs because they usurp the rights of parents. Some religious groups, such as the Moral Majority, insist on their right to endure no interference by the state and to use corporal punishment as they see fit (O'Looney, 1981).

Preventive service programs are not specifically addressed in this book, but they are implied as a prior first step and consideration during intake whenever a parent or agency requests separation of a child from his family. Even if there do not appear to be supportive or supplemental services in the community to maintain children in their own homes, practitioners should carefully assess what resources are available to the family or what adaptations of services by a community agency are possible before planning placement away from home. Most communities do not have intensive and comprehensive intervention services, such as the Homebuilders of Tacoma, Washington (Kinney and others, 1977). Nor do many communities have comprehensive emergency services, such as those provided in Nashville, Tennessee (Lockett and others, 1975). But many communities have elements of a comprehensive emergency service that can make placement, if indicated, less traumatic, or else can select and apply a range of services to a family to prevent placement. In addition, both of these programs can reduce the larger costs associated with foster care. It is unfortunate but true that the prevention of problems is not popular in the United States, although some public funding for disease prevention or health maintenance is acceptable. In social service, preventive programs are less visible than more concrete and emotionally appealing services, such as foster care, and it is difficult for the public to see that funding preventive services saves substantial money in the long run and reduces human distress.

Bibliography

Abt Associates. *Children at the Center: Executive Summary.* Cambridge, Mass.: Abt Associates, 1979.

Adams, M., and Baumbach, D. J. "Professional Parenting: A Factor in Group Home Programming." *Child Care Quarterly,* 1980, *9* (3), 185-196.

Aiken, W., and LaFollette, H. (Eds.). *Whose Child.* Totowa, N.J.: Rowman and Littlefield, 1980.

Aldridge, M. J., Cautley, P. W., and Lichstein, D. P. *Guidelines for Placement Workers.* Madison: Center for Social Service, University of Wisconsin-Extension, 1974.

Amidai, N. "Trends and Questions in Child Health." *Public Welfare,* 1977, *35* (2), 18-25.

Applebaum, F. "Loneliness: A Taxonomy and Psychodynamic View." *Clinical Social Work Journal,* 1978, *6* (1), 13-20.

Auerbach, S. "What Do Parents Want from Day Care?" In S. Auerbach and J. Rivaldo (Eds.), *Rationale for Child Care Services: Programs vs. Policies.* Vol. 1. New York: Human Sciences Press, 1975.

Baer, B. L., and Federico, R. *Educating the Baccalaureate Social Worker.* Cambridge, Mass.: Ballinger, 1978.

Baily, T. F. "Observations on Dynamics and Practice in Sexual Abuse." In W. M. Holder (Ed.), *Sexual Abuse of Children: Implications for Treatment.* Denver: American Humane Association, 1980.

Belsky, J., and Steinberg, L. D. "The Effects of Day Care: A Critical Review." *Child Development,* 1978, *49* (4), 929-949.

Belsky, J., and Steinberg, L. D. "What Does Research Teach Us About Day Care: A Followup Report." *Children Today,* 1979, *8* (4), 21-26.

Besharov, D. J. *Juvenile Justice Advocacy.* New York: Practicing Law Institute, 1974.

Blehar, M. "Anxious Attachment and Defensive Reactions Associated with Day Care." *Child Development,* 1974, *45* (8), 683-692.

Block, N. "Toward Reducing Recidivism in Foster Care." *Child Welfare,* 1981, *60* (9), 597-610.

Borgman, R., Edmunds, M., and MacDicken, R. A. *Crisis Intervention: A Manual for Child Protective Workers.* DHEW Publication No. (OHDS) 79-30196. Washington, D.C.: U.S. Department of Health, Education and Welfare, 1979.

Bowlby, M. "Grief and Mourning in Infancy and Early Childhood." In *Psychoanalytic Study of the Child.* Vol. 15. New Haven, Conn.: Yale University Press, 1960.

Boyd, P. "They Can Go Home Again." *Child Welfare,* 1979, *58* (9), 609-615.

Brager, G. A., and Holloway, S. *Changing Human Service Organizations: Politics and Practice.* New York: Free Press, 1978.

Breitbart, V. *The Day Care Book: The Why, What and How of Community Day Care.* New York: Knopf, 1974.

Breton, M. "Resocialization of Abusive Parents." *Social Work,* 1981, *26* (2), 119-122.

Brieland, D. "Mental Health and Illness in Children." In *Encyclopedia of Social Work.* (17th ed.) Washington, D.C.: National Association of Social Workers, 1977.

Brieland, D., and Lemmon, J. *Social Work and the Law.* St. Paul: West Publishing Co., 1977.

Bronfenbrenner, U. "Is Early Intervention Effective?" *Day Care and Early Education,* 1974, *2* (2), 14-18.

Bruce-Briggs, B. "Child Care: The Fiscal Time Bomb." *Public Interest,* 1977, *49,* 87-102.

Burgess, A., and others (Eds.). *Sexual Assault of Children and Adolescents.* Lexington, Mass.: Lexington Books, 1978.

Calhoun, J. "Developing a Family Perspective." *Children Today,* 1980a, *9* (2), 3-8.

Calhoun, J. "The 1980 Child Welfare Act: A Turning Point for Children and Troubled Families." *Children Today,* 1980b, *9* (5), 2-4.

Cautley, P. W., and Lichstein, D. P. *The Selection of Foster Parents.* Madison: Center for Social Service, University of Wisconsin-Extension, 1974.

Child Welfare League of America. *Standards for Foster Family Care.* New York: Child Welfare League of America, 1959.

Child Welfare League of America. *Standards for Child Protective Services.* New York: Child Welfare League of America, 1960.

Compton, B. R., and Galaway, B. *Social Work Processes.* Homewood, Ill.: Dorsey Press, 1975.

Costin, L. B. *Child Welfare: Policies and Practice.* New York: McGraw-Hill, 1972.

Crouch, R. E. "International Declaration/Convention Efforts and the Current Status of Children's Rights in the United States." In R. B. Lillich (Ed.), *The Family in International Law: Some Emerging Problems.* Third Sokol Colloquium. Charlottesville, Va.: Michie, 1981.

DeFrancis, V. "The Status of Child Protective Services: A National Dilemma." In C. H. Kempe and R. E. Helfer (Eds.), *Helping the Battered Child and His Family.* Philadelphia: Lippincott, 1972.

Dobbin, S., and McCormick, A. "An Update on Social Work in Child Care." *Child Welfare,* 1980, *59* (2), 97-102.

Ebeling, N. B., and Hill, D. A. (Eds.). *Child Abuse: Intervention and Treatment.* Acton, Mass.: Publishing Sciences Group, 1975.

Edelman, M. W. *Children: In Pursuit of Justice: On Mounting*

Effective Child Advocacy. New York: Rockefeller Foundation, 1977.

Edelstein, S. "When Foster Children Leave: Helping Foster Parents to Grieve." *Child Welfare,* 1981, *60* (7), 467-473.

Eekelaar, J., and Katz, S. N. (Eds.). *Family Violence: An International and Interdisciplinary Study.* Toronto: Butterworth, 1978.

Emlen, A., and others. *Overcoming Barriers to Planning for Children in Foster Care.* DHEW Publication No. (OHDS) 78-30138. Washington, D.C.: U.S. Department of Health, Education and Welfare, 1978.

Ewalt, P. "Book Reviews." *Social Work,* 1982, *27* (2), 194.

Fanshel, D., and Shinn, E. B. *Children in Foster Care: A Longitudinal Investigation.* New York: Columbia University Press, 1978.

Feldman, R. A. "Damaged Parents and Child Neglect: An Essay Review." *Social Work Research and Abstracts,* 1982, *18* (1), 3-9.

Fernandez, H. C. *The Child Advocacy Handbook.* New York: Pilgrim Press, 1980.

Finklestein, N. E. "Family Participation in Residential Treatment." *Child Welfare,* 1974, *53* (9), 570-575.

Finklestein, N. E. "Children in Limbo." *Social Work,* 1980, *25* (2), 100-105.

Finklestein, N. E. "Family Centered Group Care—The Children's Institution from a Living Center to a Center for Change." In A. Maluccio and P. A. Sinanoglu (Eds.), *The Challenge of Partnership: Working with Parents of Children in Foster Care.* New York: Child Welfare League of America, 1981.

Fox, E. F., Nelson, M. A., and Bolman, W. M. "The Termination Process: A Neglected Dimension in Social Work." In B. R. Compton and B. Galaway, *Social Work Processes.* Homewood, Ill.: Dorsey Press, 1975.

Fox, R., and Whelley, J. "Preventing Placement: Goal Attainment in Short-Term Family Treatment." *Child Welfare,* 1982, *61* (4), 231-238.

Furman, R. "Death and the Young Child." In *Psychoanalytic*

Study of the Child. Vol. 19. New Haven, Conn.: Yale University Press, 1964.

Galinsky, E., and Hooks, W. *The New Extended Family.* Boston: Houghton Mifflin, 1977.

Galper, J. *The Politics of Social Services.* Englewood Cliffs, N.J.: Prentice-Hall, 1975.

Garbarino, J., Stocking, S. H., and Associates. *Protecting Children from Abuse and Neglect: Developing and Maintaining Effective Support Systems for Families.* San Francisco: Jossey-Bass, 1980.

Germaine, C. B. "Child Welfare in the 1980s—Will the Graduate-Level Curriculum Prepare the M.S.W.?" Prepared for the New England Child Welfare Training Center. In *Notes from the National Center.* Ann Arbor: School of Social Work, University of Michigan, 1981.

Germaine, C. B., and Gitterman, A. *The Life Model of Social Work Practice.* New York: Columbia University Press, 1980.

Gibson, G. "An Approach to Identification and Prevention of Developmental Difficulties Among Mexican-American Children." In A. Morales and B. Sheafor (Eds.), *Social Work: A Profession of Many Faces.* Boston: Allyn and Bacon, 1980.

Goldberg, K., and Dooner, M. "Rethinking Residential Treatment." *Child Welfare,* 1981, *60* (5), 355-358.

Goldstein, J., Freud, A., and Solnit, A. J. *Beyond the Best Interests of the Child.* New York: Free Press, 1973.

Greene, M., and Orman, B. "Nurturing the Unnurtured." *Social Casework,* 1981, *62* (7), 398-404.

Halleck, S. "Family Therapy and Social Change." *Social Casework,* 1976, *57* (8), 493.

Harrell, J. (Ed.). *Selected Readings in the Issues of Day Care.* Washington, D.C.: Day Care and Child Development Council of America, 1972.

Hartman, A. "Curriculum Building for Child Welfare Practice in the '80's." In *Notes from the National Center.* Ann Arbor: School of Social Work, University of Michigan, 1981a.

Hartman, A. "The Family: A Central Focus for Practice." *Social Work,* 1981b, *26* (1), 7-13.

Heiting, K. H. "Involving Parents in Residential Treatment of Children." *Children,* 1971, *18* (5), 162-167.

Herman, M., and Callanan, B. "Child Welfare Workers and the State Legislative Process." *Child Welfare,* 1978, *57* (1), 13-25.

Hill, C. R. "Private Demand for Child Care: Implications for Public Policy." *Evaluation Quarterly,* 1978, *2* (4), 523-546.

Hill-Scott, K. "Child Care in the Black Community." *Journal of Black Studies,* 1979, *10,* 78-97.

Holder, W. M., and Mohr, C. (Eds.). *Helping in Child Protective Services.* Denver: American Humane Association, 1980.

Huessy, H. R., and Cohen, A. H. "Vulnerability of Hyperkinetic (MBD) Child to Subsequent Serious Psychopathology: A Controlled 7-Year Follow-Up." In J. E. Anthony (Ed.), *The Child in His Family.* Vol. 4. New York: Wiley, 1978.

Jacobs, M. "Foster Parent Training: An Opportunity for Skills Enrichment and Empowerment." *Child Welfare,* 1980, *59* (10), 615-624.

Jenkins, S. "Separation Experiences of Parents Whose Children Are in Foster Care." *Child Welfare,* 1969, *48* (6), 334-340.

Jenkins, S., and Schroeder, A. *The Discriminant Functions.* Publication No. (OHDS) 30259. Washington, D.C.: U.S. Department of Health and Human Services, 1980.

Jones, M. A., Magura, S., and Shyne, A. "Effective Practice with Families in Protective and Preventive Services." *Child Welfare,* 1981, *60* (2), 67-80.

Jones, M. L. "Aggressive Adoption: A Program's Effect on a Child Welfare Agency." *Child Welfare,* 1977, *56* (6), 401-408.

Jones, M. L., and Biesecker, J. L. "Training in Permanency Planning: Using What Is Known." *Child Welfare,* 1980, *59* (8), 481-489.

Kadushin, A. *Child Welfare Services.* (2nd ed.) New York: Macmillan, 1974.

Kadushin, A. "Child Welfare Strategy in the Coming Years: An Overview." In *Child Welfare Strategy in the Coming Years.* DHEW Publication No. (OHDS) 78-30158. Washington, D.C.: Office of Human Development Services, U.S. Department of Health, Education and Welfare, 1978.

Kadushin, A., and Martin, J. *Child Abuse: An Interactional Event.* New York: Columbia University Press, 1981.

Kahn, A., and Kamerman, S. *Not for the Poor Alone.* New York: Harper & Row, 1975.

Kamerman, S., and Kahn, A. *Social Services in the United States.* Philadelphia: Temple University Press, 1976.

Kamerman, S., and Kahn, A. "The Day-Care Debate: A Wider View." *Public Interest,* 1979, *54* (4), 76-93.

Keith-Lucas, A., and Sanford, C. *Group Child Care as a Family Service.* Chapel Hill: University of North Carolina Press, 1977.

Kinney, J., and others. "Homebuilders: Keeping Families Together." *Journal of Consulting and Clinical Psychology,* 1977, *45* (4), 667-673.

Klein, A. F. *The Professional Child Care Worker.* New York: Association Press, 1975.

Kline, D., and Overstreet, H. *Foster Care of Children.* New York: Columbia University Press, 1972.

Knitzer, J. "Responsibility for Delivery of Services." In J. S. Mearig and Associates, *Working for Children: Ethical Issues Beyond Professional Guidelines.* San Francisco: Jossey-Bass, 1978.

Koocher, G. P. "Child Advocacy and Mental Health Professions." In P. A. Vardin and I. M. Brody (Eds.), *Children's Rights: Contemporary Perspectives.* New York: Teachers College Press, 1979.

Krashinsky, M. "Cost of Day Care in Public Programs." *National Tax Journal,* 1978, *23,* 363-372.

Krona, D. A. "Parents as Treatment Partners in Residential Care." *Child Welfare,* 1980, *59* (2), 91-96.

Krugman, D. C. "Working with Separation." *Child Welfare,* 1971, *50* (9), 528-537.

Kuehn, B. S., and Christophersen, E. R. "Preserving the Rights of Clients in Child Abuse and Neglect." In G. T. Hannah, W. P. Christian, and H. B. Clark (Eds.), *Preservation of Client Rights.* New York: Free Press, 1981.

Levitan, S., and Alderman, K. *Child Care and ABC's Too.* Baltimore: Johns Hopkins University Press, 1975.

Lewis, M. *Clinical Aspects of Child Development.* Philadelphia: Lea and Febiger, 1971.

Liberman, P. L. "Foreword." In G. T. Hannah, W. P. Christian, and H. B. Clark (Eds.), *Preservation of Client Rights.* New York: Free Press, 1981.

Littner, N. *Some Traumatic Effects of Separation and Placement.* New York: Child Welfare League of America, 1956.

Lockett, P. W., and others. *Comprehensive Emergency Services.* (2nd ed.) Nashville: National Center for Comprehensive Emergency Services to Children, Nashville Urban Observatory, 1975.

Lowenberg, N. F. "Helping Parents to Help Their Children." *Public Welfare,* 1959, *17* (3), 115-116, 133-134.

Lynn, J. "Washington Day Care." *Day Care and Early Childhood Education,* 1979, 7 (1), 68-69.

McCarty, L. "Investigation of Incest: Opportunity to Motivate Families to Seek Help." *Child Welfare,* 1981, *60* (10), 679-689.

McDermott, J. "Divorce and Its Psychiatric Sequellae in Children." *Archives of General Psychiatry,* 1970, *23,* 421-427.

McGowan, B. "The Case Advocacy in Child Welfare." *Child Welfare,* 1978a, *57* (5), 275-284.

McGowan, B. "Strategies in Bureaucracies." In J. S. Mearig and Associates, *Working for Children: Ethical Issues Beyond Professional Guidelines.* San Francisco: Jossey-Bass, 1978b.

Magnus, R. A. "Teaching Parents to Parent: Parent Involvement in Residential Treatment Programs." *Children Today,* 1974, *3* (1), 25-27.

Maluccio, A. *Learning from Clients.* New York: Free Press, 1979.

Maluccio, A., and Sinanoglu, P. A. (Eds.). *The Challenge of Partnership: Working with Parents of Children in Foster Care.* New York: Child Welfare League of America, 1981.

Maluccio, A., and others. "Beyond Permanency Planning." *Child Welfare,* 1980, *59* (9), 515-530.

Martin, R. "Legal Issues in Preserving Client Rights." In G. T. Hannah, W. P. Christian, and H. B. Clark (Eds.), *Preservation of Client Rights.* New York: Free Press, 1981.

Matsushima, J. "Child Welfare: Institutions for Children." In

Encyclopedia of Social Work. (17th ed.) Washington, D.C.: National Association of Social Workers, 1977.

Mayer, M. F., Richman, L. H., and Balcerzak, E. A. *Group Care of Children: Crossroads and Transition.* New York: Child Welfare League of America, 1977.

Mearig, J. S., and Associates. *Working for Children: Ethical Issues Beyond Professional Guidelines.* San Francisco: Jossey-Bass, 1978.

Midwest Parent-Child Welfare Resource Center. *Interdisciplinary Glossary on Child Abuse and Neglect: Legal, Medical, Social Work Terms.* DHEW Publication No. (OHDS) 78-30137. Washington, D.C.: Department of Health, Education and Welfare, 1978.

Mishne, J. "Parental Abandonment: A Unique Form of Loss and Narcissistic Injury." *Clinical Social Work Journal,* 1979, *7* (1), 15-33.

Moss, S. Z. "How Children Feel About Being Placed Away from Home." *Children,* 1966, *13* (4), 153-157.

Murray, A. "Maternal Employment Reconsidered: Effects on Infants." *American Journal of Orthopsychiatry,* 1975, *45* (5), 773-790.

Nagera, H. "Children's Reactions to the Death of Important Objects." In *Psychoanalytic Study of the Child.* Vol. 25. New York: International Universities Press, 1970.

National Association of Social Workers. "NASW Code of Ethics." *NASW NEWS,* 1980, *25* (1).

National Center on Child Abuse and Neglect. *Child Abuse and Neglect.* Vol. 2: *The Roles and Responsibilities of Professionals.* DHEW Publication No. 75-30074. Washington, D.C.: U.S. Department of Health, Education and Welfare, 1975.

National Center on Child Abuse and Neglect. *Child Sexual Abuse: Incest, Assault, and Sexual Exploitation.* DHEW Publication No. (OHDS) 79-30166. Washington, D.C.: U.S. Department of Health, Education and Welfare, 1978.

National Center on Child Abuse and Neglect. *Family Violence: Intervention Strategies.* DHHS Publication No. (OHDS) 80-30258. Washington, D.C.: U.S. Department of Health and Human Services, 1980.

National Center on Child Abuse and Neglect. *Study Findings:*

National Study of the Incidence and Severity of Child Abuse and Neglect. DHHS Publication No. (OHDS) 81-30325. Washington, D.C.: U.S. Department of Health and Human Services, 1981.

Nolan, J. "A Brief History of Child Development in California." In S. Auerbach and J. Rivaldo (Eds.), *Rationale for Child Care Services: Programs vs. Policies.* Vol. 1. New York: Human Sciences Press, 1975.

O'Looney, J. "Child Abuse Legislation and the Moral Majority." *Checkpoints for Children,* 1981, 7 (1), 1-3.

Olsen, L. J. "Predicting the Permanency Status of Children in Foster Care." *Social Work Research and Abstracts,* 1982, *18* (1), 9-18.

Patti, R. "Limitations and Prospects of Internal Advocacy." *Social Casework,* 1974, *55* (9), 537-545.

Patti, R. "Social Work Practice: Organizational Environment." In *Encyclopedia of Social Work.* (17th ed.) Washington, D.C.: National Association of Social Workers, 1977.

Paul, J. L., Neufeld, G. R., and Pelosi, J. W. (Eds.). *Child Advocacy Within the System.* Syracuse, N.Y.: Syracuse University Press, 1977.

Perlman, R. *Consumers and Social Services.* New York: Wiley, 1975.

Pike, V., and others. *Permanent Planning for Children in Foster Care: A Handbook for Social Workers.* DHEW Publication No. (OHDS) 77-30124. Washington, D.C.: U.S. Department of Health, Education and Welfare, 1977.

Pincus, A., and Minahan, A. *Social Work Practice: Model and Method.* Itasca, Ill.: Peacock, 1973.

Polansky, N. A. *Damaged Parents: An Anatomy of Neglect.* Chicago: University of Chicago Press, 1981.

Polier, J. "Professional Abuse of Children: Responsibility for the Delivery of Services." *American Journal of Orthopsychiatry,* 1975, *45* (3), 357-362.

Polier, J. "External and Internal Roadblocks to Effective Child Advocacy." *Child Welfare,* 1977, *56* (8), 497-508.

Racher, D., and Campisi, G. "Baby Wouldn't Drown, 'So I Banged Its Head.' " *Philadelphia Daily News,* May 5, 1982, p. 24.

Rapp, C. "Effect of the Availability of Family Support Services on Decisions About Child Placement." *Social Work Research and Abstracts,* 1982, *18* (1), 21-27.

Roby, P. (Ed.). *Child Care—Who Cares.* New York: Basic Books, 1973.

Rodham, H. "Children's Rights: A Legal Perspective." In P. A. Vardin and I. M. Brody (Eds.), *Children's Rights: Contemporary Perspectives.* New York: Teachers College Press, 1979.

Ruderman, F. *Child Care and Working Mothers.* New York: Child Welfare League of America, 1968.

Ryan, W. *Blaming the Victim.* New York: Vintage Books, Random House, 1971.

Sawyer, R. "Program Design: A Method of Achieving Permanency in Foster Care." *Children Today,* 1981, *10* (5), 19-21.

Server, J. S., and Janzen, C. "Contraindication to Reconstitution of Sexually Abusive Families." *Child Welfare,* 1982, *61* (5), 279-288.

Shapiro, C. "Termination: A Neglected Concept in the Social Work Curriculum." *Journal of Education for Social Work,* 1980, *16* (2), 13-19.

Shulman, L. *The Skills of Helping.* Itasca, Ill.: Peacock, 1979.

Simons, R. L. "Strategies for Exercising Influence." *Social Work,* 1982, *27* (3), 268-274.

Simsen, C. B. "The Effect of Separation on Children and Adults." Frankfort: Kentucky Welfare Association, n.d.

Sinanoglu, P., and Maluccio, A. (Eds.). *Parents of Children in Placement: Perspectives and Programs.* New York: Child Welfare League of America, 1982.

Sinofsky, M. S. "The Process of Separation." In N. B. Ebeling and D. A. Hill (Eds.), *Child Abuse: Intervention and Treatment.* Acton, Mass.: Publishing Sciences Group, 1975.

Specht, H. "Disruptive Tactics." *Social Work,* 1969, *14* (2), 5-15.

Spitz, R. "Hospitalism: An Inquiry into the Genesis of Psychiatric Conditions in Early Childhood." In *Psychoanalytic Study of the Child.* Vol. 1. New York: International Universities Press, 1945.

Spitz, R. "Anaclitic Depression." In *Psychoanalytic Study of the*

Child. Vol. 2. New York: International Universities Press, 1946a.

Spitz, R. "Hospitalism: A Followup Report." In *Psychoanalytic Study of the Child.* Vol. 2. New York: International Universities Press, 1946b.

Star, B. "Patterns of Family Violence." *Social Casework,* 1980, *61* (6), 339-346.

Steinfels, M. *Who's Minding the Children?* New York: Simon and Schuster, 1973.

Treischman, A. E., Whittaker, J. K., and Brendtro, L. K. *The Other 23 Hours.* Chicago: Aldine, 1969.

U.S. Department of Health, Education and Welfare. *Federal Interagency Day Care Requirements.* DHEW Publication No. (OHDS) 76-31081. Washington, D.C.: U.S. Department of Health, Education and Welfare, 1968.

U.S. Department of Health, Education and Welfare. "Health, Education and Welfare Day Care Regulations." *Federal Register,* 1980, *45* (55), 17870-17885.

Vardin, P. A., and Brody, I. M. (Eds.). *Children's Rights: Contemporary Perspectives.* New York: Teachers College Press, 1979.

Wallinga, J. V. "Foster Placement and Separation Trauma." *Journal of the American Public Welfare Association,* 1966, *24* (4), 296-301.

Webster, C. D., and others. "The Child Care Worker in the Family: Some Case Examples and Implications for the Design of Family-Centered Programs." *Child Care Quarterly,* 1979, *8* (1), 5-18.

Whittaker, J. K. "Child Welfare: Residential Treatment." In *Encyclopedia of Social Work.* (17th ed.) Washington, D.C.: National Association of Social Workers, 1977.

Whittaker, J. K. *Caring for Troubled Children: Residential Treatment in a Community Context.* San Francisco: Jossey-Bass, 1979.

Whittaker, J. K. "Family Involvement in Residential Treatment: A Support System for Parents." In A. Maluccio and P. A. Sinanoglu (Eds.), *The Challenge of Partnership: Working with Parents of Children in Foster Care.* New York: Child Welfare League of America, 1981.

Whittaker, J. K., and Treischman, A. E. (Eds.). *Children Away from Home.* Chicago: Aldine, 1972.

Wilkes, J. R. "Separation Can Be a Therapeutic Option." *Child Welfare,* 1980, *59* (1), 27-31.

Williams, G. "Cruelty and Kindness to Children: Documentary of a Century, 1874-1974." In G. Williams and J. Money (Eds.), *Traumatic Abuse and Neglect of Children at Home.* Baltimore: Johns Hopkins University Press, 1980.

Wolfensberger, W. "A Model for a Balanced Multicomponent Advocacy/Protective Services Schema." In L. Kopolow and H. Bloom (Eds.), *Mental Health Advocacy.* DHEW Publication No. (ADM) 77-455. Washington, D.C.: U.S. Department of Health, Education and Welfare, 1977.

Wolins, M. "Group Care: Friend or Foe?" *Social Work,* 1969, *14* (1), 35-53.

Woolsey, S. "Pied Piper Politics and the Child-Care Debate." *Daedalus,* 1977, *106,* 127-145.

Zaphiris, A. *Protective Services to Abused and Neglected Children and Their Families.* Official Proceedings, National Institute for the Training of Trainers, December 16-20, 1974, Denver: University of Denver Graphics Department, 1975.

Index

237